Dance Delights

A collection of diverse inventions

by John Gardiner-Garden

Privately published by the author
Dr John Gardiner-Garden
Canberra, Australia
October 2020

ISBN 978-0-6450216-3-9

Please contact the author via john@earthlydelights.com.au or www.earthlydelights.com.au if you would like to make comments, ask questions, receive supplements/corrections or extend an invitation to teach, lead or talk.

Also by and available from the author:

Lost Dances of Earthly Delights, Vol. 1: *Pleasures for Four Seasons*, Canberra, 2000 & 2005 (with 4 CDs)

The Christmas Carol Dance Book, Canberra, 1st edition 2002, expanded 2nd edition 2020

Lost Dances of Earthly Delights, Vol. 2: *Favourites for Four Settings*, Canberra, 2005 (with 4 CDs)

Dancing through the Ages, being a series of 31 books on the dance and dances of the 1400-1900 ballroom, Canberra, 2020.

Illustrations:
Front cover: At top Robert and George Cruickshank 'Tom, Jerry, and Logic making the most of an evening in Vauxhall' in Pierce Egan's *Life in London*, London, 1821 and at bottom William Heath's 'Tom & Bob sporting their figures at a fancy dress ball' in *Real Life in London*, London, 1821/2. Inside the letters are a fragment of an image from the Stuttgart manuscript *Cod. Pa. germ. 142, Pontus and* Sidonia, from 'Bal de Saint Cécile', in Charles Vernier's lithograph collection *Les Bals de Paris*.
Rear cover: A detail from a card promoting the University of Ghent Students Society' series of masked and dress balls for February 1845.
Title page: 'Minuet de la Cour', possibly by William Heath, London, Tegg, c.1817 and an extract from 'Princely amusements or The humors of the family' by George Cruickshank, London, 1812.
The exact provenance of the pictures between the Preface and Contents is unknown to me but the illustrations on *page 10 are:* at top Anton Möller c.1600 depiction of dancing in Danzig and a detail from a 1610 painting by Dutch artist David Vinckboons, in middle Carlotta Grisi and Lucien Petipa in a scene from the 1845 ballet *Le diable à quatre* and a Paris image of a mazurka trio, and at bottom J. Brandard's illustration for *Julien's First set of Lancers entitled the English Lancers* and a 'Ball given by the troopers of the Second Life Guards at St. James's Ball', *The Graphic*, 1 March, 1884, p.197.

Preface

I'm pleased to have at last had a chance to revise and improve most of the 20 odd dances and dance instructions presented in my 2015 and 2016 *Odd Delights* editions, to add to them 33 new dances that I have composed in response to different needs, challenges and inspirations over the last 5 years, and to offer directions for 29 daring medleys that dancers in my home scene have enjoyed the challenge of dancing.

As the original work has undergone many changes and a great expansion, and as the title *Odd Delights* was a little cryptic, I have named this new work *Dance Delights*—thus linking it with the earlier name while making it clear that the work pertains to dance. To flag the broad ranging and original nature of the choreographies I have added the subtitle *A collection of diverse inventions.* The elements in this subtitle have all enjoyed distinguished historical use—the second (1630) issue of Fabritio Caroso's 1600 *Nobiltà di dame* being called *Raccolta di varij balli* ('A collection of various [or diverse] dances') and the second (1604) edition of Cesare Negri's 1602 *Gratie d'Amore* being called *Nuove inventioni di balli* ('New dance inventions').

As it is still of relevance, here is the Preface of my 2015 *Odd Delights.*

> The collection is a mixture of recently 'unearthed' dances Bordonian dances and tunes by ancient scholars such as Jan d'Honger, and of dances (some to historical some to original tunes) that I have composed in between other projects in response to requests, challenges, needs, whim and inspirations. Some of the dances have become popular requests that I have simply not to date published elsewhere. A couple of the dances are so new they've not yet been danced and several of the compositions are so old I had forgotten about them until I found them recently. Together they might well have been called the 'nearly-lost dances'.

> The different dance entries and tunes are pretty well as I first set them out so are not all in a consistent format. To capture them in this little booklet before any more decide to go astray I decided to not wait till I have time to retest and rewrite them, but to publish them as they are.

> Though the style of these dances range from that of 1500 to that of 1900, to decorate the cover [the old cover illustrations have been reproduced in black and white on the title page] I have chosen two c.1800 hand coloured etchings from my own personal collection which I feel set the right tone for this collection of curiosities.

> Wishing you happy dancing, *John G-G* 22 March 2015

Occasionally in this new 2020 *Dance Delights* I refer to three other works I have authored. One is my just published 31-book study of historical dance, *Dancing through the Ages,* usually referring to it when I want to point the reader to further details on a particular dance form or dance (there being nearly 1,000 dances there described). The second is my two Volume *Lost Dances of Earthly Delights* collection from 15 to 20 years ago (each with 64 'recovered' dances)—some of the first dances in my *Odd Delights* were ones that just missed out on getting into those *Lost Dances* collections so have similar sources (left unexplained in this work but explained fully in the earlier work). The third is my *Christmas Carol Dance book* (with the 2020 edition having the 64 dances from the 2002 edition plus 8 extra ones). Some medley-like dances in this book include all or part of dances presented in my *Lost Dance* or *Christmas* collections, and when that is the case I don't always redescribe the dance in this book. So although nearly all the entries in this book include all you might need to know, it is not always the case and I hope the reader will eventually acquire copies of all my other works in order to have my full world of dance open up to them.

I would like to thank Sally Taylor for chording nearly all the tunes here presented, the dancers who in small groups have helped me try out draft versions of all the dances here presented, and all the dancers and musicians in our wider 'Earthly Delights' scene for supporting my continual introduction of new material, both my new historical reconstructions and my own new 'inventions'.

John G-G
25 August 2020

by John Gardiner-Garden

Abbreviations have been kept to a minimum. A1, A2, B1, B2 etc denote successive playings of successive tune strains or part strains—and their corresponding dance section. 1M, 1W etc denotes the first man and woman in a set, with the identity of 2M, 3W etc depending on set formation and number system specified. acw=anti-clockwise, cw=clockwise, l.o.d.=line of dance that runs acw around or straight up dance space, dsd=do-si-do (*dos à dos*). If and when used, l.f.=left foot, r.h.=right hand, l.sh.=left shoulder, etc, and step and figure abbreviations are derived from the first letters of the relevant period term.

Contents

~ On the dances ~

The 55 dances in this book range from the very simple to the very challenging, and range across many styles. Unlike in my *Lost Dances* collections, but as in my *Dancing through the Ages,* the dances in this book are arranged alphabetically so are not arrange from the easiest to the most challenging. In the table that follows, I try to group the dances by their level of challenge but how easy or otherwise any one person or group might find a dance will depend on many circumstances. The period style to which I have allocated dances is also very rough, as the dances are all original and I was usually not intending to channel a particular period style in every respect (i.e. formation, mechanism, figures and steps).

Style	Relatively easy	Moderately challenging	Challenging
16-17th century	Bright star Pastime in good company Schiarazula's Hey The Spanish Brawl	Branle de Montirande Ferrareze Fantasy Pavan & Galliard medley Die Zwelf Monet	Galliard Dating Mirror Measures—Heaven and Hell
18th century	Easter Thursday Rough Seas	Emma's Song Parlour Games The Recurring Dilemma Sechs Deutsche *or* Crossed Conversations	The Conundrum The Fleeting Moments Minuet The Social Obligations Minuet Wachet auf / Sleepers awake
19th century	Arcades and Alleyways The Corona Polka Sweet Bunch of Daisies Waltz Futsal	Carmen Habanera The Short Country Bumpkin The Lacework Mazurka Mazurian Anglaise or Courland Fancy Mazurian Ecossaise or Livonian Lilt Missing the Neighbours Polka Nationale Sechs Ecossaisen *or* Perpetual Motion Tempest through a looking glass The Waratah Polka Mazurka	The Australian Polka Mazurka The Bordonian National Polka (1) & (2) Five Steps to Heaven The Grand Polka Medley Holiday Holubiec The Marathon Mazurka medley Mazurka country dance medley The México Varsovienna medley My Markowski Mixup The New Iolanthe Schottische medley The Russian Gypsy Queen The Waratah Polka Mazurka The Wind-Up Galop The Zig-Zag Mazurka
Time-less	The Battle of Waterloo Lobster Quadrille	Knot à Trois The Rewind Waltz Stars of Joy	The Hambo Sandwich The Philosopher's Stone

~ On the music ~

The dances in this book are set or intended to be set to a wide range of different kinds of music, ranging across the centuries. Sometimes the dance is tailored to a particular tune or suite, and sometimes any tune of a certain type will do. The two are not mutually exclusive as sometimes even though I have set the dance to a particular tune, the dance could equally well be set to a different tune with the same feel and structure and sometimes even though I have said the dance can go to any tune of a certain kind I have preferences which I have recommended. Here is the list.

To Renaissance tunes or songs:

Branle de Montirande (in Michael Praetorius' 1612 *Terpsichore*)

Bright star ('Chiara Stella' in Fabritio Caroso's 1581 *Il ballarino*)

Ferrareze Fantasy Pavan & Galliard medley ('Pavane Ferrareze' and 'Gaillarde Ferrareze' in Pierre Phalèse's 1571 *Premer livre de danseries*)

Galliard Dating ('La Volta' tune collage from Michael Praetorius' 1612 *Terpsichore*

Mirror Measures—Heaven and Hell (Hieronymus Bosch's 'Garden of Earthly Delights' tune)

Pastime in Good Company (song ascribed to Henry VIII early 16th century)

Schiarazula's Hey (Giorigio Maniero's *Schiarazula Marazula,* published 1578)

The Spanish Brawl (form of *Gagliarda di Spagna* in 1581 and 1602 works of Caroso and Negri).

Die Zwelf Monet (a traditional Breton 'An Dro')

To Bach:

The Conundrum (bourrées 1&2 in movement 5 of cello suite no.4)

The Fleeting Moments Minuet (minuets 1&2 in movement 5 of cello suite no.1)

The Recurring Dilemma (bourrées 2 movement in no.5 in cello suite no.4)

Wachet auf / Sleepers awake (part of 1731 *Cantata*)

To other 18th century music:

Easter Thursday (unknown composer)

Emma's Song (George Frideric Handel's *Non lo dirò col labbro*)

Parlour Games (Jig in 1st Sonata of *Il Pastor Fido,* once ascribed to Vivaldi, now to Nicolas Chédeville).

To Beethoven:

Arcades and Alleyways (Contradance/Contredanse/Contretanz no.1 and 8 of WoO 14)

The Battle of Waterloo (Contradance/Contredanse/Contretanz no.4 of WoO 14)

Sechs Deutsche *or* **Crossed Conversations** (Deutsche no.1 to no.6 of WoO 42)

Sechs Ecossaisen *or* **Perpetual Motion** (Ecossaises no.1 to no.6 of WoO 83)

Stars of Joy ('Ode to Joy' / European Anthem- derived from Beethoven's Ninth Symphony)

To 19th century music:

The Australian Polka Mazurka (Armand Roekel, c.1860s)   cont. overleaf…

— John Gardiner-Garden, *Dance Delights*, 2020 —

The Carmen Quadrille (the 'Habanera' from George Bizet's 1875 *Carmen*).

Five Steps to Heaven (Conner, in *Home Circle*, 1857)

The Marathon Mazurka medley (4 tunes from Joseph Hart's c.1830 'First set of mazurkas')

Mazurka country dance medley (as above)

The México Varsovienna medley (Luis Abadie's 'México. Varsoviana', 1854')

My Markowski Mixup (Alfred St.Julien 'La Sicilienne', late 1850s)

The New Iolanthe Schottische medley (Popplewell Royle's mid-1890s 'Iola')

Polka Nationale (anonymous mid-19th century composer)

Sweet Bunch of Daisies (Anita Owen's 1894 song)

The Waratah Polka Mazurka (Daphne, possibly 1878).

The Wind-Up Galop (Charles Godrey, c.1871/2)

To any (though I may make suggestions):

The Corona Polka (32-bar polkas)

The Short Country Bumpkin (32-bar reel and/or jigs)

The Hambo Sandwich (32-bar hambos)

Holiday Holubiec (32-bar mazurkas)

Knot À Trois (32-bar landler, quick waltz or triple-time bourrée)

The Lacework Mazurka (32-bar mazurkas)

Mazurian Anglaise or Courland Fancy (32-bar mazurkas)

Mazurian Ecossaise or Livonian Lilt (32-bar mazurkas)

Missing the Neighbours (32-bar reels, jigs etc)

The Philosopher's Stone (one recommended tune is 'The Emperor of the Moon')

The Rewind Waltz (32-bar waltzes)

Rough Seas (32-bar hornpipe, e.g. The Sailor's Hornpipe' and 'Soldier's Joy')

The Russian Gypsy Queen (32-bar mazurkas)

The Social Obligations Minuet (24-bar minuet, e.g. 'Mr Priest's Minuet', 1711)

Tempest through a Looking Glass (32-bar reels, jigs etc)

The Zig-Zag Mazurka (32-bar mazurkas)

Waltz Futsal (any waltzes)

To tunes by myself (John Gardiner-Garden):

The Bordonian National Polka (1) & (2) (my 'Dudeslac Dawn', 'Lost Valley Day', 'Nenjira Sunset' and 'Tersichorean Night')

The Grand Polka medley (recommend my *Lost Dances of Earthly Delights* Court 7 'The Layman's Advice, The Madman's Counsel and the Idiot's inspiration'—but any set of 32 bar polkas should do).

Five Steps to Heaven (my 'Five Steps to Heaven', or any other five step waltz)

Lobster Quadrille (my namesake tune).

The Philosopher's Stone (one tune I recommend is my 'Earth Maiden's ruse')

~ On the medleys ~

Nearly all the 55 dances that have entries in this new *Dance Delights* edition are standalone dances featuring a sequence that can be enjoyed many times over. Six of the dances are, however, medleys of other dances by myself which I have tailored to a historical tune suite which might only be played through just once (or an adaptation of a tune set by myself). The six are as follows:

Ferrareze Fantasy Pavan&Galliard medley—dances from *Lost Dance* Volume 1&2 and *Christmas Carol Damce Book* to 'Pavane Ferrareze' and 'Gaillarde Ferrareze' (Pierre Phalèse's 1571)

The Grand Polka medley—dances from *Lost Dance* Volume 1&2 and *Dance Delights* to a structurally adapted playing of my *Lost Dances of Earthly Delights* Court 7 tunes.

The Marathon Mazurka medley—dances from *Lost Dance* Volume 1&2 and *Dance Delights* to 4 tunes from Joseph Hart's c.1830 'First set of mazurkas'.

Mazurka country dance medley—dances from *Dance Delights* to 4 tunes from Joseph Hart's c.1830 'First set of mazurkas'

The México Varsovienna medley—all from *Lost Dance* Volume 2 to Luis Abadie's 'México. Varsoviana', 1854'

The New Iolanthe Schottische medley—which mixes new ideas with 4 dances from *Lost Dance* Volume 1&2 all set to Popplewell Royle's mid-1890s 'Iola'

Most of the dances used in the above medleys are from my *Lost Dance* volumes (2015 edition), but some are from my *Dance Delights* (2020 edition) and from my *Christmas Carol Dance Book* (2002—with a new edition due late 2020). As these source works are presently available, as I hope you will one day acquire them all, and as I don't want to overload this book, I do not in five instances in this book redescribe the constituent already-published dances. In one instance, **Ferrareze Fantasy Pavan&Galliard medley**, I do redescribe the constituent parts because half the time the arrangement of the action in the parts is different from in the original.

Beside the above six medleys, I have over the years enjoyed putting together many other dance medleys in order to create fast moving displays and ballroom challenges. These medleys have been of two types.

The first type are medleys of historical dances that I have crafted to fit a historical tune or tune suite. I have included none of this kind in this book but have included in this book **My Markowski Mixup**, in which I combine modified version of half-a-dozen historical couples dance sequences to go to a historical tune suite. Because the constituent parts have been modified and designed to go to a single tune suite, I have described the parts, and the combination in is not so much a medley as a single original work.

The second type are short medleys of my own dances to my own music. As they have all proved thrilling additions to dance entertainments and in a way constitute 'Dance Delights' in their own right, I will summarise 29 such medleys on the next two pages. Most of these medleys were designed by myself between 2005 to 2008 and used in public performances by my group 'The Bordonian Heritage Dancers'. Others are medleys which I put together more recently and which have been performed in public by dancers from my Earthly Delights Historic Dance Academy. I hope you and your friends enjoy trying some! Please remember that full instructions for the dances that make up these medleys are available in the various indicated works, here I am offering just outlines.

In the outlines that follow the <u>underlining</u> indicates the tune set recommended, *italics* means I play on hurdy gurdy (rather than bagpipes), (sh) means a short choreography and 'P' means 'progressive' (i.e. unless decided otherwise, the dancers end the sequence progressed onto new partner). 'Spring', 'Summer', 'Autumn', 'Winter' refers to collections in *Lost Dances* Volume 1: Pleasures for Four Seasons. 'Village', 'Country', 'Town' and 'Court' to collections in *Lost Dances* Volume 2: Favourites for Four Settings. CCDB stands for *Christmas Carol Dance Book*, and *Dance Delights* refers to this book in hand.

The medleys described as 'for couples' include ones with dances that might normally include a progression onto a new partner. If you have a circle of couples you might want to preserve that progression, but if you don't or don't want the dancers changing partners partway through the medley, there is normally an easy obvious action you can do with your partner in lieu of progressing. Where the medley is mainly of couples dances but some of those dances require going into a group circle formation I have referred to the dance as 'for a circle of couples'. Where the dance is of a set nature I simply call them a 'Medley for x or y couples'.

With some of the outlined medleys that follow it is not just the constituent dances that are original but the way they connect to each other, and when that is the case (as for example with my '6 couple improper longways' contra medley) I have tried to briefly explained the transition mechanism.

~ Mazurkas for couples ~

Opposite foot MAZURKA
Boots and Blades (Autumn 14) x 2
Blackforest Mazurka (*Village 5*) x 2
Askance Romance (Town 13) x 2
(sh) Conjuring L'Amour (Cntry 12) x 2 P

Opposite foot MAZURKA
Regatta Room Grapple (*Country 15*) x 2
The Washing Machine (Court 14) x 2
Footloose Gypsy (Court 12) x 2
The Cavalier's Mazurka (Winter 14) x 1

Mixed foot MAZURKA 1
Barabarous Elegance (Court 2) x 2 (opp.f)
Ad Absurdam Sur Place (Vill. 15) x 2 P
Russian Tour (Town 4) x 2 (l.f.) P
(sh) Vulgarian Salut. (Vill. 2) x2 (l.f.) P

Mixed foot MAZURKA 2
(tune set never decided)
Russian Gypsy Queen (*Dance Delights*) x 2
Lacework Mazurka (*Dance Delights*) x 2
Zig Zag Mazurka (*Dance Delights*) x 2.

~ Polkas for couples ~

Opposite foot POLKA
(Option of couples galloping onto floor out of phase)
Loose Cannon Galop (Winter 7) x2
Grapevine Polka (*Village 3)* x2
Hot Cross Polka (Country 1) x2
Pyrotechnic Polka (Autumn 1) x2

Opposite foot 'Dance Delights' POLKA
The Corona Polka (*Dance Delights*) x 2
Wind-up Galop (*Dance Delights*) x 2
Bordonian National Polka 1 (*Dance Delights*) x 2
Bordonian National Polka 2 (*Dance Delights*) x 2

Mixed foot POLKA
Fast Forward (Cntry 7) x 2 (outside to l.f.)
Peek-a-boo Polka (Town 15) x 2 (l.f.) P
The Courtship Polka (Aut. 13) x2 (l.f.)
Wrong foot Polka (Aut. 10) x 2 (r.f.) P

~ Schottisches for couples ~

Left foot SCHOTTISCHE
Southern Highland Schott. (Cntry 4) x2
The Showdown Schott. (Town 10) x2
Switch, Swish and Swing (Court 13) x2
Reprise of Southern Highland Schott. x 1

~ Schottisches for circle of couples ~

Left foot group SCHOTTISCHE
Potluck Welcome (*Village 7*) x 2
Riverbank Ramble (Autumn 11) x 2
Taking Turns (Town 1) x 2
Reprise of Potluck Welcome x 1

Opposite foot SCHOTTISCHE
Short Easy Sotiisi (*Village 1*) x 2
Rise up Shepherd (CCDB) x2
Rudolph the Red-Nosed ... (CCDB) x2
Santa Clause is Coming … (CCDB) x 1
and dance off with the final turning step-hops.

~ Waltzes for couples ~

Left foot WALTZ
What Child is This (CCDB) x 1 P
Two to Twirl (Winter 6) x 1
The Little Landler (Country 3) x 2 P
The Grand Illusion (Town 2) x 2
Reprise of What Child is This x 1

Opposite foot WALTZ
The Alexandrina Waltz (Town 9) x 2 (P)
Hands off Waltz (Village 10) x2 (p)
Even Handed Ländler (Village 12) x 2 (P)
I Wonder as I Wander (CCDB) x2

~ Varsovienna for couples ~

Mixed foot VARSOVIENNA
La Va ouvert (Country 6) x2
La Va melangée (Court 9) x2
La Va croisée (Town 11) x2
La Va ouvert (Country 6) x1

~ Medleys for 3 or 4 couples ~

3 couple ROUND
Past, Present and Future
(Winter 4 ea. tune x1) x3
Northern Stars, Southern Skies
(Town 16 ea. tune x1) x 3

4 couple LONGWAYS 1
The Maze (Country 11) x 2
The Tapestry (Town 3) x 2
Snowball Slalom (Court 3) x 2

4 couples LONGWAYS 2
That Broad Road (Autumn 5) x 2
The Devil's Mill (Summer 9) x 4
A Delightful Play (Winter 9) x 1

4 couple SQUARE 1
There and Back Again (Court 1) 2 x each part
Longway Home (Summer 1) x 2 P
Where is Santa (CCDB) x 4

4 couple SQUARE 2
Four Baskets (Spring 15) x 2
Beau between Belles (Town 5) x 2

4 couple SQUARE 3
Turning the Table (Winter 5) x 2
Tangled Web (Winter 13) x 2 P

4 couple SQUARE 4
The Sweetheart Quadrille (Aut. 16) x 2
Birthday Treat (Country 8) x 2

~ Medleys for 6 or 7 couples ~

6 couple improper LONGWAYS
(start with column of 3 couples facing down
improper towards 3 couples proper facing up)
Middle facing couples start propagating **Alcuin's
Contra** (Village 16) and when they reach the end of
column, after waiting out 1 tune playing, one couple
re-enters introducing **Catapult Contra** (Country 14)
and the other re-enters introducing **Contra Quintain**
(Town 8) so for a moment 3 different contras are
danced simultaneously. When starting couple face
each other again they stop and others continue till
the snowball unravels.

6 or 7 couples KNOTTY SET
Lotsi's Spell (Spring 11) x 2
Ariadne's Thread (Village 14) x 2
Bridges of Konigsberg (Spring 10) x 2

~ Medleys for 8 couples ~

8 couple BECKETT to CIRCLE
Running the Gauntlet (Autumn 4) x 2
Jesus Born in Bethny (CCDB) x 2
then with the final promenade change set from
column to double circle for…
Sun and Moon Allemande (Cntry 16) x 2
Three Baskets (Village 4) x 2

8 couple SPOKES to CIRCLE
Great Roundabout (Town 12) version 1 x 2
Great Roundabout (Town 12) version 2 x 2
then transition into double circle for…
Choreographer's Fancy (Winter 1) x 4 P

8 couples proper LONGWAYS
The Battering Ram (Autumn 7) x 2
The Giant's Backbone (Country 2) x 2
Round with Corners (Court 10) x 3

8 couple BOURRÉE
The Labyrinth (Autumn 12) x 2
then break into 2 squares, each of 4 couples for….
Quarter Short Square (Winter 3) x 2
Burley Griffin Bourrée (Country 13) x2

8 couple GALOP
(We nick named this medley the 'Suicide Galop')
Near Miss Galop (Autumn 8) x 2
ending 'squashing' set into shape for…
Baltic Crossing (Village 13) x 2
ending in 'beckett' column for…
Daring Damsel (Village 11) x 2
ending 'squashing' into close facing lines for…
The Dashing Dragoon (Court 15) x 2

Right foot MINUET
My Lady's Minuet (Town 14) x 2 P
My Lord's Minuet (Court 11) x 2 P
Whirl of Memories Minuet (Court 16) x 2
Whirl of Memories Waltz (Crt 16) x 2

~ Hambos for circle of couples ~

(sh) Handfasting Hambo (Country 10) x 2
(sh) Harmony Hambo (Town 7) x 2 P
(sh) Honeymoon Hambo (Court 5) x 2
Repeat pattern until end of music.

The
dances

~ Arcades and Alleyways ~

Form a meszolanze set, with each downward facing rank of as many couples as will (the 1s) facing an upward-facing rank (the 2s)—all ranks with the same number of couples, women on right of partner.

Start either foot.

Dance as a giant mescolanze.

Middle ranks propagating out the following figure:
A1 All r.sh. dsd. opp. *while* line 1 arch over 2s / the 2 long lines join hs in circle and circle l. (cw) as far as will with 8 steps
A2 groups circle b. to r. (acw) w. the same / all l.sh. dsd. opp. *while* line 2 arch up over 1s
B1 W advance to M; take 2 hs and draw M toward her line / 2h cw t.
B2 M slip right; M fall b. *while* W advance into wave / M slip left *while* W fall b. into holding hs in rank, all advance and pass opp. by r.sh. to face new rank.
N.B. When a cpl. reach the end of column they should wheel about.
All x n.

Play any double-time 32 bar AABB tune x n. I particularly recommend Beethoven's Contredances no.1 and no. 8 from his Twelve Contradances for small orchestra (WoO 14), the relevant extracts from *Zwölf Contretänze von L. van Beethoven*, Ludwig van Beethoven's Werke Serie 2. No.17a, Breitkopf & Härtel, Leipzig, 1864, appearing at the end of this entry. For no.1 the violin 1 line offers the clearest melody, but for no. 8 both the oboe and the violin 1 offer strong melodies, so I have written them both out in this transcription below of no.8, either for part playing or for use on different playings. For more variety still, add to the medley Contredanse no. 4 from the same Beethoven collection, used for **Battle of Waterloo** (in this same book).

No.1

No.8

— John Gardiner-Garden, Dance Delights, 2020 —

A1	All <u>right shoulder do-si-do opposite</u> but downfacing <u>rank 1</u> do so *while* <u>holding hands and arching over those in line 2</u> <u>facing long ranks join hands in circle</u> and circle as far to left as possible (cw) with 8 steps
A2	<u>Circle back to the right</u> (acw) with 8 steps <u>All left shoulder do-si-do</u> *while* those facing up in rank 2 hold hands and <u>arch</u> over original opposites
B1	With 4 steps <u>W advance to opposite M</u> then <u>take 2 hs and with 4 steps draw M toward her line</u> With 8 steps <u>2 hand cw turn the same opposite</u> (in jagged line so each pair has an overlapping alignment with partner's pair beside them) ending ready to catapult M on reverse trajectory and let go
B2	<u>Men take 4 sliding steps (one man's position) to right</u>, passing with his back to the front of his partner *while* passing the one man who was opposite his partner belly-to-belly, <u>then with 4 steps men fall back while the women go forward and take hands in a giant wave</u> along the middle of the set The <u>men take 4 slip steps back to left</u> passing behind partner's back *while* women <u>push off each other and fall back and let their hands be taken by the men to each side</u> (her palms down his up, her partner back on her left side) <u>then with 2 steps the ranks advance</u> towards each other <u>and</u> letting go <u>with 2 steps all pass the opposite by the right shoulder.</u>
AABBxn Continue till all back in original position or till music stops.	

This dance was partly inspired by the *Tempête* in Th. Helmke's *Allgemeine Tanzkunst,* Stralsund, 1836 (presented in my entry on **La Tempête (2)** in Volume VIII of my *Dancing through the Ages* book series), partly inspired by the 'Arcaden-dos à dos' figure which Eduard Friedrich David Helmke calls for in a *La Tempête* choreography in his *Almanach der neuesten Modetänze fur das Jahr 1832*, Merseburg, 1832 pp.273-75, and partly inspired by **The Gothic Dance** in Elias Howe, *American dancing master and ball-room prompter,* Boston, 1862, p.129, which I presented in Volume IX of my *Dancing through the Ages* and which I saw as using the same 'Arcaden-dos-à-dos'. My first incarnation of the dance 5 years ago was called 'Arcade Encounters' (in my 2015 *Odd Delights* edition) and turned into my 2015 **The Battle of Waterloo** (see entry further below). This dance has ended up different from both of those dances, but as with the latter I've decided to recommend setting it to a Beethoven contredancetune. Indeed, you can do this dance in the same giant *mescolanze* formation that I recommend for **The Battle of Waterloo** and if you like you can for this dance make a medley of the two Beethoven contradances, both being 32 bars long with an AABB structure.

I call the dance a *mescolanze* (from Greek for 'mix-up') because that was the name of the early 19th century dance form which crossed the newly popular quadrille with the progressive longways country dance. Like a quadrille, a *mescolanze* involved couple-facing-couple figures, and like a country dance it involved passing though couples above or below to repeat the sequence from progressed position. In a normal *mescolanze* there are just 2 couples in each rank, but I thought, if you have the right figures and a large dance crowd, why contain a rank to 2 couples? Why not have the rank stretch all the way across the room. So as in **The Battle of Waterloo**, I have designed the figures in this dance to work in ranks of many couples as you like. Although it is possible to start this dance in the same snowball way as in that dance, as we are not trying to recreate a battle I recommend beginning with every rank facing another and start the dance with simultaneous action.

I called this dance 'Arcades and Alleyways' as in the A1 and A2 the dancers make use of Helmke's 'Arcaden-dos à dos' figure, rank 1 making the arches when doing the right shoulder do-si-do and the rank 2 making them when doing the left shoulder do-si-do, and as in the B1 and B2 the dancers move through narrow spaces on both a vertical and a horizontal axis as if slipping through side alleys. I'm pleased how I managed to use the offsetting of couples in the first half of A1 to give an opportunity to two hand turn the opposite with more space than you would if all in the original ranks as well as position dancers perfectly for the sideways box the men are about trace as individuals cw about own partner. I'm please how that box starts with the women helping the men reverse momentum from the preceding 2 hand turn (as if she is catapulting him into sideways action) and I'm pleased how the box ends with the man's hands collecting the women's hands from behind and below. I'm also pleased how the women have an opportunity to overlap with the men's sideways box, a going into and pushing back out of a women's wave in the space between the two ranks.

Although the dance was conceived of as one for a large number of dancers, if you only have enough dancers for 2 ranks of 2 couples, you can still enjoy it. After passing through, you vert quickly resume inside hand hold with partner and wheel with your partner about—but rather than wheeling 180 degrees about to repeat with same opposites, wheel 90 degrees to face former neighbours and to take hands in a new vertical rank with former opposites. This way each couple gets to dance with 2 other couples, as dancing couples progress cw or acw around the set (for those progressing acw the wheel will feel natural with the woman going forward but for those progressing cw the wheel will feel a little unnatural as the man needs to go forward so in that as you may want to manoeuvre as individuals to face new direction but not take hands till doing so.

Below are Contradance no.1 and 8 as Beethoven arranged them for small orchestra and as published in *Zwölf Contretänze von L. van Beethoven*, Ludwig van Beethoven's Werke Serie 2. No.17a, Breitkopf & Härtel, Leipzig, 1864. These were among the nine contradances from this collection for which Beethoven later wrote piano versions (not included here). No.1 is said to date from c.1791 and no. 8 possibly from c.1802.

1.

8.

~ The Australian Polka Mazurka ~

Form couples in ballroom hold.

Start opposite feet, man left woman right.

Dance as appropriate to chosen music.

Play Armand Roeckel's 'The Australian Polka Mazurka', Sydney, J.R. Clarke, 1863, transcribed below, full score (with 12 -bar coda) at end.

A1 *Waltz* 7 cw turning polka-redowas along l.o.d. then 'and-hold-' to present sh. & r.f. to the l.o.d. **A2** Cnterpart starting over sh. w. other f.

B1 *Prom.* w. long hobble sequence x 2 but instead of last polka redowa do 2 stamps-pose to present sh. to l.o.d. **B2** Cnterpart (still cw)

A *Waltz* with 7 polka-redowas and step-pivot.

C1 *Prom.* w. polka redowas in open waist-sh. hold but on last bar 2 M pass W across and take 2 stamps **C2** Cnterpart starting new outside f.

D1 *Mazurka holubiec* wheel acw in waist-sh. hold w. M as pivot doing 2x deep *assemblé-plié-sissone* (w. *rond de jambe*) *while* W f. w. 2 x 2 quick steps-hop; 3 steps to pass to other arm and 2 stamps--point new out. f. / cw M again the pivot **D2** Repeat acw & cw (or cnterpart cw&acw w. W as pivot)

C3 *Prom.* w. polka redowas but last bar step & strike outside f. w. ptner's.

Repeat all then A again plus 4 bars during which you do slow step together while turning W out under M's raised l.h. to face then 2 steps as you bow.

♩ = 140

A1	*Waltz* (fig.1) 7 cw turning <u>polka-redowas</u> (i.e. glide-cut-leap x 7 along l.o.d.) then '<u>and-hold-'</u> <u>to present shoulder and right foot</u> to the l.o.d.
A2	<u>Counterpart starting over shoulder with other foot</u>
B1	*Promenade* with <u>long hobble sequence</u> (3 glide-cut-hop + 1 glide-cut-leap turning cw) x 2 but instead of last polka redowa do <u>2 stamps</u>-pose to present shoulder to l.o.d.
B2	<u>Counterpart, still cw</u>
A	*Waltz* with 7 <u>polka-redowas</u> and <u>step-pivot</u>.
C1	*Promenade* with <u>polka redowas in open waist-shoulder hold but on last bar 2 M pass W across and take 2-stamps</u>
C2	<u>Counterpart starting with new outside foot</u>
D1	*Mazurka* <u>holubiec</u> wheel acw in waist-sh. hold with man as pivot doing 2x deep *assemblé-plié-sissone* (with *rond de jambe*) *while* W f. w. 2 x 2 quick steps-hop, then 3 steps to pass to other arm and 2 stamps--point new outside foot
	Wheel cw with the same footwork (but starting on other foot) and M again the pivot
D2	<u>Repeat acw & cw *or* counterpart cw and acw with W as pivot</u>
C3	*<u>Promenade</u>* <u>with polka redowas but in last bar step and strike outside foot with partner's.</u>
AABBACCDDC again — Repeat all then A again plus 4 bars during which you do slow step together while turning W out under M's raised left hand to face then 2 steps as you bow.	

The dances in this collection are arranged in alphabetic so being the second dance in this book does mean it's the second easiest. If you are used to couples dancing and are up for a very pleasant challenge then do try it but if you are not then I suggest you just enjoy reading the notes that follow. Every dance tells a fascinating story, so I'm all for reading about dances even if not dancing them! For pointers to dances you can try that are relatively easy or only moderately challenging, please see the table in my introductory 'On the dances' section.

As I have discussed under 'The Mazurka' in Part 1b of my *Dancing through the Ages* Volume VII and VIII, in Western Europe the mazurka evolved not just quadrille forms but also different turning couples dance forms. The 'Polka mazurka', as I discuss under 'The Polka Mazurka' in Part 1b of *Dancing through the Ages* Volume IX, was the couples dance form in which the mazurka enjoyed most widespread popularity.

There are many descriptions of the 'Polka mazurka' from the last years of the 1850 and from throughout the 1860s, and I have presented half-a-dozen of these in my on **Polka Mazurka (2)** in *Dancing through the Ages* Volume IX, but those descriptions are all of a short sequence that has 1 or 3 mazurka-like hobble travelling steps followed by 1 polka-like steps to turn half about, so it seems strange that that dance in that late 1850s-1860s period is called a 'Polka mazurka' when the mazurka element comes before the polka. Indeed, Friedrich Zorn called the tune he supplied for that dance and which I offered as a possible setting in my **Polka Mazurka (2)** entry, 'Mazurka-Polka'. Even if a simple inversion of the parts doesn't quiet explain the name, as the 'glide-cut-hop', though somewhat mazurka-like, is not the most typical of the mid-19th century mazurka steps. More typical mazurka travelling steps in the mid-19th century were hop-glide-hops or hop-glide, cuts, and more distinguishing still of the mazurka was the *tour sur place* and there's no sign of that in either the short or long version of the **Polka Mazurka (2)**. The clue as to why the dance was called Polka Mazurka may lie in the earliest description I have found of the dance. That is one found in J. Kurth, *Der gewandte Ball-und Vortänzer*, Erfurt, c. 1854, pp 32-34 (facsimile from my collection at the end of this entry).

Kurth's Polka Mazurka is a much longer sequence than the alternation of hobbles and half-turns that came to be associated with the name just a few years later. That was effectively just the middle ('promenade') figure in Kurth's three-part dance. Kurth's first figure was an uninterrupted turning of the couple as if polka-ing in triple time, and his last figure was a side-by-side wheel (which he calls 'waltz') in place, as if doing the *holubiec* from the mazurka. Thus we have the Polka and a truly characteristic Mazurka in the right order. Curiously, the two figures that most gave rise to the name of the dance seem to have faded from the dance which ended up surviving under that name. How quickly the first and the last part faded is hard to determine. Kurth noted that the **Musik zu diesem Tanz ist in jeder guten Musikalienhandlung zu finden** ('The music for this dance is found in any good music shop') and there are indeed dozens of good polka-mazurka piano scores that survive. Many of these are suggestive of patterns that go well beyond the simple alternation of one or three hobbles and a half-turn. I offer in transcription above and facsimile below a score in my collection that seems capable of being a setting for all four of the figures Kurth describes (he names three figures but gives alternate for the 2nd figure). It is Armand Roeckel's 'The Australian Polka Mazurka', published in Sydney sometime in the 1860s (transcription above, full score below). Its different parts seem ideal settings for the different figures Kurth describes—its A strain for Kurth's Figure 1 'Waltz' (turning polka-redowas), its B for Kurth's Figure 2 'Promenade' using combinations of 3 glide-cut-hop hobbles and 1 turning polka-redowa), its C for Kurth's Alternate Figure 2 'Promenade' using polka-redowa steps, and its D strain for Kurth's Figure 3 'Waltz' as in wheeling mazurka *holubiec*.

I'll not here offer my transcription and translation of Kurth's instructions nor reconstruction of the dance they suggest—for that see my entry on **Polka Mazurka (1)/The Australian** in of my *Dancing through the Ages* Volume IX. Here I will offer my own polka mazurka sequence inspired by Kurth's figure order and tailored to fit Roeckel's score.

In my dance above I've tried to contain myself to variants of Kurth's figures and start every new part with the man on the proper side, with opposite feet free and with any turning about to go cw. In order to make a satisfying dance that compliments the music I've punctuated some sequences with a 2-stamp *'pas finale'*, contriving to have counterparts start on opposite foot (even if going same way) and, to the D strain. I've also introduced the possibility that turning (waltz) in A2 may go in the opposite direction to in A1 and that the wheeling (mazurka) in D2 may go in opposite direction to in D1. With respect the D strain *holubiec* the combination of starting foot and music have led me to suggest three differences between the *holubiec* here and that I have described under Mazurka figures in Part 1c of *Dancing through the Ages* Volume VIII and under **Mazurka (2)** of that same Volume. For a full discussion of these difference see my entry on **Polka Mazurka (1)/The Australian** in of my *Dancing through the Ages* Volume IX.

If you want more choreographies to set to Armand Roeckel's 'The Australian Polka Mazurka' you might use my 32 bar 'Black Forest Medley' and 'Askance Romance' (Village 5 and Town 13 respectively in my *Lost Dances of Earthly Delights*, vol.2: *Favourites for Four Settings*) to the AABB and CCDD respectively of Roeckel's tune, with the reprise of the A being 8 plain polka-redowas and the reprise of the CC being 8 plain short polka-mazurkas. If you play the tune another time you could set to it my 'Cavalier's Mazurka' (Winter 14 in *Lost Dances of Earthly Delights*, vol.1: *Pleasures for Four Seasons*), which is also based on polka-mazurka footwork and any other of my 32 mazurka sequence (even if not based on polka-mazurka footwork). For descriptions of the Polka Mazurka once it shed its opening polka-redowa and concluding *holubiec*, and for more tunes that can be enjoyed, see my entry that follows on **Polka Mazurka (2)**.

For another interestingly structured Polka Mazurka tune to which I have set an adventurous (but *holubiec*-free) sequence, see my entry und **The Waratah Polka Mazurka** in this *Dance Delights*.

— 32 —

Da nun die Figuren oder Touren nach Zeichnungen sich leichter erkennen lassen, als nach Beschreibung, so verweise ich auf folgende Abbildungen.

1. La Polka à la Paris.

Paris, Jeunnin, Editeur, place du Louvre 20.

Wien, bei L. T. Neumann.

Berlin, bei Gebrüder Rocca.

2. La nouvelle Polka à la Berlin.

Berlin, Lith. Anstalt von Stentz.

---

7. Polka Mazurke. ($^3/_8$ Takt.)

Siehe Tafel IV. Fig. 3.

Ist der Polka mit Figuren ganz ähnlich, indem auch jedes Paar für sich die Figuren ausführt, in Abwechselung von 16 Takten im Kreise herum.

Die Touren sind:

1. Polkabewegung in Walzerform.
2. Promenade.
3. Valse.

3 Arten Pas kommen vor. Pas zur 1. Tour: Der Herr fängt mit dem linken Fuß an und die Damen mit dem rechten Fue, wie zur Polka. Die 3 Tempo dieses ersten Pas

Fig 3

Beschreibung Seite 52.

— 33 —

bestehen 1stens aus einem degagé des l. F. des Hrn., für die Dame des r F., indem man schief vorwärts gleitet. 2tens aus einem coupé dessous mit dem r. F für den Herrn, für die Dame des l. F. 3tens aus einer Bewegung mit dem l. F. der Herr und die Dame mit dem rechten Fuße à la jeté, und sich eindrehen der Hr zum Walzer, wodurch die Dame auf die andere Seite des Herrn kömmt. Nun fängt der Herr mit dem rechten und die Dame mit dem linken Fuße an u. f. w.

N. B. Das Eindrehen zur Walzerbewegung hat allemal dasjenige, welches auf die Herrenseite gekommen ist.

Pas zur 2. Tour: Der Herr fängt mit dem linken Fuß, indem er die 2 ersten Tempos des einfachen Walzers begleitet, von einem fouetté nach rückwärts ausführt, und ganz ebenso mit demselben Fuße die 3 Bewegungen des einfachen Walzer beginnt, und 6 Tempo also 2 Takte vervollständigt.

Zu dieser Promenade kann man auch Pas 1. nehmen

Pas zur 3. Tour: Wird gemacht, indem man sich auf dem Platze herumdreht, wie in ur Mazurka, d. h. im entgegengesetzten Sinne, doch links. Diese Herumdrehungen auf dem Platze, werden mit dem l. F. für den Herrn und mit dem rechten Fuße für die Damen ausgeführt

— 34 —

Diese 3 Arten von Pas zur Polka Mazurke folgen und wechseln ab ins Unendliche.

Musik zu diesem Tanz ist in jeder guten Musikalienhandlung zu finden.

The AUSTRALIAN Polka Mazurka ROECKEL.

AUSTRALIAN POLKA
MAZURKA

ARMAND ROECKEL

2
ff
Ped
ff
grazioso
Expressione
TRIO
dolce
mf
Australian Polka Mazurka

ff
fff Ped ff
Ped p
ff
ff
1a
2a
Expressione
dolce
Ped
Ped
ff
Allegro
staccato
Ped
Ped
Ped
Ped
Ped
Ben marcato
ff
ff Ped
fff Ped
ralian Polka Mazurka

~ The Battle of Waterloo ~

Form a grand mescolanze with 2, 3 or 4 ranks of 4, 6 or 8 side-by-side couples (W on right of M) on one left side of hall (1s) facing same on right side of hall (2s), middle ranks facing each other across a gap that runs down centre of hall, others lined up behind. Identify and don't hold hands in centre of ranks so dancers know who should lead behind on grand *chassé croissé*. Ideal, is 4 ranks of 8 couples on one side of hall facing same on other (i.e. 64 couples, 128 individual dancers).

Middle ranks propogating out:

A1 F & clap 2 hs w. opp.; fall b. & take hs w. neigh / grand *chassé croissé* (inside M leading behind)

A2 F & clap w. same opp.; fall b. & taks hs / *chassée* home

B1 Dsd opp. r.sh. / pass r.sh. catching hs in sh.-height wave w. opp.s; push b.

B2 Dsd same l.sh. dsd. under / pass into wave w. opp.s; push b. 2 counts and pull f. & thru w. 2 counts.

All x n.

Start either foot.

Dance with middle facing ranks followed by all the others snowballing to opposite wall, turning about as couples when waiting out near wall, back through middle towards own wall, turning about again, then heading back toward middle and stopping when they arrive home.

Play any double-time 32 bar AABB tune till all back in place, my preference being Beethoven's Contredanse no.4 (WoO 14 no.4), and if you have 3 ranks on each side, play the tune x13 for front ranks to start, then action to snowball and unravel till all are back in original place on original side.

Here is a freely available piano transcription of the same:

— John Gardiner-Garden, *Dance Delights*, 2020 —

A1	With 3 walking steps and pause go <u>forward directly towards opposite and clap 2 hands with them,</u> <u>then</u> (with same steps as before) <u>fall back and take hands with neighours in two long facing lines</u>. Grand *chassé croisé* <u>with</u> each rank dividing so upper and lower halves can slip past each other (with 7 little glissades and a step-close), <u>whichever half is led by man going behind</u>.
A2	<u>Same as in A1</u>: forward, clap, fall back into broken lines and *chassé* home (<u>other half being led by</u> <u>inside man behind</u>)
B1	With 8 walking steps <u>do-si-do opposite by right shoulder</u> With 4 walking steps and with hands held at shoulder-height side (nearly pass) opposite by right shoulder *while* catching right hand with that opposite and left hand with corner to all have all elbows bent and arms pressing in a wave, then (with same steps) push back
B2	<u>With same steps as in B1 do-si-do opposite by left shoulder</u> then forward into left shoulder raised-hand wave, but just push back for only one bar (with 2 steps) and retain hands so as to be able to swing them down and pull through (with same step) in last bar
	Continue till all back in original position, stopping when you arrive there.

This dance came out of the need for a whole-hall involving dance for a '200 years since the Battle of Waterloo' ball we were holding at Canberra's Albert Hall on the 11 April 2015 as part of our Jane Austen Festival Australia. I conceived of a dance that could bring everyone in that magnificent historic hall into one set and orient them as if drawn up for battle—and I thought of a grand mescolanze turned on its side (much as I had already conceived of for **Arcade Encounters** written earlier and presented above. Instead of ranks of just 2 couples as in a normal mescolanze, we would have ranks of 4, 6 or, hopefully, 8 couples, and instead of the ranks being oriented across the hall as normally expected, they would run the length of it—so from the stage it should look like two arms lined up for battle. To suggest a battle, I have had the engagement progress from an opening volley of claps to some side slipping manoeuvring involving a 'grand-scale' *chassé croissé* with 2, 3 or 4 side-by-side couples go each way, followed by a repeat of this, then on to a full engagement with do-si-dos and a push back to place, then a repeat which ends in a breaking through to next rank.

Envisaging the dance as one for a very large crowd, recommend simple walking steps when not slipping sideways on the *chassé croissé.*

With respect the figures I have made them simple ones that can be done with very long ranks—and indeed suggest that ranks of 8 couples (16 dancers—the limit for a grand *chassé croissé*) would be ideal. This means the opening engagement would be between 32 dancers—coincidently the number of dancers in the special large-formation quadrille which the Hereditary Prince of Orange enjoyed at his February 1815 party in Brussels. This dance was reported on by both Lady Caroline Capel (*The Capel Letters*, ed. by The Marquess of Anglesey, 1955, p.83) and Lieutenant Colonel Basil Jackson (*Notes and Reminiscences of a Staff Officer: Chiefly Relating to the Waterloo*, chap.1)—see my discussion in my 2020 *Dancing thorough the Ages* Volume VII, Part 1.

With respect the music, I wanted the dance to commemorate the battle rather than celebrate it, so wanted to avoid music with any nationalistic or martial overtones. My choice fell to a Beethoven *contretanz*. Beethoven had lived through the Napoleonic war era, was a man with utopian political ideals, his *An die Freude* ('Ode to Joy') was chosen in 1985 to be the European Anthem, and his *contretänze* are in a dance form popular at the time and eminently danceable. Although my choreography could go to any double-time 32 bar played AABB tune, my strong preference is for Beethoven *contretanz* no.4, from his series of 12 *contretänze*. These compositions have been dated between 1791 and 1802 with No. 4 date to late 1801, some 14 years before the Battle of Waterloo and perhaps 20 years ahead of the height of the mescalanze craze in Britain, but close enough to be an appropriate setting. Note, the above scores have the 'e' in the upbeat at the beginning of and half-way through the B strain natural, but some transcriptions leave it flat, and that works fine as well.

Here is a transcription for small orchestra published in *Zwölf Contretänze von L. van Beethoven*, Ludwig van Beethoven's Werke Serie 2. No.17a, Breitkopf & Härtel, Leipzig, 1864.

~ The Bordonian National Polka (1) & (2) ~

Form couples in ballroom hold.

Start outside f.t, M's left foot W right foot

Dance each variant x 4 or *ad.lib.*

Play ea. tune x 2

1) perhaps x 4 to 1st 2 tunes
- **A1** Point-tap, polka ½ cw; again / 2 galops, 3 polkas **A2** Cntrprt (start sh.)
- **B1** M (on inside) drop to knee and lassoo W cw / 3 polkas, 2 pivots
- **B2** Cntrpart: M (on outside) to knee and lasso W cw / start polkas over sh.

All x n

2) perhaps x 4 to 2nd 2 tunes
- **A1** *Balonné* kicking free out&b., polka ½; 2 slow glissades / t. w. 4 step hops/clicks **A2** Repeat starting over sh.
- **B1** W rev. M; M t. W under raised l.h. to swap places / M rev. W; M pir. W over l.sh., both tremble **B2** W flees, he follows and taps her r.sh. w. his l.h., she t. over r.h. to be caught in ballroom hold / 2 polkas; W t. out, M drop to knee&spring up

All x n

Dudelsac Dawn

♩ = 120

2/4

Gm B♭ F C Gm B♭ F C

B♭ F D C Gm F Gm F E♭ F Gm D

1.   *2.*

Lost Valley Day

Dm C B♭ A Gm C C A

Gm C Gm B♭ A Dm A Edim A A⁷

1.   *2.*

Nenjira Sunset

G G C C G G C C

Em⁷ Em⁷ Am⁷ Am⁷ Em⁷ Em⁷ Am⁷ Am⁷

G G C C F G G C C

Terpsichorean Night

Cm G Cm Dm D Cm Gm Cm D Cm A♭

1.   *2.*   end only

G G Cm A♭ G G G Cm

— John Gardiner-Garden, *Dance Delights*, 2020 —

or with fuller piano chords:

Dudelsac Dawn

Lost Valley Day

Nenjira Sunset

Terpsichorean Night

	~ Part 1 ~
A1	In 1st bar, point outside foot out to 2nd position, then cut it back in and up to tap against the inside of partner's foot, with next bar polka as a couple ½ cw, then with next 2 bars do same back starting with other foot.
	With next 4 bars do 2 galops along l.o.d., closing rear to front foot after the second, and with the next 3 bars polka as a couple 1½ cw, to finish in exchanged places presenting shoulders to l.o.d.
A2	Repeat on other foot, back to place

B1	M drops to his r.knee (weight mostly on l.foot) retaining W's right hand in his left and W goes (or is 'lassoo-ed') with 4 polka steps behind then in front of him and goes cw around him back to place, M rising transferring weight on to his r.f. on 4th bar With the next 3 bars to polka as a couple 1 ½ then on last bar to pivot once around with 2 steps, finishing in exchanged places presenting shoulders to l.o.d.
B2	Repeat on other foot—M dropping to l.knee (weight mostly on r.f.) retaining W's right hand in his left, W going (again) cw around him, then M rising transferring weight onto l.f. to starting the couples polka with r.f. over the shoulder and finishing either with 2 pivots if going to repeat part or a dramatic *assemblé* and hop on r.f. and fouetté with l.f. if going to go on to Part II.
	~ Part 2 ~
A1	Kick outside foot out to raised fourth, cut back in to raised 3rd to *balonné*, polka ½ way, 2 slow slides over sh. along l.o.d. then do 4 step-hop clicks to turn twice around and with each hop do a heel click, finishing cutting new free foot up to raised 3rd ready for kick out.
A2	Repeat above but in exchanged roles, starting with opposite foot and finishing M swinging a little further forward across in front of woman so as to start to present back to the l.o.d.
B1	With 2 polka steps W reverses (or 'backs') M on his l. diagonal *while* W advances on her r.diagonal, then M goes back on his r. *while* W advances on her l., then next 2 polka steps M turns W under his raised l.h. (her r.h.), and goes acw ½ around to exchange places. With 2 polka steps M reverses (or 'backs') W, M forward on his l.diagonal *while* W back on her r.diagonal, then M forward on his r. *while* W back on her l., then with 1 polka M turns W under his raised l.h. (her r.h.), but instead of changing places, they face each other, W back to l.o.d. M facing l.o.d., release hands and *polka tremblante* bouncing 3x on toes.
B2	With 4 polka steps W turns back over her r.sh. and goes off along the l.o.d. pursued by the M, who on the 3rd bar taps the W on her r.sh. with his l.h. and she responds on the 4th bar by raising her r.h. and starting to turn cw over her r.sh. M then he takes her right hand with his left and they take ballroom hold and with 2 polka steps they turn cw as a couple and then with 1 polka step she turns out under his raised l.h. (her r.h.), and on final bar they face each other with a dramatic stomp M with r.f. W's l.f.—and as he does so M drops quickly to l. knee then bounce back up onto r.f.) cutting l.f. back to shin as they hop on same back foot and take ballroom hold.
N.B.	If man does not want to do the drop to the knee in Part 2's B2 he might just do as woman does, i.e. stomp back foot (right for him, left for her) then standing dramatically tall draw front foot back to shin, ready to recommence Part 2 with its A1 *balonné* or recommence Part 1 with its point and cut.

[**N.B.** These dances just missed out on getting into the 2005 *Lost Dances of Earthly Delights* Volume 2, so for the background that is assumed in the 2015 notes that follow, see my *Lost Dances volumes*]

No Bordonian dance has had a greater influence abroad. These polkas came to influence the work of many 19th European and American dancing masters. The opening foot work of each part/version came to be echoed in dances such as 'Zulma l'Orientale' (see entry in *Dancing through the Ages* Volume IX). We see Part 1's 2 galops and 3 polka turns and drop to the knee figures in the Esmeralda (2) and mazurka figures respectively (see *Dancing through the Ages* Volume IX). We see Part 2's *coup de talon* in the 'Polish Galop' recorded by Gilbert in 1888 (see *Dancing through the Ages* Volume X) and the reversing of each other and the W fleeing in 'The Pursuit' and 'The Coquet'—two polkas found in many late 19th century manuals (see *Dancing through the Ages* Volume VIII and IX).

In Bordonia itself there was no dance, indeed no issue, that caused more dissention and communal division. It brought the Bordonians close to civil war. There was never any disagreement about figures, music or origins. The figures were danced identically in both Nenjira centred west Bordonia and Dudelsac centred east Bordonia, the dance went equally well to regular length hurdy-gurdy or bagpipe polkas, and all agreed the dance was composed in the capital Terpsichore by the mid-19th century dancing master Jan D'Honger at a time when Bordonians were at some risk of losing their identity under a wave of foreign influences. Coming from neither the west or the east but from the centrally located capital the dance initially had an unify effect on Bordonians—but then people started to argue over which part came first. It was not simply that all those from the one side or other of the country wanted the music suited to their favoured instrument played first, for some of them though it more prestigious if it were played last. The divide on the issue did not therefore translate into open warfare between regions, but it did start to divide members of the same town district, same village, same workplace, same dance school, same family, and the soon families were splitting, dance schools breaking in two, workplaces becoming dysfunctional and a large sector of the population found themselves on the move. But where were they to move to? A resolution had to be found, and it was decided it would be in the form of a competition to decide once and for all which order of parts worked best—a competition in the form of a dance off. Angry, displaced and aggrieved folk from all over Bordonia descended on the capital, and those who could not squeeze into one side or other of the palace ballroom took to one side or other of the cities central square. In both venues musicians converged on a medley of polka tunes equally suited to the abundant bagpipes and hurdy-gurdies—with the other string and reed players all prepared to play along. When it came to the appointed hour to commence, everyone realised one matter had remained unresolved, who, out of the bagpipers and hurdy-gurdy players, should go first. By that stage however, it was too late. The musicians inside and outside the palace started playing and everyone started dancing the polka in the order they preferred. Dancers almost immediately started bumping into each other. Those dancing the Part 2 three slides bowling over those doing the second Part 1 point and tap. Those dancing the Part 2 pursuit were reversing into those doing the Part 1 kneeling man, those doing the final Part 1 pivot were skittling those doing the final Part 2 assemble and fouette. By a third of the way through the set, however, something miraculous started to happen. Dancers started to enjoy the challenge of avoiding each other, and were taking pleasure in doing the chasing coquette around those doing the genuflection, and were enjoying the syncopations resulting from the rising sounds of overlapping steps. In the last third of the dance, people were so enjoying the ordered chaos that they were adding to it by break from doing the bended knee of Part 1 to chase a passing lady doing the coquette in Part 2, and men who should have been pursuing a lady were dropping to their knee before women preparing to orbit someone else. So much fun was had that the overlapping of the two parts became the most requested form for the dance at subsequent balls, and out of this near disaster the Bordonian National Polka was born anew as a unifying force. Years later, when a learned council, considering new manuscript evidence that had come to life, quietly published their findings that Jan D'Honger had originally intended Part 1 and Part 2 be as presented here above (Part/Variant 1 x 4 to the first 2 tunes each played twice, then Part/Variant 2 to the second 2 tunes each played twice), no-one was interested. People at balls were positively disappointed if there were not equal numbers of Part 1 and Part 2 starters. Harmony had been restored and the issue was dead. Has anyone noticed, however, how some people do the final stamp at the end of Part 2 with two feet and some with one foot? I recently asked some émigré Bordonians which was traditional and couldn't agreed. On the dance floor I found musicians pulling in different directions with respect chordal accompaniment, so have included two different scores (the first seeming to be a more traditional arrangement, the latter seeming to be influenced by the later introduction of the piano).

~ Branle de Montirande ~

Form an in-facing hand-holding circle of as many as will, no partner necessary.

Start left foot free.

Dance non-progressive sequence as many times as will.

Play intro. then tune xn *either* in Gm

A1	Shade l&r in place w. *fleuret* l., *fleuret* r.; all f. to centre as joined hs slowly rise w. S l.-lift r. across, S r.-lift l. across
A2	Repeat back (i.e. 2 *fleuret* in place, 2 S b. as hs are lowered)
B1	Double l. and divided double r. **B2** Repeat
C1	S l.-close, S l.-close w. stomp r. (releasing l.); bal. f&b / S l.-close, S l.-close w. stomp; t.s. l along l.o.d. w. *2 fleurets*
C2	Repeat
All x n	

or in Cm

A1	<u>Shade left then right shoulder back with *fleurets* left and right</u> (each 3 quick steps or kicks), <u>then all forward toward centre as joined hands slowly rise with step left and lift right high across, step right and left across</u>
A2	<u>Same step pattern back to place: 2 *fleurets* in place while hands are raised, then 2 singles back *while* hands slowly lower</u>
B1	<u>Double left (left-together right-left-lift right) then</u> <u>divided double right (i.e. right-close left together, kick left-right-left)</u>
B2	<u>Repeat</u>
Long C1	<u>Single left-close right, single left-close right with a stomp (that releases left foot); balance forward toward centre with a single left-lift right, balance back with a single right-lift left /</u> <u>repeat singles sideways and balance, then releasing hands turn single left along l.o.d. with 2 quick *fleurets* and rejoin hands</u>
Long C2	Repeat C1
AABBCC x n.	

The above tune is from period sources and seems to have once been popular and to have once been danced

— John Gardiner-Garden, *Dance Delights*, 2020 —

to. No dance, however, survives in period manuals to match this tune, so I made this one up. I included the dance in my *Dancing through the Ages* Volume II: 1550-1600 to stimulate readers to consider what might go into a period branle choreography, and I include it again in this work featuring my original dances. I might also include here in this work some of the notes from *Dancing through the Ages* Volume II on the origin of the tune. See that work for more than I include here.

The name Montirande may come from the name of the town Montier-en-Der in the Haute Marne region of north-eastern France. Michael Praetorius in his *Terpsichore* (Wolfenbüttel, 1612), when mentioning a Branle 'Montirande' says it **Hat den Namen von dem Mesister der ihn gemacht und erdacht hat** ('Has the name of the master who made and conceived it'), but although it is possible that a dancing master might have a name that is a place name, given that there does seems to be many different dances and tunes under variants of the name Montirande, it does seem more like that the 'Montirande' in extant dance and tune reference is derived directly from a place name and was recognised as such by French dancers and musicians. I might quickly introduce the half a dozen times in late 15th early 16th century that the place name occurs in association with mention of branle tunes or branle dances.

The earliest occurrence is Arbeau's reference in his entry on the **Branle du Haut Barrois**. Towards the end of that entry Arbeau says **vous debvroit suffire, si ne laisserayje a vous en donner une sur l'air d'un branle de Monstierandel** ('I might give you one arranged to the tune of a branle of Montierandel'), but an explicit 'branle of Montierandel' tune or dance does not appeared in Arbeau's surviving *Orchesographie* (though as I will discuss Arbeau's **Branle de Malta** tune starts with almost the same first two bars as the Praetorius branle de Montirande tune offered above).

A second occurrence is when two tunes appear under the name Branle de Montirandé in the first branle medley offered in lute tablature in Anthoine Francisque 1600 lute anthology *Le trésor d'Orphée*. The first of these two tunes is very similar to the Praetorius one transcribe above. Here below is Henri Quittard's c.1900 piano transcription of both tunes:

Premier Branle de Montirandé 31.

Second Branle de Montirandé 32.

The third occurrence is when Michael Praetorius on p.4 and 5 of his 1612 *Terpsichorea* offers two tunes by the name *Bransle de Montirande* toward the end of a grand branle suite (just before the two concluding gavottes. They are both structured 4 bar A x 2, 8 bar B x 2 and are different from Francisque's tune, though like that tune and Arbeau's Branle de Malte, and like Praetorius later separate *Bransle de Montirande* (see 'the fourth occurrence below') the first of his suite *Bransle de Montirande* starts with bars of 4 quavers followed by 2 crotchets.

The fourth occurrence is when Michael Praetorius on p.21 of his 1612 *Terpsichore* offers a tune similar to Anthoine Francisque's in 4-part arrangement credited to Pierre Francisque Caroubel. The tune is structured 4 bar A x2, 4 bar B x 2 then 8 bar C x 2 and is the one I present above transposed from Praetorius key of Gm into C minor:

The fifth occurrence is when Antoine Emerauld, in his c.1610 *Instruction pour dancer* offers not a tune but a few words of instruction for two different branles by this name, one 'le branle de Montiranday a 11 pas' the other 'Le double de Montirande'. In many instances I have found it possible to match Emerauld's dance instruction manuscript with tunes in Praetorius' printed book and it seems both go back to manuscripts left together by the French dancing master Emerauld with Praetorius in the German court town of Wolfenbüttel, but in this instance I have been unable to match either of Emerauld's branle description with any of Praetorius' Montirande tune. For more see my entry in *Dancing through the Ages* Volume II.

The sixth occurrence is really a possible unnamed one. Francoise de Lauze's 1623 *Apologie de la dance.* offers neither a tune nor dance under any variant of the name 'Montirande' but at the point in his branle medley that Emerauld offers *le branle de Montiranday a 11 pas* De Lauze offers a description **Du Cinquiesme Bransle** ('of a fifth branle'). For more see my entry in *Dancing through the Ages* Volume II.

The seventh occurrence is the 'Bransle de Montirande' tune that appears in Father Marin Mersenne's 1636 *Harmonie universelle*, 2nd book. The tune appears as the last in a branle suite, and is different from the Francisque and Praetorius tunes. Mersenne characterises the music and dance as follows:

> **Le cinquiesme se nomme *bransle de Montirandé*,**
> The fifth is called the '*Branle* from Montirande'
>
> **sa mesure est binaire, mais elle est fort viste.**
> Its rhythm is duple, but it is very fast.
> **Il a huict mesure, & seize mouvmens, & est divisé en trios parties differentes de pas, dont la premier en a unze, la seconde douze, & la troisiesme en a dix.**
> It has 8 bars and 6 movements, and is divided into three different step parts, of which the first is in 11, the second 12 and the third 10.
>
> **Son exemple est de l'onziesme mode transpose un ton plus bas, & se peut rapporter au mouvements Anapestique. - - —**

It's example is in 11th mode transposed done a tone, and it can be directed to Anapestique movements - - — [i.e. short, short,long].

In my entry *Dancing through the Ages* Volume III **Branles—opening suite (2a&b)** I tried to corollate the 5-branle medley texts and tunes found in the early 17th century works by Emerauld, Praetorius, de Lauze and Mersenne (and I offer facsimiles of all the relevant texts) and although I was tempted by some correlations for the first four branles in the medley, I found it almost impossible to correlate the texts and tunes offered for the fifth and I presented just. Left with slender hope of confidently reconstructing any historical branle de Montirande, but not wanting to let the good tune which is in common to Francisque and Praetorius go undanced, I have devised the above tabulated dance in a style that is in the flavour of other contemporary branles, while not being cliché.

To make my above dance sequence as easy as possible to remember, I have provided for the repeat of each strain to be accompanied with an exact repeat of the matching dance sequence, without any starting on a different foot and doing in counterpart. To make the dance intellectually satisfying (in a subconscious way) I have given it a story-line that develops from a first part that involves dancing just a little to each side on the spot, to a second part that has dancing further to the left than to the right, and to a third part that has nothing but dancing to the left, and introduced an in and out dimension. To make the dance physically rewarding I have attempted to match the steps exactly to the music, called for simple steps to simple parts of the tune, and busy steps to busy parts of the tune, and contrived to finish the sequence with a somewhat dizzy turn single on along the line-of-dance.

This dance does not need partners, but if partners are taken it can be done in a medley with 'The Spanish Brawl', a dance presented later in this *Dance Delights* that does need partners.

~ Bright Star ~

Form a circle of couples, men facing acw women cw.

Start left foot free.

Dance sequence as the progressive circle mixer as many times as will.

Play the 16th century Italian tune 'Chiara Stella' as many times as will in a pattern AABCC

A1	l.D f. to press r.hs; r.D b.; t.s. l.D l.
A2	Counterpart
B	Slip to own l. ending M touching l. hs in a star in the middle *while* W 'twinkle' fingers of raised l.h.); b. into line
C1	Clap slow r, l; quick r-l, both high
C2	Clap slow r, l; take l.h. and ½ t. w. r.D to prog.
AABCCxn	

♩. = 120

A1 (6 bars)	With right hand raised Double left into right shoulder side partner till right palms are pressing, then Double right back, then Double left turn single left
A2 (6 bars)	The counterpart, with left hand raised, starting with right foot, into left shoulder side pressing left hands, push back and turn single right
B (4 bars)	All slip 4 steps to own left (men going into circle and touching left hands in a star *while* women go out of circle and 'twinkling' the fingers of their raised left hands), then with 4 slip steps slip the other way back into line and to face.
C1 (4 bars)	Slow clap right-and, left-and, then quick clap right-left-high brushing both hands with partner and then arc own hands out wide and back
C2 (4 bars)	Slow clap right-and, left-and, then retaining the left hand clapped ½ left hand turn with a right double to progress on to a new partner.
AABCC x n. Repeat sequence as many times as will	

This is a simple circle mixer set to the lively Renaissance Italian tune 'Chiara Stella', which means 'Bright star'. For the dance Fabritio Caroso presented to the tune in his 1581 *Il ballarino* see my entry on **Chiara Stella** in my *Dancing through the Ages* Volume II.

I devised this simple dance for a school Renaissance event and it worked well even though it was an all-girls school. It's conceivable that the dance could work equally well with all boys, because offsetting the delicate 'twinkling' are the more physical pressing and pushing of palms. The ideal is, however, a mixed circle, and we've used it as such at a Christmas event.

~ The Carmen Quadrille ~

Form 4 couples in front skater's hold (left over right) in a square (numbered cw).

Start right foot, end every *chassés* with a high lift and give weight with every turn.

Dance sequence twice, once with heads active, once with sides.

Play Georges Bizet's 'Habanera' 'L'amour est un oiseau rebelle' from 1875 opera *Carmen*. For piano score see end of entry.

A1	Leads & opp. zigzag f&b / chain W across
A2	Side same
A3	Leads and sides simultaneously f&b / chain W home.
B1	Lead W flirt inside set
B2	Lead M fetch ptnr / prom. her way home
B3	Lead & opp. cpl meet, ½ circle and fall b. into exchanged places / all set to & 2h t. cnr
B4	Repeat home / all set to and cross h. swing ptner then kiss and transition into front skater's hold facing in.

AAABBCC x Repeat w. next cpl leading.

♩ = 75   bass line continues thus till last bar of piece

[music notation]

A1	Lead couple and opposites *en avant quatre* (that is, advance <u>with partner towards opposite</u>) <u>with 2 zigzag *chassés* forward and 2 zigzag *chassés* back</u> <u>Same opposites *chaîne des dames* W's chaining across giving right hand to each other and left hand turn opposite man</u>, all with 4 forward travelling *chassés*
A2	<u>Sides do same</u>
A3	<u>All 4 couples repeat, chaining the women home, where men courtesy turn partner (left in left out front, her right in his right behind her waist... lead man ready to send his woman forward)</u>

— John Gardiner-Garden, *Dance Delights*, 2020 —

B1	Lead woman improvise in the middle, flirting with other men, but her flirting stops on the last bar when her partner starts after her.
B2 var.	Lead man catches up with his partner on 4th bar, takes her in any hold he likes (inside hand hold, back-skater's hold, high promenade hold, waist-shoulder hold etc) and promenade her to and wheel her back into home place
B3	Lead couple and opposite couple meet with 1 travelling *chassé*, ½ circle with 2 travelling *chassé* then fall back into each other's place with 1 *chassé* and turn to face corner All *balancé et deux mains*: set right and left to corner; 2 hand (open hold) cw turn with 2 *chassés* at the end of which heads need to release corner and retake partner
B4 var.	Lead couple repeat home All 4 couples set to partner and cross hand cw swing partner, without letting go of hands pull into a kiss on first pause, relax arms into front skater's hold facing across set on second pause.
AAABBCCx3 Repeat all the above with 2s, 3s and 4s taking turn to lead.	

This dance is based on a choreography I prepared for a production in 2017 of Elizabeth Scott's play *The Rational Dress Society*. The request was for a period style dance set to the 'Habanera' from Georges Bizet's 1875 opera *Carmen*. Given the availability of 8 dancers and the need to set the dance in the late 19th century, I proposed a 4-couple square set quadrille with figures that all have historical pedigree. To match the passionate nature of the music and opera story I suggest dancing with dramatic schottische-like *chassés* step with a high lift, and giving lots of weight with every turn. I have improved the original choreography in several respects, introducing in A3 an overlapping of what I have the heads do in A1 and the sides do in A2, and introducing in B1&B2 where the music has some dramatic stresses, I suggest a figure that was inspired by the 'La Coquette' which Carlo Blasis' presented at the 3rd figure of in a set of quadrilles he published in 1828, and in which in the middle of each couple's turn to lead the figure the woman goes off flirting with other men before returning to her partner for a joint promenade and the 'La Jalouse' 4th figure in the same quadrille when the man does the flirting and his partner seems to come out to fetch him home (see my entry on **Blasis' new set of Quadrilles** in Part 2a of my *Dancing through the Ages* Volume VIII: 1825-1850). The music stress should correspond with when the man alarms his partner by coming after her at the end of B1 and when he catches up with here in the middle of B2. It doesn't matter in what hold the man promenade's the woman home but they need to open out on inside hand to transition easily into B3. The neighbour turn at the end of B3 should be with 2 hands wide-open so dancers can open out easily back beside partner and take with them an inside hand to transition into. The partner turn at the end of B4 should be with 2 hands crossed and go twice around so dancers can pull into the kiss, and, if they are one of the couples needing to recommence, they can transition easily into the opening low front skater's hold.

In the score transcription above I have marked the point Carmen and the choir sing. I appreciate that not every dance band will have a female vocalist and choir on hand, but if you do here below is the lyric they might sing and if you don't you might be able to use these as the same markers for when different instrument combinations feature. In the opera the song 'L'Amour est un oiseau rebelle' fills just two playings of the above transcribed tune, but to give all four ladies a chance to flirt, this dance requires four playings of the tune, i.e. two times through the whole song.

Georges Bizet set his lyric to an aria he adapted from the 'habanera' in *El Arreglito ou la Promesse de mariage* by the Spanish Basque musician Sebastián Iradier, first published in 1863. 'Habanera' was a term used in Spanish America for a form of dance music derived from the 18th century French *contredanse*. Like the latter it usually consisted of just two strains, each of 8 or 16 bars. Bizet had believed the melody to be a folk one and only learnt later that it had been composed by Iradier. Below is the lyric and a rough translation. Beware, if dancing to a recording of an opera performance where some notes are held for a long time, you need to be prepared to improvising a filling pose or action and contain your laughter!

— John Gardiner-Garden, *Dance Delights*, 2020 —

1A1	L'amour est un oiseau rebelle Que nul ne peut apprivoiser Et c'est bien en vain qu'on l'appelle S'il lui convient de refuser	Love is a rebellious bird That none can tame, And it is well in vain that one calls it If it suits him to refuse
1A2	Rien n'y fait, menaces ou prières L'un parle bien, l'autre se tait; Et c'est l'autre que je préfère Il n'a rien dit mais il me plaît	Nothing to be done, threat or prayer. The one talks well, the other is silent; And it's the other that I prefer He says nothing but he pleases me.
1A3	L'amour!... L'amour!... L'amour!... L'amour!... [choir echoes of lyric of 1A1]	Love... Love... Love... Love... [choir echoes of lyric of 1A1]
1B1	L'amour est enfant de Bohême Il n'a jamais, jamais connu de loi Si tu ne m'aimes pas, je t'aime Si je t'aime, prends garde à toi! [choir echoes last phrase]	Love is a gypsy's child, It has never, never known the law; If you do not love me, I love you; If I love you, take guard yourself [choir echoes last phrase]
1B2	Si tu ne m'aimes pas Si tu ne m'aimes pas, je t'aime! [choir echoes last phrase] Mais, si je t'aime Si je t'aime, prends garde à toi!	If you do not love me, If you do not love me, I love you [choir echoes last phrase] But if I love you, if I love you Take guard yourself!
1B3	[Choir echoes 1B1 together with last phrase]	
1B4	[Carmen repeats lyric of 1B2 and choir again echoes last phrase]	
2A1	L'oiseau que tu croyais surprendre Battit de l'aile et s'envola ... L'amour est loin, tu peux l'attendre Tu ne l'attends plus, il est là!	The bird you hoped to catch Beat its wings and flew away ... Love is far, you can wait for it You no longer await it, there it is
2A2	Tout autour de toi, vite, vite Il vient, s'en va, puis il revient... Tu crois le tenir, il t'évite Tu crois l'éviter, il te tient.	All around you, swift, swift, It comes, goes, then it returns ... You think to hold it fast, it flees you You think to flee it, it holds you.
2A3	L'amour! L'amour! L'amour! L'amour! [Choir echoes lyric of 2A1]	Love!... Love!... Love!... Love!... [Choir echoes lyric of 2A1]
2B1	L'amour est enfant de Bohême Il n'a jamais, jamais connu de loi Si tu ne m'aimes pas, je t'aime Si je t'aime, prends garde à toi! [echo]	Love is a gypsy's child, it has never, never known the law; if you love me not, then I love you; if I love you, take guard yourself
2B2	Si tu ne m'aimes pas Si tu ne m'aimes pas, je t'aime! [garde à toi] Mais, si je t'aime Si je t'aime, prends garde à toi!	if you love me not, if you love me not, then I love you but if I love you, if I love you, take guard yourself!
2B3	[Choir echoes 1B1 together with last phrase]	
2B4	[Carmen repeats lyric of 1B2 and choir again echoes midway phrase]	

Here is a public domain piano score of the song:

HABANERA.
Georges Bizet
Allegretto quasi Andantino. (♩ = 72)
CARMEN.
Nº 5.
pp
CHŒUR.
p
CARMEN.
p

30
35
CHŒUR.
f
CARMEN.
pp
40
f
CARMEN.
pp
cresc.
mf
CHŒUR.
mf
45
50
f
CARMEN.
p
55
CHŒUR.
CARMEN.
p
cresc.
f
ff

~ The Conundrum ~

(a cotillon to Bach's cello suite 4 bourrées)

Form couple facing couple

Start right foot free.

Dance sequence as arranged.

Play Bach's c.1720 suite for solo cello no.4 movement 5:
Bourrée no.1
ABBC x2
DEFGHIJK x2
Bourrée no.2
AABB x1
Bourrée no.1
ABCDEFGHIJKx1

Bourree no.1 with each half repeated

A   T.s. over l.sh., clap r-l-both; t.s. over r.sh (M 1¼ W ¾) to ptner clap l-r-both

B1 w. ptner take r., l. over top; 1/2 cw t. end facing opp. / **B2** w. opp. cntrprt;

C   in crossed hs lead opp. out; lead b. in / same w. ptner up or down

A-C Repeat home

D   R.sh. dsd opp. 1¼ to end r.sh. near; r. elbow-l.h. into r. b. allemande t.

E   Grand chain starting r. w. opp. / side same r.sh. into line-of-4, push b.

FG L.sh. dsd, into l. allem. hold, t., chain starting. / l.sh. side into line, push b.

H   All set r-l on final & open to; ½ circle r w. 4 *chassées*

I   All bal. r-l; t. b-to-b. over r.sh. w. D r. / bal. l-r; t. out l.sh. w. D l.,

J   All in circle take slow r-l b., D r. f.; slow l-r b. then circle 1½ with 8 *chassées* last unclosed and turn out with a l.D., ending all swing r.side in

K   M step in w. r-tog. to take & shake r.hs, W in w. same to take and shake r.; ½ r. mill, quick *pir.* about over l.sh.   **D-K** Repeat to home

Bourree no.2 with internal repeats x 1:

A1 F&b. to opp..; r.sh. dsd same   **A2** F&b. to ptner; l.sh. dsd same

B1 r.sh. gyp. opp; ½ cw 2h t. / ½ *chassé croisé* ptner ; f&b. to opp.; ½ r&l

B2 Cntrprt: l.sh. gyp. ptner; ½ acw t. / ½ *chassé* opp. / f&b to ptner; ½ r&l

Repeat Bourrée no.1 (A-K) with no repeats

Bourrée no.1 with internal repeats:

— John Gardiner-Garden, *Dance Delights*, 2020 —

Bourrée no.2 with internal repeats

then Bourrée no.1 *with no internal repeats.*

— John Gardiner-Garden, *Dance Delights*, 2020 —

	Bourree no.1, each time with internal repeats
A	Turn single forward over left shoulder, clap hands with opposite right-left,-both;
	Turn single over right shoulder (M 1¼ W 3/4) to face partner with 4 steps, clap left-right-both with partner
B1	With partner take r.h., take l.h. (loosely) over top; 1/2 cw turn on crossed hands and open out side by side facing opposite /
B2	with opposite do counterpart take l.h., take r.h. over top and 1/2 acw turn;
C	in crossed hands right over top of left) lead opposite out of set, swivel about and lead opposite back into set ending sliding into cross hands hold (right over top of left) with partner;
	lead partner (2s) up or (1s) down, swivel about and back into set ending sliding releasing hands
ABBC	Repeat all back to place
D	Right shoulder do-si-do opposite 1¼ to end right shoulder's near
	Give right elbow then take left hand behind in allemande hold, 4 count right allemande turn 3/4 ready to slide out facing originl direction
E	Grand chain (4 counts per hand, starting sliding out of allemande hold to take) right, pull-past and give left; Pull on and give right, pull on and give left
	side right shoulder into line-of-4 till pressing raised hands palm-against-palm with partner/neighbours) and (push) back
F	Left shoulder do-si-do opposite
	Give left elbow then take right hand behind back in left allemande hold, 4 count left allemande turn 3/4 acw
G	Grand chain (4 counts per hand starting) left, right; Left, right
	side left shoulder till pressing raised in line-of-four and (push) back into holding hands in circle
H	All set right and left, ending on the upbeat take weight on r.;
	then with 4 counts ½ circle right with 4 (together-right) *chassées* the last delaying the 'right' to)
I	All balance right and left then turn back-to-back over right shoulder with double right
	balance left and right then turn out left shoulder with double left
J	All retire into large circle with slow step right— left, and all forward with double right (right-left-right) then retire into large circle with slow step left–right ending on upbeat taking weight on l.
	circle 1½ to left with 8 (together-left) *chassées* and turn single with a l.D (left-right-left) ending where you started earlier circle right, right side and hand of all swinging forward ready for...
K	Men step in on diagonal with right drawing left up to close to take and shake right hand, women do same *while* men retain their right hand so a mill is formed,

	½ right-hand mill, turn out with quick 2 count pirouette over left shoulder (acw).
D-K	Repeat all back to place
Bourrée no.2 with internal repeats	
A1	Holding partner's inside hand meet opposite with 4 steps forward and 4 steps falling back; with 8 steps right shoulder do-si-do opposite on vertical axis ending facing across set
A2	Holding opposite's inside hand meet partner with 4 steps forward, 4 steps falling back; with 8 steps left shoulder do-si-do partner on horizontal axis.
B1	Right shoulder gypsy opposite; 1/2 cw 2h turn same, and momentarily retain 2hs slip sideways towards other pair dropping hands at last 1/2 *chassé croisé* partner *while* looking at opposite Forward and back along l.o.d. towards opposite; starting with opposite 1/2 r&l chain to home place
B2	Counterpart of B1 starting left shoulder gypsy partner; 1/2 acw 2h turn same, 1/2 *chassé croisé* opposite / Forward and back across l.o.d.; starting with partner 1/2 right and left, momentarily retaining the left hand with the opposite past whom you've just chained in order to transition into a turn single left before them to recommence the Bourrée no. 1 sequence.
N.B.	[If extracting this Bourrée no.2 sequence out to be a stand-alone progressive improper duple-minor contradance figure, instead of following the 'right' in the ½ right and left with a 'left', follow it with a turn single left, man once about, woman once and a half, so man arrives facing in original direction with his right hand held out palm-up slightly ahead of woman, who then drops her left hand into the man's right ready for the forward and back towards new opposites at the beginning of the reprise of the A1 of the sequence.
Bourrée no.1 with no repeats	
A-K	Repeat all the above without any repeat

The two bourrées in the 5th movement of Bach's c.1720 Suite for solo cello, no.4 in Eb major were arranged by Bach into a delightful whole. For dance purposes it might be tempting to abbreviate or do without bourrée no.1's second part as it is very long and seems to just play with ideas already introduced in the first part of that tune, but musically the end of the first part of tune 1 requires the second part and the second part would not be the same if not played in its entirety. Accordingly, my default choreography (given above) matches the whole of both tunes performed in the arrangement Bach seems to have intended.

To match the short first part of the cheerful Bourrée no.1 (A-C) I have choreographed a sequence punctuated, when the music seems to suggest, by claps and glissades, while trying to mirror most action done with opposite in that which is done with partner. To match the longer second part of Bourrée no.1 (D-K) I have suggested a sequence which has no figures in common with the first part choreography, but which as in the first part, and although, as in the first part, starts with action done with opposite being echoed in the same done with partner, to the H, I and J strain I decide to offer by way of respite from the alternation some all in communal action (trying to match the music with something of a palindrome because you dance roughly in place (*pas de basque* setting) and circle right; balance and turns back in; balance and turn out; then dance again roughly in place (open, close and open the circle) and circle left (plus turn out). I then use the break-cum-momentum from the turn out of the circle to go into an alternation not of opposite/partner but men. women, before a final communal figure and climactic pirouette.

To match the simple, beautiful and romantic Bourrée no.2 I have offered a flowing choreography that though essentially simply has like figures set to like parts of the melody (for example, a simple forward and back to the first 2 bars of its A1, A2 and penultimate 2 bar of its B1 and B2), has dancers pay all their attention to opposite gender dancers in their minor set (and none to same gender), has dancers share their attention equally between partner and opposite, has a development of intimacy from meeting, to do-si-do-ing, to gypsying, has the action in A2 and B2 the counterpart of that in A1 and A2 respectively, has the action in the A1 and A2 foreshadow that in B1 and B2, and has the action in B1 and B2 start on the same axis as that in A1 and A2, but has the action in the B parts more intimate, busier and longer than in the A parts.

To fit the way Bach has arranged these tunes in the 5th movements of his cello suite no.4, wherein each of the two bourrées is played one with internal repeats than the first bourrée played again but without internal repeats (the same as for the minuet 5th movement of his cello suite no.1), I have ended the C and K of his Bourrée no.1 with figures that can either transition back to the A or D respectively, or forward to the D or Bourrée no.2 respectively. To make the most of the different transition possibilities I recommend the dancer be alert to what is coming up!

If you have an outstanding cellist willing to play these tunes solo in Eb major as Bach originally intended them please enjoy that, but if, as is more likely, you need to have your cellist supported by other musicians, you may prefer the tunes as I have presented them above transposed down to C major. To give different musicians in such an ensemble a range of starting options I have presented a bass-clef line, an identical treble clef line, and chords (kindly provided by pianist friend Sally Taylor).

The tune for Bourrée no.2 is so beautiful that it is almost impossible to not wish to hear it again after the sole playing through provide for in the fifth movement of his Suite no.4 cello suite. If you find this the case, then you might want on some occasion to extract it from the suite and play it over and over for a progressive (improper) duple-minor contradance. This is possible musically as it does not need to transition immediately back to Bourrée no.1 and it is possible dance-wise by making just a slight adjustment to the above suggested cotillion figures. For a progressive *contradance* (country-dance) sequence (rather than a return-to-home cotillion sequence), see my separate entry on **The recurring dilemma**.

Dance-wise it is also possible to turn the first part of Bourrée no.1 into a progressive contredanse (for the 2nd half of C you simply 1/2 r.h. mill and then pull through by the right shoulder, ready to repeat the A-C sequence with a new facing couple) but it does not work so well musically as the tune wants to eventually modulate after the C to D strain that opens the second half of the tune, and once you start on the D strain you don't want to miss anything on your way to the K strain and a matching dance sequence becomes too long (even if you don't repeat D-K) to warrant being repeated in contradance fashion.

My working title for this dance **The conundrum**, references three circumstances— firstly, the way dancers seem not able to decide with whom they want to do minor figures (which they invariably do both with opposite and partner) and from which side they want to do major sequences (most of which they end up doing from both sides); secondly, the challenge involved in doing all the figures of this dance in the right order, with the right people and from the right side; thirdly, the fact that matching this movement of this Bach suite with a dance which used nothing but period figures and was physically, socially and emotionally satisfying for the dancers, was like trying to solve a giant puzzle-without the sure knowledge that there was a solution.

~ The Corona Polka ~

Form a large circle of scattered couples, partners not touching or holding each other

Start left foot.

Dance sequence as a mixer, as many times as will.

A1	W has M follower her acw around space then turns over her r.sh. / gypsy cw about each other ending with W facing back along l.o.d. M facing along l.o.d.
A2	l.heel&toe, w. 1 polka each individually turn ¼ acw to present backs to each other across l.o.d.; r.heel&toe, w. 1 polka t. another ¼ acw to face along l.o.d. (i.e. from exchanged places) / repeat to get home.
B1	Tap right toes, tap left toes; tap right-left-right-left / hit right elbows, hit left elbows; turn signal over left shoulder with 1 polka step and stomp 3x
B2	Heel&toe no-hand grand-chain (l. heel&toe, pass not touching right hand; r.heel&toe then pass not touching left hand / repeat)
AABBxn	*Recommence* chasing new person each time.

Play any 32-bar polka (e.g. the 'Wrong-Foot Polka' set which I wrote years ago and recorded with my band as Autumn 10 in *Lost Dances of Earthly Delights*, Vol. 1).

	~ The coquette ~
A1	With 4 travelling polka steps <u>woman coquettishly leads man (or M chases W) acw around dance space then she turns over her right shoulder to face</u> back towards the <u>man</u> <u>Pair gypsy cw about each other</u> ending with W facing back along l.o.d. M facing along l.o.d.
	~ Balance en carré ~
A2	<u>left heel&toe and 1 polka polka step each individually turning ¼ acw to present backs</u> to each other across l.o.d., then <u>right heel&toe and 1 polka turning ¼ acw to face</u> along l.o.d. (i.e. from exchanged places) <u>repeat till</u> in <u>home</u> position having traced a square (diamond) around partner.
	~ Social distance greetings ~
B1	<u>Both make a small leap onto left in order to tap right foot with each other, leap onto right to tap left toes; tap right-left-right-left</u> <u>Both take a polka step shading left shoulder back in place in order to hit right elbows with each otehr, polka shading right shoulder back to hit left elbows; with 1 polka step turn signal over left shoulder and then make 3 stomps in place</u>
	~ No-hand grand chain ~
B2	<u>Left heel&toe, pass by right shoulder feigning giving but not touching right hands, then right heel&toe and pass not touching left hand</u> <u>repeat</u>
AABBxn Repeat sequence as many times as will, each time with a new opposite/partner.	

On the eve of Canberra's Corona Virus shutdown in March 2020, I cancelled all my dance classes and I invited just 3 of our 16 regulars to come around to video some dances we had been working on, lest we forget our choreography during the shutdown. Before we got stuck into capturing the dances we had been working on, they allowed me to try out this new dance I'd written and it was a lot of fun. All the figures can be found in actual mid-19th century polka variants. See for example, 5th figure of the London Polka Quadrille, presented in my entry on **Polka Quadrille/ London Polka Quadrille** in Volume VIII of *Dancing through the Ages,* Canberra, 2020.

— John Gardiner-Garden, *Dance Delights*, 2020 —

~ Easter Thursday ~

Form longways for as many as will, right foot free.

Start either foot.

Dance as progressive duple minor.

Play intro. then AABBxn

A1	1s dsd below w. 6 counts (possibly just walking); dsd ptner w. same; 1s w. 2s star r. w. 6 hop-steps
A2	w. same step pattern 1s 2h t. below; 2h t. ptner; circle w. 2s
B1	1M, 1W, 2M, 2W in t. take *contretemps* and *ass.* to form single upward-facing file then w. 6 hop-steps cast indiv. to place
B2	starting r.h. to ptner w. 3 hop-steps ea. h. full r&l & 1s cast off
All x n.	

A1	With 6 walking steps 1s and 2s right shoulder do-si-do each other on the side of the set

With same 1s right shoulder do-si-do partner

with 6 *demi-contretemps* (hop-steps) 1s and 2s right hand mill all the way. |
A2	Using same step pattern as before 1s 2 hand turn the 2s below, then 2 hand turn each other, then circle cw all the way :
B1	1M, 1W, 2M, 2W in turn take 1 bar of a 1 *contretemps* and an *assemblé* (a hopstepstep&jump) to go into the middle to form a single upward-facing file, then, in last 2 bars, perhaps using 6 *demi-contretemps* (hop-steps) cast off as individuals (in a fountain) back to respective places.
B2	Starting right hand to partner and with 3 *demi-contretemps* (hop-steps) each hand, rights and lefts the whole way round, then, with 6 *demi-contretemps* 1s cast off into progressed place.

As I observed in my entry on this dance in my *Dancing through the Ages* Volume V: 1700-1750 Part 2a, this beautiful tune may have been as admired in its day as it is today and for this reason publishers were keen to include it in their collections. These publishers include John Walsh and John Johnson, with the dance and tune **Easter Thursday** appearing in *Caledonian country dances,* [Volume 1] Book the second, London, Walsh, c.1737, in *A choice collection of 200 favourite country dances*, vol.2, London, John Johnson, c.1742, and in *Caledonian country dances,* London, John Johnson, c.1750. The figure set for this dance was, however, an impossible fit for this tune. It was virtually the same set of figure as given for 'Katherine Street' in *Dancing master* Volume 2, c. 1710 and 'Sadler's Wells' in *The dancing master*, Volume 3, 17th edition of 1728—where the tune structure is very different to 'Easter Thursday'. 'Easter Thursday's' figure instructions read:

> **The 1st cu. back to back with the 2d cu. and then with their partners .**
> **The 1st cu. turn the 2d cu. and turn their own:**
> **Meet all four and sett, then turn single and clap hands all four going quite round .**
> **Then the 1st Cu. go the figure thro' the 2nd Cu. and cross over and turn their own partners :**

I won't here go into why this figure set is an impossible fit to the Easter Thursday tune, or indeed why the figures that are most commonly danced today in the modern English country dance scene are also a poor fit for this tune, for that discussion see my entry on the dance in *Dancing through the Ages* Volume V: 1700-1750 Part 2a. Here I will just offer a set of figures that I think can fit the beautiful tune well, and which even start paying homage to the Walsh / Johnson figures. I might explain myself as follows.

In A1 and A2 I retain all the figures given by the publisher Johnson, but contain the back-to-back and 2 hand turn figures inside 2 bars, the same number of bar allocated to such figures in a dance such as **Mr Beveridge's Maggot**, and to add on at the end of A1 and A2 a figure which I feel compliments both the bouncy quaver-full melody of these bars and complements the action of the preceding figures—that is a 6 step-hop right hands across (or right hand star) at the end of A1 and an a 6 step-hop cw circle at the end of A2.

In B1, I replace Johnson's figures with the forming and dissolving of an upward-facing file (a figure we find in different forms in such contemporary dances as **The Toast** and **Mr Priest's Minuet**, also presented in this Volume). To make the most of the similarity between the first 4 bars of the strain I propose dancers take it in turn falling into the line (as they are called to do in the dance **Nonesuch**, presented in Volume IV— although there the dancers aren't all facing up). In the last 2 bars the dancers can all cascade back to their starting place (just as they do in 4 bars in **The Toast)**. I use a somewhat similar figure in my **Wachet Auf** in this collection.

In B2, I replace Johnson's figures with something with 4 actions in 4 bars such as rights and left all around, and then using the last 2 bars for a cast off to progress.

With respect the steps for the first 2/3s of the A1 and A2, in my *Dancing through the Ages* entry I suggest one possibility is *demi-contretemps* (hop-steps), just as I recommend for the last 1/3 of each of these strains, and another possibility is 3 *fleurets* across each 2 bars of music. My preference, however, is to just use plain walking steps. The contrast with the hop-steps and hopstep-steps in other parts of the dance offers the dance some pleasant colour and offers the dancer an opportunity for some foot respite, and if you want further respite you can make the B2 plain walking steps as well.

Graham Christian in his 2015 *The Playford Assembly* notes that the tune later appeared as a 'Polonese Dance' in the 1763-4 pantomime *Perseus and Andromeda*, attributed to Thomas Arne, and that the dance title might refer to the ancient English custom of the monarch on Easter Thursday, in emulation of Jesus' washing of his disciples feet after the last supper, washing the feet of the poor and distributed gifts of clothing and money.

Below is a facsimile of the dance-instruction from two of the above discussed texts:

Easter Thursday. Longways for as many &c.

160

The 1ft Cu. Back to Back with the 2d Cu. and then with their Partners : The 1ft Cu. turn the 2d Cu. then turn their own : meet all four and fett . then turn S. and clap Hands , all four going quite round : Then the 1ft Cu. go the figure throuh the 2d Cu. & crofs over & turn their own Partners :

J 88
Eafter Thurfday.

The 1ft Cu. Back to Back with the 2d Cu. and then with their Partners : The 1ft Cu. turn the 2d Cu. then turn their own : Meet all four and fett, then turn fingle and clap hands all four going quite round : Then the 1ft Cu. go the figure thro' the 2d Cu. and crofs over and turn their own Partners :

D. C.

~ Emma's Song ~

Form longways duple minor set of 4 couples, every second couple (i.e. 1s and 3s) improper.

Start right foot.

Dance sequence once through.

Play Arthur Somervell's song *Silent Worship* set to *Non lo dirò col labbro* from Handel's 1728 opera *Ptolemy*.intro. then ABCAB

A	1&4W cnr trios circle / W under arch to take next W's place (she moves up/down) and men switch (end M under & inside middles over & outside) // Set r&l, b. / ends 2h t. ½, middles 2 cpls circle ½
B	Repeat all above to invert set
C	All ½ circle, dsd / ½ circle, gypsy
AB	Repeat A&B to place

Did you hear my lady	A	1M, 1W & 2M take hands at one end while 3M, 4W and 4M take hands at other end of set, then these <u>trios circle left</u> once around
Go down the garden singing		Men make an <u>arch and send W under</u> 'singing' & turning single over right shoulder into place of middle woman who moves to end *while* end M go under same arch to middle men's place while the latter mover up, <u>to all progressed one place.</u>
Blackbird and thrush were silent		All <u>set</u> right and left then <u>fall back</u>
To hear the alleys ringing		All <u>advance and</u> then new <u>ends 2h turn 1/2 way</u> *while* new <u>middles</u> take hs and <u>circle left 1/2</u> with men letting go with their left hand before completing 1/2 circle ready for corner circle
Who saw you not my lady Out in the garden there Shaming the rose and lily For she is twice as fair	B	<u>New ends lead the same</u> figures above <u>till set is fully</u> <u>inverted</u>—1s and 4s now in each other's places, 2s and 3s in each other's places.

— John Gardiner-Garden, *Dance Delights*, 2020 —

Though I am nothing to her	C	All 8 dancers take hands and circle the rectangular set left 1/2 way till all back in original place
Though she must rarely look at me		Right shoulder do-si-do partner
And though I could never woo her		All circle left 1/2 way again till set is again inverted
I'll love her till I die		Right shoulder gypsy partner
Surely you heard my lady Go down the garden singing Silencing all the song birds And setting the alleys ringing	A	Repeat the original A
But surely you see my lady Out in the garden fair Riv'ling the glitt'ring sunshine With glory of golden hair	B	Repeat the original B till all arrive back in place

	Libretto by Nicola Francesco Haym, after a libretto by Carlo Sigismondo Capece, for George Frederic Handel's three act opera Tolemeo (Ptolemy).	Possible literal translation of Italian libretto, not for singing.	Arthur Somervell's song *Silent Worship.*
A	**Non lo dirò col labbro** **Che tanto ardir non ha;** **Non lo dirò col labbro** **Non lo dirò col labbro**	I will not say it with my lips Which don't have sufficient passion;	Did you hear my lady Go down the garden singing Blackbird and thrush were silent To hear the alleys ringing
B	**Che tanto ardir non ha;** **Che tanto ardir non ha;** **Non lo dirò col labbro** **Che tanto ardir non ha.**		Who saw you not my lady Out in the garden there Shaming the rose and lily For she is twice as fair
C	**Forse con le faville** **Dell' avide pupille,** **Per dir come tutt'ardo,** **Lo sguardo parlera**	Perhaps the sparks Of my burning eyes, Revealing my passion, My glance will speak	Though I am nothing to her Though she must rarely look at me And though I could never woo her I'll love her till I die
A	**Non lo dirò col labbro** **Che tanto ardir non ha;** **Non lo dirò col labbro** **Non lo dirò col labbro**		Surely you heard my lady Go down the garden singing Silencing all the song birds And setting the alleys ringing
B	**Che tanto ardir non ha;** **Che tanto ardir non ha;** **Non lo dirò col labbro** **Che tanto ardir non ha.**		But surely you see my lady Out in the garden fair Riv'ling the glitt'ring sunshine With glory of golden hair

The words to this song were sung in the 1996 movie *Emma* by the characters Gwyneth Paltrow, playing Emma Woodhouse, and Ewan McGregor, playing Frank Churchill. The music is from George Frederic Handel's three act opera Tolemeo (Ptolemy)—first performed at the King's Theatre, London, 30th April 1728. Libretto was by Nicola Francesco Haym, after a libretto by Carlo Sigismondo Capece. In the work, the banished co-ruler of Egypt, Ptolemy IX, lives on the island of Cyprus accompanied by his wife Seleuce, known as Delia. The sister of the despotic Araspe, King of Cyprus, Elisa, is in love with Ptolemy, while her brother pursues Seleuce. Ptolemy is eventually, after various intrigues, re-united with Seleuce and restored to the throne by his younger brother Alessandro, who had taken his place. *Non lo dirò col labbro*, the *cavatina* of Alessandro in the 1st act. Here, with an English translation, are the opening words.

Arthur Somervell (1863-1937) gave the aria the English 'Silent Worship' lyric which you hear in the move and to which I have set my dance in the tabulation table above.

The dance attempts to echo Somervell's lyric with the corner ladies going under a dancers' arbour **into the garden** while her partner goes behind the hedge spying on her, with all falling back when the birds fall **silent,** with garden alleys moving with the **ringing**, and with partners going back-to-back to the words 'Though she must rarely look at me' and doing a forlorn gypsy to the words 'I'll love her till I die'. The dance also attempts to be socially and choreographically satisfying—with different hands being taken all the way through, with the dance hinging on a grand communal round, and with the set inverting in the course of the first third of the song, and reverting in the course of the last third.

~ Ferrareze Fantasy Pavan & Galliard medley ~

Form as many couples around space as will, man on inside holding inside hands with woman on outside, ready to promenade as couple along l.o.d.

Start left foot

Dance sequence once through.

Play the Phalèse-published 'Pavane Ferrareze' 1 (ABAB) and 2 (CDCD), all x 2 then 'Gaillarde Ferrareze' (ABAB) and 2 (CDCD), all x 2 (with C strains of both the pavan and galliard modified from original printed form):

Pavan

Basic pavan:

A   f. w. l.f. sequence; sideways singles r&l, double 'en reprise' b.

B   f. w. l.f. sequence; sideways singles r&l, *reverence*

AB Repeat ending turning more towards partner

CDCD The Cloved Orange pavan (M f.; W f / prom. W twirl; prom. M twirl // repeat led by W starting r.f.)

ABAB Albert Hall Pavan with progression (set&t.s. x2 / r.&l.h. t. // prom. along & b. / swing; bal., fall b.) with progression

CD   **In the Bleak Mid-Winter** pavan (prom.; M cw around W / into circle & b.; W acw around neigh. and ch. hs to progress)

CD   Repeat 'In the Bleak…' with progression

Galliard

ABAB The Cloved Orange galliard (M 2 *gall.*; W 2 *gall.* / fig. 8 // W 2 *gall.*; M 2 *gall.* / ½ fig. 8; ¾ l.sh. gyp. into single circle

CD   **Remember O Thou Man** (M, W; M, W / M t. about, W same; ½ 2h t. neigh. to progress, bow.

CD   Repeat 'Remember' but ¾ 2h t. to end M again on inside.

ABABCDCD Repeat both Galliards but w. W leading everything.

♩ = 60   [Pavan] [A]

(Pavan A strain — key signature of Gm; chords: Gm, F, Gm, D)

[B]

(chords: Gm, C, F, Gm, D⁵, Gm)

[C]

(chords: Gm, F, Gm, D)

[D]

(chords: Gm, C, F, Gm, D⁵, Gm) → 6/4

♩. = 65   [Galliard]   [A]   6/4

(chords: Gm, F, Gm, D)

[B]

(chords: Gm, C, F, D⁵, Gm, D Gm)

[C]

(chords: G, F, Gm, D)

[D]

(chords: Gm, C, F, Gm, F Gm, D Gm)

— John Gardiner-Garden, *Dance Delights*, 2020 —

	~ **The Pavan** ~
	The basic **Passing measure pavyon (or Quadran Pavan)** and variant
1A	Forward as a couple with a left foot pavan sequence (single left, single right, then double left) Single sideways right, single sideways left and reprise with a double right
1B	As above but instead of reprise, make a *reverence* looking at each other but without turning towards each other.
2AB	Repeat above, but ending towards each other with the *reverence*
	Pavan from **The Cloved Orange** (*Lost Dances*, Country9)
1C	M, with one l.f. pavan sequence, those who drift away from partners can do so in any direction and try hiding behind other dancers and those seeking an even occasionally steal the hand of someone else's partner, glides away from W, finishing facing away and leaving weight on the final l.f. then W, with one l.f. pavan sequence, glides off after her M, leaving weight on her l.f.
1D	Both travel forward together with a single r., single l., and M takes r.f. double in place *while* W turns cw (over r.sh.) with r.f. double under M's raised r.h. Both travel forward with a single l., single r., and W takes l.f. double in place *while* M turns acw over l.sh. under own r.h.
2C	W, with one r.f. pavan sequence, glides away from M, finishing facing away and leaving weight on the final r.f. then M, with one r.f. pavan sequence, glides off after his W, leaving weight on his r.f.
2D	Travel forward together with a single l., single r., and W takes l.f. double in place *while* M turns acw (over his l.sh.) under his raised own r.h. Both travel forward with a single r., single l., and M takes r.f. double in place *while* W turns cw over r.sh. with r.f. double under M's raised r.h.
	Albert Hall Pavan (*Lost Dances*, Summer 7)
3A	Take 2 slow steps towards partner and with 3 quick steps (l, r, l) turn single over l.sh. back to place Repeat starting r.f. and, letting r.h. drift up to shoulder height, turn back over r.sh. following extended r.h. and finishing r.h. reaching out towards partner
3B	With l.f. pavan sequence r.h. turn partner 1/2 way round With r.f. pavan sequence l.h. turn partner 1/2 way back
4A	Turn to face along l.o.d., take skater's hold by joining r.hs under joined l.hs and starting l.f. with l.f. pavan sequence promenade forward along l.o.d., about facing on last step. With r.f. pavan sequence promenade back against l.o.d. and face each other.
4B	In crossed 2h hold starting l.f. take l.f. pavan sequence to turn each other once cw With hands still held and elbows bent balance with a right step forward and left step back, then with 2nd half of pavan sequence (double right) back away from each other on a right diagonal, M against l.o.d., W along l.o.d, to face new partner across l.o.d. (i.e. **end progressed**)

	The Pavan **In the Bleak Mid-Winter** (*Christmas Carol Dance Book*)
3C	All <u>promenade forward</u> along the l.o.d. with l.f. pavan sequence With r.f. pavan sequence <u>M goes cw ¾ around W</u> *while* <u>W turns</u> acw on the spot <u>under M's raised r.h.</u>1¼ <u>till both facing in;</u>
3D	Holding hs in circle, all take <u>singles</u> left and right <u>into centre,</u> all <u>retire with l.double.</u> With a r.f. sequence <u>W goes cw ¾ around</u> r.side <u>neighbouring M</u> *while* <u>M turns</u> acw on the spot under <u>W's raised r.h.</u> 1¼ <u>finishing M</u> back on inside <u>facing W</u> on outside, <u>changing hands so W's left goes back into Ms right hand and couple open out to again face along the l.o.d.</u> **(end progressed)**
4CD	<u>Repeat all but last time end releasing hands and facing across l.o.d.</u>
	~ The Galliard ~
	Variant of galliard from **The Cloved Orange** (Lost Dances, Country9)
1A	Facing partner <u>M improvises 2 bars of galliard</u> (e.g. plain, bell or cross kicks either on the spot, forward and back, or turning—plain galliard step being kick r, 1,r ,1, spring in air and land weight mostly on l.f., r.f. in front, then kick 1, r, 1, r, spring and change to weight back on r.f., l.f. in front). <u>W responds</u> with same or different steps.
1B	With both dancing, with 4 plain galliard steps do a figure of 8: that is <u>½ r.sh. gypsy, loop over own left shoulder, then ½ l.sh. gypsy, loop over own r.sh.</u>
2A	As in 1A
2B	<u>As in previous B but</u> after ½ r.sh. gypsy and loop over own l.sh., then <u>3/4 l.sh. gypsy into facing each other in single circle,</u> M facing along l.o.d. W against l.o.d. (i.e. **transition to single circle)**
	Remember O Thou Man (*Christmas Carol Dance Book*)
1C	<u>M</u> (facing acw around circle) <u>take 1 galliard step</u> (kick r, l, r, 1 spring in the air, switch to pointing r.f. as you land on r.f.) <u>in place</u> directly towards partner, then <u>W</u> (facing cw around circle) make <u>1 galliard step.</u> <u>Repeat</u> starting <u>on other foot</u> (M then W)
1D	<u>M take 1 galliard step</u> on original foot <u>to turn about</u> ½ acw over l.sh. <u>clapping own hs upon the switch of feet,</u> landing back to partner weight on l.f., pointing r.f., then <u>W same</u> as M above, finishing facing new partner. Take <u>2hs</u> with 1 galliard step <u>turn new partner ½ way</u> cw to finish in progressed position on original foot, then holding l.f. freee all make a flourishing <u>bow</u> to one just turned, i.e. to new partner.
2CD	Repeat above, but **(N.B. transition)** <u>end turning 2h ¾ back into double circle with back M on inside W on outside</u>
	Remember both Galliards with women leading
3AB 4AB 3CD 4CD	*Repeat* both **The Cloved Orange** and the **Remember O Thou Man** galliards but with the women leading all the actions, and end making last 2 hand turn again just ½ way to with communal bow in circle. If the dance is participatory man retains woman's left hand in his right to open out after 2 hand turn to face in for bow, but if the dance is display with surrounding audience man retains woman's right hand in his left to open out to face outward for bow.

I first started making a medley of some of my individual pavan and galliard choreographies when preparing a long display for a concert with 'Bush Baroque' and theorbo player Nick Pollard at the Festival of Early Dance my Earthly Delights Historic Dance Academy organised in Canberra on 7-9 June 2014. The tunes they played did not include the above, but the pair of tunes I have used as a setting for my above medley of pavan and galliard variants have long intrigued me and deciding to use them for this dance has obliged me to finalise my thinking on the tunes. The original source for the pavan and galliard I've used is the *Premier livre de danseries* ('The first book of dances') published in 1571 in Leuven (the Netherlands) by Pierre Phalèse (whose Dutch name was Peeter van der Phaliesen and Latin name Petrus Phalesius), but in that source the C strain of both the Pavan and the Galliard have problems. As I discussed in my *Dancing through the Ages* Volume II Part 1b section on 'The Pavan', the problems are as follows.

Firstly, Phalese's original Pavan's C strain has 2 more beats than all the other 3 strains, so is not 4 bars like the other but 4½ bars long and, for a Pavan that is found in a book said to be of *danseries*, there seems no conceivable reason why the composer would consciously introduce something so awkward for dancing as an extra ½ bar in one of 4 strains.

Secondly, the galliard's C strain does not echo the Pavan's C strain either harmonically or melodically, and this is exceedingly strange given that the contents to Phalese's work lists this suite as a **Pavane Ferrareze avec leur gaill.** ('Ferrarese Pavan with its galliard'), giving us the expectation of a relationship between the Pavan and the Galliard.

I proposed to pianist friend Sally Taylor that we might take 2 counts off the Pavan's C strain, and she suggested to me a way the Galliard's C strain could then be brought into alignment melodically and harmonically with the Pavan's C. Initially I proposed taking the 2 counts out of the middle of Phalese's Pavan C strain, but on later hearing the band La Rossignol recording of the 'Pavan e Gaillarde Ferrareze' on their album *Canti e danze alla corte Estense,* I realised it is much more sensible to do as they do and take the 2 counts off the front of the Phalese's Pavan C strain. La Rossignol did not propose any amendment to Phalese's Galliard C strain but that Sally had proposed and which I have incorporated into my rendering of the Galliard above, seems to echo the revised Pavan C strain perfectly. When it comes to melody, the 2nd bar of both is a lower pitched repeat of the 1st bar and the 3rd bar a passage that runs down-up-down. When it comes to harmony, bother progress from Gm or G in the first bar (the former in the Pavan the later in the Galliard) to F in the second bar, to Gm in the third bar and to D in the 4th bar.

It might be objected that what I (and La Rossignol and perhaps others as well) have seen as a mistake in the top line of the first strain of the 2nd Pavan is unlikely to have been a mistake as it appears (in a related form) in the Contratenor, Tenor and Bass parts published to go with the 'Superior' or descant line. I would suggest, however, that finding the same curiosity in three other texts does not lessen the chances that it was a mistake. Phalèse, even if having a great interest in music, was above all a printer. He gathered and borrowed tunes and did not himself write this music. The three other parts may have been derived somewhat by rote from the first part and the error reproduced. Similarly, it might be objected that we shouldn't tamper with Phalese's Galliard when it does on face value work, but by Phalese's own description the Galliard was meant to be the Pavan's Galliard, that is pertain to, echo the pavan, and whoever wrote it would have been responding to the pavan above... so it is not surprising that when a mistake entered the C strain of the Pavan above an unlikely C strain was produced for the Galliard. I think adjusting both C strains in the way we have may actually bring us closer to original intent, not further from it.

One other respect in which I have decided to diverge from Phalese' original, is in adding a sharp at the end of the penultimate bar of the Pavan's B and D strain. This is very much optional but both I and my collaborator Sally, feel it helps link slightly more closely the Pavan and Galliard, for although there is no F# in the penultimate bar of either the B or D strain of the Galliard, there is at the very end of each of those strains, and by having it come in at the end of the penultimate bar of the matching pavan strains helps to foreshadow this.

Below is a facsimile of fol. 3r and 3v of Phalèse's 1571 *Premier livre de danseries*.

It's not clear if whoever wrote Phalèse's above pavan had intended it to be danced with 1 single to a bar and 1 double to two bars as with Arbeau's Belle qui tiens ma vie' pavan, or danced with 2 single to a bar and 1 double to 1 bar, as with Caroso's 'Pavan Matthei', but as the tune is very busy and said to be in a Ferrara (Italy) style, I suspect the latter and have designed my choreography accordingly. Even if we are to step 2 singles to a bar and 1 double to a bar, and even though the tune is busy, I don't think the pavan needs to be played a slow as many bands interpret it (and could be played a little quicker even than La Rossignol play it). The pavan needed to be stately and aristocratic, but it needed to be danced. The 'Gaillarde Ferrareze' like both Arbeau's and Caroso's above-mentioned galliards, can be danced with one '5-step' sequence to a bar, and within the figure structure my choreography provides I'm happy to allow for improvisation of the actual galliard step. For a discussion of historical galliard step variants see my entries in Part 1c and 2 of my *Dancing through the Ages* Volume II and III.

Coincidently, my medley requires the same playing structure as offered by the La Rossignol recording:
(Pavan 1 (AB)x2 Pavan 2 (CD)x2)x2 then (Galliard 1 (AB)x2 Galliard 2 (CD)x2)x2

To set the mood and to come out onto the dance floor, to **Pavan 1** when played the first 2 times (i.e. 1AB 2AB) I have set the pavan sequence which once appeared at the beginning of the Inns of Court Old Measures Suite and which sources referred to as the **Passing measure pavyon, Quadran Pavan** or simply **The Payvan** (see my *Dancing through the Ages* Volume II), together with a slight variant which replaces the final *reprise* with a *reverence*. To **Pavan 2** when played the first 2 times (i.e. 1CD 2CD) I have set the pavan from **The Cloved Orange** (*Lost Dances*, Country 9) and although the whole sequence is not repeated the second CD is effectively a repeat of the first CD's action but a counterpart lead by the woman.

To **Pavan 1** when played the second 2 times (i.e. 3AB 4AB) I have set the sequence I choreographed for the **Albert Hall Pavan** (*Lost Dances*, Summer 7). It naturally ends with a progression (which you may as well leave in as then the medley starts to develop) and it fills the whole playing so can't be repeated. To **Pavan 2** when played the second 2 times (i.e. 3CD 4CD) I have set the mixer Pavan I wrote to go with the carol **In the Bleak Mid-Winter** (*Christmas Carol Dance Book*). You can do the sequence twice, then end back in a double circle, but instead of both facing forward ready to promenade, face partner across l.o.d. ready for the galliard.

To the **Galliard 1** the first 2 times (i.e. 1AB 2AB) I have set a rearranged version of the progressive galliard I wrote for **The Cloved Orange** (*Lost Dances*, Country 9), ending with a transition to single circle. To **Galliard 2** the first 2 times (i.e. 1CD 2CD) I have set the progressive galliard I set to the carol **Remember O Thou Man** in my *Christmas Carol Dance Book*, danced twice. To the repeat of **Galliard 1** and **2** (i.e. 3AB 4AB 3CD 4CD) I have proposed repeating the same galliard sequences.

If dancing as a participatory dance I recommend ending with a ½ 2 hand turn (in Galliard 4D) and open out woman on right of man to all bow facing into the middle of the circle. If dancing as a display surrounded by an audience perhaps end with a ½ 2 hand turn and open out with woman on left to all bow facing out.

~ Five Steps to Heaven ~

Form couples in offset ballroom hold, woman back to l.o.d., man facing

Start outside foot.

Dance as many times as will.

Play intro. then the following tune devised by myself (i.e. John G-G) AABBCCDD xn then AA., with or without another five step waltz.

Simple version (every 1 bar of action repeated, every 4 bars in cnterpart):

Variant 1

  A1 M b. W along l.o.d. w. 4 steps-lift, repeat; t. cw as cpl w. waltz plus step-lift, repeat

  A2 Same as A1 except W b. M and t. acw

Variant 2

  B1 Glide-cut-hop-stomp-stomp, repeat; glide-cut-hop-glide-lift & t.½ cw as cpl, repeat

  B2 Same as B1 but t. acw.

Variant 1 without internal repeats

  C1 The whole of A1&2 without the internal repeats.

  C2 As above but ending in open waist-sh. hold facing f.

Variant 3

  D1 M pass W in acw arc to l.arm w. step-*chassé*-step-close-point, M cw pass W b. to r. arm w. cntrpt; wheel 2x cw (i.e. M f.) w. 4 steps-lift x2

  D2 As before but wheel acw (i.e. M b.).

All x n then return to AA to end.

A1	**Variant 1**
bar 1 &2	<u>Man backs woman with 4 steps and lift</u> (pointing free foot), then <u>repeat</u>
bar 3&4	Turn as a couple with 3 waltz steps to turn ½ cw and 1 single step on count 4 and a lift on count 5 to turn another ½ cw, then <u>repeat</u>
A2	<u>Repeat A1 but starting M going back along l.o.d.</u> W going forward <u>and making turns acw</u>.
B1	**Variant 2**
bar 1&2	Both <u>go along l.o.d w. glide-cut-hop-stamp-stamp,</u> then go along l.o.d. with glide-cut-hop <u>hobble mazurka step and on count 4 and 5 glide forward and lift to turn as a couple ½ cw</u>
bar 3&4	<u>Repeat</u> starting M on W's side, doing 'hobble' over shoulders and ending turning back to own side.
B2	<u>Repeat B1 making all ½ turns acw.</u>
	Condensed Variant 1:
C1	the whole of that in A1&2 but without the internal repeats.
C2	As in C1 but ending in open waist-sh. hold facing f.
D1	**Variant 3**
bar 1&2	M pass W in acw arc to l.arm w. 1 step, 1 chassé, 1 step to close and point outside foot, then M cw pass W back to right arm with counterpart
bar 3&4	wheel as a side-by-side couple 2 times cw (i.e. man forward) with 2 sequences of 4 steps and lift
D2	As before but wheel acw (i.e. M b.).
AABBCCDDx n. Repeat all as many times as will.	

— John Gardiner-Garden, *Dance Delights*, 2020 —

Signature 'Five Steps to Heaven' tune by myself (i.e. John Gardiner-Garden):

Possibly in medley with another tune such as the 'Five Step Waltz' by Conner in *Home Circle*, vol.1 Boston, 1857, pp.202-203, ABCD x n then A to end. In order to better support the above dance, I have departed from Connor's original tune by doing without the original's repeats on the A and D strain and by breaking into a pair of quavers the crochets on the second beat of the first, second, fifth and sixth bars of the D strain.

— John Gardiner-Garden, *Dance Delights*, 2020 —

If your body and mind equally enjoy a good whirl you might like this pleasant challenge. The sequence makes use of two the mid-19th century 'Waltze à Cinque Temps' variations which I identified in my *Dancing through the Ages* Volume VIII but the ideas surrounding and colouring them are my own—as are the tune, chorded by pianist friend Sally Taylor, whose advise on earlier versions I also valued.

My A1 Variant 1 features in its second half (i.e. bars 3 and 4) the mid-19th century 4 weight-change turning sequence which I have presented under **The Five Step Waltz (1)** in my *Dancing through the Ages* Volume VIII. I have preceded it with a 4 step-in 5-count 'yale-position' backing-promenade of my own devising, and A2 is then just an acw turning counterpart developed from that.

My B1 Variant 2 features in bar 2 and 4 the mid-19th century short-polka-mazurka-like 'hobble' and turn sequence which I have presented under **The Five Step Waltz (2)**. I have preceded each of those bars of turning with a bar of sideways hobble that doesn't change feed—and which has stomps called for in the music (supported by the melody). B2 is then just an acw turning counterpart developed from that.

My C1&2 is just a repeat of A1&2, it flowing well, with an extra ¼ turn twist, out of the acw turn which concludes B2—but, to offer something different in response to the new musical theme, I recommend that by omitting all the repeated action you condense the 16 bars of Variant 1 into the 8 bars of C1, and then you repeat those 8 bars in C2.

My D1 Variant 3 features in its first half (bars 1 and 2) the weight-change pattern of the late 19th century sequence I have presented under **The Five Step Waltz (3)** in my *Dancing through the Ages* Volume X. That sequence involves a quick *chassé* (together-step) on count 2, and you will hear that supported by the rhythm suggested by the melody in bars 1 and 2 of this strain. Here, however, rather than doing the step-*chassé*-step to close-step-step to close-lift forward and turning as the late 19th century source descriptions you need to do it sideways, and as you may be doing it to a five step waltz played quicker than possibly envisaged for **The Five Step Waltz (3)**, you will need to dance this passage in this dance lightly on your toes. In bars 3 and 4 we fall back to the recurring 4 steps and lift pattern to do a side-by-side wheel cw twice about, with a nice *ronde de jambe* of the outside foot, as in a mazurka *holubiec*. D2 starts with the same switching of sides but then has the wheel go acw—offering a good weight-trajectory for transitioning back into A1's Variant 1.

There were many other elements I experimented with in attempting to craft a five step waltz sequence to a 5/4 tune set, but I ended settling the above as each of the 4 sequences offers a balance between dizzy turning and restful along or across l.o.d. action, brain teasing developments and forgiving counterparts, zesty reversals and flowing-on transitions, and the sequence combination as a whole makes use of all three of the historic variations.

FIVE STEP WALTZ.

CONNER.

Dances. **203**

FIVE STEP WALTZ, Concluded.

TRIO.

D.C. al Fine.

~ The Fleeting Moments Minuet ~

(a cotillon allemande)

Form 2-couple cotillion, start facing partner holding left hands.

Start right foot free.

Dance as arranged with minuet steps throughout.

Play Bach's cello suite no.1, movement 5 Minuets 1&2 ea. x1 then 1 again with no repeats.

Minuet 1: **A1** Sideways r; l / W ½ r.h. t. opp.; ½ l.h. t. opp. M
A2 Facing opp. r; l / M ½ r.h. t.; ½ l.h. t. ptner on opp. side
B1 joining r.hs over l.hs M b. ptner ½ acw / dropping l.hs r.h. t. same // ½ r. / l. mill **B2** l.h. t. opp. / joining r.hs over l. W b. opp. // drop l.hs and starting opp. chain r; l / r; l
Minuet 2: **AABB** Repeat all to return to starting place.
Reprise Minuet 1 with no repeats: **A** ½ hey home (starting W giving r.sh.) **B** w. *bal.* f&b; W ¼ l.h. t *while* M solo prom. ¼ acw / repeat // full l.h. t. / joining r.hs over top cross hs swing cw into reverence.

Minuet 1

Minuet 2

Repeat Minuet 1 with no repeats.

— John Gardiner-Garden, *Dance Delights*, 2020 —

Here is a score for those who want the option to read a treble line one or two octaves above the cello.

Minuet 1

Minuet 2

Repeat Minuet 1 with no repeats.

— John Gardiner-Garden, *Dance Delights*, 2020 —

	Minuet 1
1A1	Facing partner and retaining left hand <u>set right</u> (1 minuet) <u>and left</u> (1 minuet) ½ W's chain (<u>W ½ r.h. turn with opposite woman, then ½ l.h. turn opposite M</u>)
1A2	Facing opposite from improper side (left hands still held) <u>set</u> 1 minuet sideways <u>right and</u> 1 <u>left</u> ½ M's chain (<u>M ½ r.h. turn with opposite man, then ½ low l.h. turn partner</u>) <u>to all end in home</u>
Long 1B1	Facing partner and joining right hands (in wide arc) over left hands to make cross hand hold <u>M backs W 1/2 acw around set ending dropping left hands and retaining right hands</u> <u>Full</u> right-hand turn partner with 2 minuet steps 4-person <u>½ right-hand mill</u> with 2 minuet steps 4-person ½ <u>left-hand mill home</u> with 2 minuet steps ending retaining left hand
Long 1B2	<u>Full left-hand turn opposite</u> Facing opposite and joining right hands (in wide arc) over left hands to make cross hand hold <u>W backs M 1/2 acw around set ending dropping left hands and retaining right hands</u> <u>Starting with opposite full right and left around set,</u> with 4 minuet steps, 1 per hand, <u>ending retaining left hand with partner</u> and turning 1/4 acw to face partner
	Minuet 2
2AA BB	<u>Repeat</u> from progressed position as many times as will
	<u>Reprise of Minuet 1 without repeats</u>
3A	With 4 minuet steps ½ linear hey home, starting M with their left hand guiding W in to pass each other right shoulder in the middle, left shoulder pass opposite, M pass right shoulder in middle and then pass partner left shoulder, with no hands given till the very end when hands are taken in a vertical axis wave, women holding right hands with each other and men left hands with partner.
Long 3B	all balance in the wave with 1 *balancé* forward and 1 *pas de balancé* bace; release partner and women ¼ left hand turn *while* men solo promenade ¼ acw / repeat till all home // full left hand turn partner / joining right hands over top of retained left hands cross hand swing cw once around into reverence.

I have written this short 'couple-facing-couple' cotillion to go to two minuets in the 5th movement of Johann Sebastian Bach's solo cello suite no.1 in G major. In the dance I have tried to do four things (apart from complement the music).

Firstly, I have tried to include, even if in a somewhat disguised form, all of the figures of a standard ball-opening *menuet à deux*, and to include them in the expected order. The expected opening and changing of sides is represented by the going to right and left and ½ women's chain in A1 and then the counterpart in A2. The expected presentation of right and left hand is represented by the action in the last ¾ of B1 and first ¼ of B2. The expected climatic presentation of both hands is represented by the final cross-hand 2 hand turns

— John Gardiner-Garden, *Dance Delights*, 2020 —

in the B of the Reprise. In the figure variants, to avoid brain strain while avoiding cliché I have tried to use commonplace elements but in uncommon ways.

Secondly, I have tried to achieve an evenly balanced alternation of action between opposite and partner. Anything you do with your partner you will either do with your opposite or will have done already with your opposite. This holds for the single-sex chaining in 1AA and 2AA, and for the backing and hand-turning in the 1BB and 2BB. There is also an even handedness in the grand chain in the second half of 1&2B2. I've allowed the title of the dance to allude to this alternation of attention and to what you might say to one about doing the same with the other.

Thirdly, I have tried for lots of cross-hand action, so that the dance might be technically termed a *contredanse allemande,* the late 18th century French term for a square cotillion with lots of right and left hand turning, and a recurring feature of a left hand acw turn followed by cross-hand cw turn. This hybridisation of a 'German' with a minuet might not be inappropriate considering the dance is set to minuet music composed by a great German composer, Bach. Although it is possible, as in a couple's *allemande* to use 2 *fleurets* to a bar at some points in the dance (especially in the first half of B1 and B2 in each tune before the reprise) I recommend using the '1-and-a-*fleuret*' minuet step throughout the dance.

Fourthly, I have opted to match the no internal repeat reprise of the first tune without figures that are more communal and thrilling but can be danced well with minuet steps throughout and which echo to some extent the opening part of the main sequence. In the 3A, we don't have the time we had in the 1AA or 2AA to send first the women and then men across, so I decided on a ½ hey in which, inside 4 minuet steps, without any introductory or intervening setting the women then men cross the set. In 3B I decided to balance in a wave on the vertical axis and then horizontal axis, and when home to echo the left hand acw turn into cross hand cw turn that features earlier in the dance. As earlier, I recommend you describes a wide arc with the right hand as you bring it over the left to make the cross hand hold, and that just as the left hand hold creates an 'S' down the length of the joined dancers left arms, the cross hand creates two mirror 'S's. In other word, don't cramp yourself or partner with any of these hand holds and arm dispositions—make everything comfortably curved.

At what tempo should these Bach minuets be played? I am in agreement with Chung-Hui Hsu, who in her Doctoral thesis *The solo string works of J.S. Bach: The relationship between dance, and music elements,* submitted to the Graduate Faculty of the Louisiana State University and Agricultural and Mechanical College in May 2012, wrote 'Many dance pieces are performed too slowly, especially in Bach's solo works for strings'. She suggested that the main program which leads to the slow tempo is the 'romantic' performance practice: 'frequently, we hear too many beats in a bar'. She notes that it is difficult to decide a good starting tempo, as Bach includes no marks for a metronome (which had not yet been invented) and terms which might be included which we might today take as indications of tempo were then intended more as indications of character ('mood' or 'manner' rather than speed)—and on this point she cites Leopold Mozart, *Versuch einer grundlichen Violinschule*, Augsburg, 1756). Chung-Hui Hsu suggests, however, that there are three constants of relevant to Bach's solo violin and cello *partitas* that can help a player decide tempo. I'll summarise these briefly.

One constant is the alternation of slow / fast (or fast / slow) movements. Hsu observes (p.50) that although Bach varies the dance movements used he invariably intended an alternation between slow and fast, and this does indeed seem to be borne out by an examination of all the relevant suites (once past the preludes)- even though her suggestion that there is also an alternation between duple and triple time dance movements is not strongly borne out, there being too many triple time movement possibilities compared to duple minor to always separate the former with the latter.

A second near constant is an expectation that some types of movements will be faster or slower than others in the same tempo. Hsu suggests, from slowest to fastest, movements in duple meter are Allemande, Gavotte, and Bourrée, in triple meter, Courante, Sarabande, Chaconne and Menuet, and in compound meter, Loure and Gigue. By this analysis the Bourrée and Menuet are the fastest in their metre group, and when she goes through the suites allocating 'moods' she describes the Menuet I & II in suite no.1 in G Major to be 'Joyful' and the Bourrée I & II in Suite no.4 in E flat major to also be 'Joyful'.

A third constant is one Hsu derives from consideration of bowing options open to the Baroque musician playing the baroque instrument in baroque positions, and which she expresses it by quoting Robert Donington, *String playing in Baroque music*, New York, 1977), p.78:

> As a good working rule for baroque music, take quick movements less quickly than might be thought; and take slow movements less slowly than might be thought.

I would concur with the above observations and suggestions, but suggest there is a reasons that Hsu overlooks for considering the minuets be played at a tempo that might be considered 'joyful'. It is that nearly all the surviving minuets from around the time of Bach that were clearly intended for dance serve the dance best with a tempo mark of crochet equals 140 to 180. The ball-opening *menuet à deux* works best at around the 140 mark, while some special choreographies set to special tunes, such as the **Menuet d'Alcide**, seem served best at around 180. It is very difficult to dance a minuet at a tempo that is a lot slow than 140, especially if interleafing *contretemps de menuet* steps or any step with a *jeté* or *demi-jeté*, as there is a limit to how long you can stay in the air. Although it is unlikely that Bach intended his solo string instrument suites be danced to, it is a fact that every movement of every suite (beyond the occasional prelude) carried the name of a social ballroom dance. It is even possible that Bach, in the order he introduced the dances, was imagined the order they might be encountered at a ball: *Allemande, Courant, Sarabande* and *Gigue* possibly meant to reflect the opening you might enjoy with a communal German processional, the elegant couples dance you might enjoy from Italy/France, the sultry/sexy/contemplative dance you might indulge in from Spain, and the lively all-in finale you might enjoy from England, with minuets, gavottes and bourrées, all associated with France, being added occasionally between the Saraband and the Gigue. Given this, it seems unlikely that he intended tempos that were entirely alien to or inappropriate for the named dance.

Turning again in particular to Bach's cello suite no.1 Menuet I&II, these are much fuller melodies than that for 'Menuet d'Alcide' so is clearly not going to sit well at 180 beats-per-minute, but if the tempo is too-far below 140 and I believe the music loses its intended connection to the minuet dance and the joyfulness that seems called for following the 'Sarabande' earlier in that suite. I have accordingly proposed a compromised tempo of a crochet equals 136. This is not too fast for playing comfort and not too slow for dancing. It would be nicer for dancing if the tempo was 140, but the busy tune does not seem to want that, and nor is it necessary to get to fast during the minuet as excitement can be left to the gigue that follows in that suite. Because of the modest tempo, I have avoided calling in my choreography for any fancy in the air steps such as *contretemps de menuet* steps, indeed for anything other than plain minuet steps which I am happy for dancers to make of the non-hemiolic 'one-and-a-bourrée' variety, which I believe best suited to the music.

To reflect the structure scholars seem to believe Bach intended, I have devised a dance with a main figure sequence which leaves the dancers in inverted position after the first minuet played AABB, returns them home when danced again to the second minuet played AABB, and which is followed by a final figure sequence that inverts then reverts the set in the course of a reprise of the first minuet played AB.

As an aside, I might note that I do not concur with the curious suggestion in Hsu's thesis (p.38) that the first short strain (8 bars of 3/4) of a court minuet in Bach's time was danced by the man, its repetition by the woman, and that the longer strain that followed (16 bar of 3/4) was played more quickly for them to dance together. For my addressing of this issue see my section on the Minuet in V.

It might be in keeping with period practise to following the above minuet dance, though a stand-alone one, with something more lively, be it a jig (as in **Mr Holt's Minuet and Jig**) or a gavotte (as with **Menuet de la Cour**) you may want to follow this minuet cotillion with my **The Conundrum Bourrée**, which is in the same formation and has the same running theme of alternation-of-attention.

~ Galliard Dating ~

Form upward facing rank of 6 dancers, 3 side-by-side men and 3 side-by-side women, where 1M & 1W at each end are novices, 2M & 2W in middle of own-gender half are moderately capable, and 3s next to each other in centre are most capable. If top of page is the presence, then: 1W2W3W 3M2M1M.

Start left foot free

Dance as many times as will.

Play 24 bar 6/4 tune such as the following French 'Volte' that is presented as tune CCX in Michael Praetorius' *Terpsichore*, Wolfenbüttel, 1612 x4.

1A1	All bow to presence / 1M&W f. w. their travelling step 1 (doubles)
1A2	2M&W f. w. their travelling step 2 (*cinque passi*) / 3M&W advance w. their travelling step 3 (*fioretti & cad.*x 2)
1BB	1M display 1a (*trabs & finto*) / 1W display 1b ('bell' kicks).
1CC	2M display 2a ('double cut') / 2W display 2b ('toe-heels').
1D1	3M display 3a ('knot') / 3W display 3b ('together' combo).
1D2	In up-facing rank all *ruade* l&r / in facing files *ruade* to own l&r.
2A1	1M w. his travelling step displaces 3M / displays his variant to 3W
2A2	3W displays same; both same tog. and prepare to pair but
2BB	1W up w. her travelling step and displays her var. to 1M
2CC	1M echos same; both same tog. and prepare to pair but…
2D1	2M up to w. his travelling step and displays his var. to 1W
2D2	1W echos same; both same tog. and prepare to pair but…
3A1	2W comes up with her travelling step and displays her variant
3A2	2M echos same; both same tog.and prepare to pair but…
3BB	3M up with his travelling step and displays his var. to 2W
3CC	2W echos same; both same tog. and prepare to pair but…
3D1	3W up w. travelling step 3 and displays her variant to 3M
3D2	3M echos same; both same tog. and prepare to pair
4A1	3s, 2s & 1s in turn *scorsi* to pair & arc acw into up-facing rank.
4A2	1s display tog. their variants
4BB	2s display tog. their variants // **4CC** 3s display tog. their variants
4D1	1s retire w. their travelling step 1 / 2s retire w. their travelling step
D2	3s retire w. their travelling step / all bow to presence

	~ 1st playing ~
A1	<u>All bow</u> to the presence (or audience) <u>1M&W</u> (from respective ends) <u>advance with travelling step 1</u>: 2 x '3 steps' (i.e. doubles)
A2	<u>2M&W</u> (from middle own side) <u>advance with travelling step 2</u>: 2 x '5 steps' (*cinque passi*) <u>3M&W</u> (from inside) <u>advance w. travelling step 3</u>: 2x'7 steps' (2 *fioretti & cadenza* all x2)
B1	<u>1M display his variant 1a</u> (perhaps *trabuchetti* left & right, *finto* back, tog., forw. & stamp. <u>1W display her variant 1b</u> (perhaps a 5 step 'bell' or 'campanella' step starting swinging l. b., r. f. under, l. b., r. under, *cadenza*, then counterpart.

— John Gardiner-Garden, *Dance Delights*, 2020 —

B2	2M display his variant 2a (perhaps a 'double cut', cutting r.f. twice infront of l.shin, l.f. twice in front of r.shin, *cadenza*, then counterpart). 2W display her variant 2b (perhaps 'toe-heels', pointing in front r.toe, r.heel, l.toe, l.heel, *cadenza* then counterpart).
CC	3M display his variant 3a (perhaps a 'knot' or *groppo* variant: cut r.f. up behind, l.f. up infront, r. behind again, l. infront again, *fioretto* l., *fioretto* r., t.s. l. w. 2 two count *passi*). 3W display her variant 3b (perhaps a 'together' combination, that starts with a jump together to the left, swing r.f. f.-b-cut under-*cadenza*, then counterpart).
DD	In single rank facing presence, all *ruade* to left and right finishing M turn ¼ cw W ¼ acw. In facing files all *ruade* to left and right (M toward and away from presence, W opposite).
	~ 2nd playing ~
A1	1M come up to in front of 3M with his travelling step 1 (forcing him to step back a bit) and display his variant 1a (trabs & *finto*) to 3W
A2	3W does same display; both same together and prepare to bow and take inside hand but …
B1	1W comes up (on audience side of file, calling out 'wait') to in front of 3W with her travelling step 1 (i.e. doubles) *while* other W are 'forced' back a little and displays her variant 1b (the 'bell-kick') to 1M
B2	1M echos same; both same together and prepare to bow and take inside hand but…
CC	2M comes up to in front of 1M with his travelling step 2 (i.e. *cinque passi*) and displays his variant 2a ('double cuts') to 1W
DD	1W echos same; both same together and prepare to bow and take inside hand but…
	~ 3rd playing ~
A1	2W comes up with her travel steps 2 (*cinque passi*) and displays her variant 2b ('toe-heels')
A2	2M echos same; both same together and prepare to bow and take inside hand but…
B1	3M comes up to in front of 2M with his travelling step 3 (*fioretti*) and displays his variant 3a (the 'knot') to 2W
B2	2W echos same; both same together and prepare to bow and take inside hand but…
CC	3W comes up to in front of 2W with her travelling step 3 (i.e. *fioretti*) and displays her variant 3b (the 'together' sequence) to 3M
DD	3M echos same; both same together and prepare to bow and take inside hand
	~ 4th playing ~
A1	3s, 2s and 1s in turn *scorsi* (scurry) to meet, pair off, lead up, turn off to left and arc acw till all in upward facing side-by-side-rank, from left to right: 3s, 2s, 1s.

A2	1s display their variants 1a & 1b (i.e. 'trabs' & 'bell-kick')
B1	2s display their variant 2a & 2b (i.e. 'double-cuts' and 'toe-heels')
B2	3s display their variants 3a & 3b (i.e 'knot' and 'tog.')
CC	1s retire with their travelling step 1 (i.e. 2 doubles) 2s retire with their travelling step 2 (i.e *cinque passi*)
DD	3s retire with their travelling step 3 (i.e. *fioretti*) All bow to presence

Having been encouraged by dancers in our scene to compose a grand 'massed' galliard, I thought it wouldn't be right to just have a single long sequence, as flashy as one might be able to make such sequence—firstly because you might limit the sequence to only be realisable when you have all expert dancers, and secondly because galliards were not historically about everyone doing the same thing at the same time, but about dialogue and competition. I decided to work out a dance that gave opportunities for dancers to rise to (or rest at) different levels of competency, while competing with each other for the admiration of members of the opposite dancing gender. I was also determined to have the dance equally fun to watch as to do, and to give it a storyline that would amuse the audience as much as it would dancing participants. I came up with the idea of 'galliard dating'. Dancers can choose if they want to dance a level 1, 2 or 3 role, and then join one of as many ranks as numbers and space permit (men on one side, women on the other, lower level dancers on outside ends and higher level dancers in centre). Dancers form ranks facing up to the presence/audience, no-one holding hands, all 'singles' ready to find partners. The dance leader can recommend to and practice with the men and woman of the different levels 3 different ways of advancing (way 1, 2 & 3) and 6 different ways of displaying (1a&b, 2a&b, 3a&b).

The dance runs as follows. After introducing themselves to the audience with their solo advances and displays (as if registering their availability) they do in unison a figure that ends with all facing towards the opposite gender dancers. Starting with the lowest level outside dancers, all shuffle positions in their effort to impress opposites. On each occasion the one who comes up from the end of rank placing their back to the one of same gender on inside of rank so as to block them out (even force them back a little) and be able to display their own variant to the opposite gender dancer opposite them. That opposite catches on and they seem to be getting on well, but before they have a chance to pair off there is another blocking out their co-gender dancer in the centre and offering their display. Eventually, when there are no more challengers, the 3s, followed by the 2s and 1s, all pair-off and cast off as couples, so when an upward facing line is again formed, they are this time sorted by galliard competence, level 1 dancers on the left end, level 2 in the middle and level 3 on the right. Each couple in turn then happily display, partly to the presence/audience and partly to each other, the variants each had started with, and each couple in turn fall back with their common 'advancing' step. The dance then ends as it began, with a *riverenza*.

We had a lot of fun when we debuted this dance. We thought it might be just for those with experience, but ended up everyone in the room who wasn't playing music, taking one or other role in one of multiple upward facing ranks. I as the leader took a 3M position in the front rank, and we found by having slightly more competent dancers in all the front-rank positions, all the ranks that followed were able to catch on quickly. The dancers had a great time and the musicians reported that it looked great. Hope you too have fun with it.

You could set this dance to any 24-bar galliard or la volta tune. I have offered above a chorded single melody-line transcription of one of the French *Volte* tunes in Michael Praetorius' 1612, *Terpsichore*. For Praeotorius' 5-part version of that tune from p.116 of 1930s Friedrich Blume edition see my entry 'La Volta' in my Volume II Part 2b of my 2020 *Dancing through the Ages* 31 book series. For some reason we used to play this tune with the second strain as the final strain—the tune and dance work equally well either way.

— John Gardiner-Garden, *Dance Delights*, 2020 —

~ The Grand Polka medley ~

Form couples around dance floor

Start outside foot free.

Dance either short or long version as arranged

Play any set of 3 polka tunes (such as my Country 7 set in *Lost Dances of Earthly Delights* Volume 2- 'The Layman's Advice', 'The Madman's Counsel' and 'The Idiot's Inspiration'), each tune two times, repeat all then back to first tune once.

7 mins 32b.x13	*foot*	*Dance sequence x 1*	*Prog-ress*	*source*
Tune 1	opposite	**The Corona Polka**	yes*	*Dance Delights*
2nd x		**Fast Forward 1st variant**	no	Country 7
Tune 2	left	**Fast Forward 2nd variant**	no	Country 7
2nd x		**Peek-a-boo Polka**	no	Town 15
Tune 3		**The Courtship Polka**	no	Autumn 13
2nd x	right	**Wrong foot Polka**	yes*	Autumn 10
Tune 1	opposite	**Loose Cannon Galop**	no	Winter 7
2nd x		**Grapevine Polka**	no	Village 3
Tune 2		**Hot Cross Polka**	no	Country 1
2nd x		**Bordonian Nat. Polkas (1)**	no	*Dance Delights*
Tune 3		**Bordonian Nat. Polkas (2)**	no	*Dance Delights*
2nd x		**Pyrotechnic Polka** **Drive the cold winters away**	no yes*	Autumn 1 *Christ.C.D.B.*
Tune 1		**Wind-up Galop**	no	*Dance Delights*

As with all the other 19th century couples dances, I have been teaching couples polkas since the late 1980s, and in those 33-plus years have captured many historical and imagined step and figure variants inside many sequences. As with the Mazurkas that are featured in my **Marathon Mazurka medley** below, polkas are meant to be improvised but I, like many teachers over the centuries, have found it useful to present students with possible improvisation ingredients in sequences. Medleys can also be useful for showcasing variants. For both reasons many dancing masters composed polka medleys in the mid-19th century—see, for example, my entries on **Polka (1)** and **Polka (2)** in *Dancing through the Ages*, Volume VIII, where I present two of the earliest ways some particularly popular polka figures were sequenced in Paris and London in the 1840s, and which I re-sequenced in my **Polka Nationale** in this **Dance Delights** book. Sometimes dancing masters in the 1840s even use the term 'Grand' for their polka sequences—see my entry in that work under **Polka (3) / Grand Polkas**, so the title of my above medley is in a good tradition.

To offer background to the medley proposed above I might note that I've choreographed more than a dozen polka sequences, most 32 bars long but some just 16 bars long, and each usually consisted of about 4 different step or figure ideas. I designed each sequence so that if the dancer didn't want to deconstruct it for their own purpose, they could repeat it over and over as a self-sufficient dance. I wrote tune sets for all the polkas that appeared in my *Lost Dances* Volume I: *Pleasures for four seasons* and Volume II: *Favourites for four settings*, and between 2005 and 2008 and I had a great display team called the Bordonian Heritage Dancers who loved to include short medleys of my polkas in performances (in between medleys of other dances). In 2018 their successor, the Earthly Delights Historic Dance Academy dancers, wanted the challenge of dancing all my *Lost Dance* polkas together with

5:20 mins 32b.x10	*foot*	x 1 (except Pyrotechnic Polka)	*source*
Tune 1	oppos.	**Wind-up Galop**	*Dance Delights*
2nd x		**Fast Forward 1st variant**	Country 7
3rd x	left	**Fast Forward 2nd variant**	Country 7
Tune 2		**Peek-a-boo Polka**	Town 15
2nd x		**The Courtship Polka**	Autumn 13
3rd x		**Wrong foot Polka**	Autumn 10
Tune 3	right	**Loose Cannon Galop**	Winter 7
2nd x	oppos.	**Grapevine Polka**	Village 3
3rd x		**Hot Cross Polka**	Country 1
Tune 1		**Pyrotechnic Polka** x2	Autumn 1

— John Gardiner-Garden, *Dance Delights*, 2020 —

my post-*Lost Dances* 'The Wind-up Galop', and at the Australian National Folk Festival in Canberra at Easter 2018 we debuted the following 10 dance medley.

After the display some dancers suggested that although the under-arm twirl-out of the woman that is possible at the end of the Pyrotechnic Polka can be a very effective finale, 'The Wind-up Galop' might offer an even more thrilling finale as it involves lots of travelling pivoting. Accordingly, when I revised this medley with a small group in the middle of the 2020 pandemic, I took the opportunity to rearrange the medley so that it would finish with the Wind-up Galop. I also took the opportunity to add into that 5:20 minute suite four of my polka choreographies that were not in that original grand medley—three in this *Dance Delights* edition (the **Bordonian National Polka 1 & 2** and **The Corona Polka**) and one polka presented in my *Christmas Carol Dance Book* (**Drive the Cold winters away**). The result is a medley of 14 dances (with none repeated) that takes about 7 minutes to dance. It's as thrilling and showy—and although dancing it takes almost as long as the **Marathon Mazurka** medley (also presented in this book) it is little less exhausting as you tend to have you feet more often on the ground in a polka than in a mazurka.

I decided to start my new Grand Polka medley with one which captured the no-contact spirit of the time this new Grand Polka medley was being put together, a dance I'd debuted in my very last class before the great shutdown of March 2020, **The Corona Polka**, and build up from there with other sorts of heel&toe polkas before getting into polka that have more travel in them. The figures, steps and character of the constituent polkas change constantly, so it is not only a physical challenge, it is a mental one as well! It is however possible to dance and remember with minimum prompting, and although the pandemic has prevented us debuting this medley in public, three couples have successfully danced it at my home studio.

As with my other grand medleys of dances I've already written and published, I'll not here write out the instructions for all the constituent dances, but the instructions for all can be found in this *Dance Delights* and for the other 13 in my *Lost Dances* Volume I and II (2000 and 2005), and in my *Christmas Carol Dance book* (2002, with 2020 edition forthcoming). I'll not go into detail about the particulars of every transition but I might here briefly note how, if you want to, you can avoid the progressions that are in the original versions of three of the above constituent dances.

The Corona Polka (*Dance Delights*) instead of doing a heel&toe no-hand grand-chain past 4 people, just do the pretend right- and left-hand chain past 2 and then turn in and do the no-hand chain back past those same two dancers.

Wrong foot Polka (Autumn 10)—instead of starting A1 with 2 hands of a grand chain, just turn right and left-hand turn partner, then do rest of dance with same partner.

Drive the cold winters away (*Christmas Carol Dance Book*)—when the man turns solo over outside shoulder in B1 he should come back to the same partner, not progress on to a new one.

I've left out of the above choreography the polka I wrote to the carol **The Old Year now away is fled** (see my *Christmas Carol Dance Book*). Although it is a lot of fun and different again in its feature figures to any of the others named above, it feels a little bit more like a circle dance than any of the other sequences, so not wanting to go beyond the 8:00 minute mark, I decided to leave that one out.

Don't expect to learn this whole medley from scratch in one go! Although a wonderful sense of achievement is to be had once mastered, I suggest you introduce it to dancers with no prior knowledge of any of the component dances only a half or quarter at time (in between gentler dances) and wait till most are comfortable with one section before introducing another section, possibly spreading out the building up the whole medley over half-a-dozen classes. Once mastered, however, you will have enough polka ideas at your toes disposal to last you the rest of your life. Have fun!

~ The Hambo Sandwich ~

Form a line of 3 same-way-facing dancers, with a dancer of either gender in the middle but ideally with a M on the left, a lady on the right.

Start with dancers on left and in middle with l.f. free, and dancer on right with r.f. free.

Dance as many times as will.

Play any hambo tune.

A1	F. w. 3 waltz bal., w. 4 hambo steps (r-l-tog. / tog.-r-l / l-tog.-r) form basket & t. 3 times, then 1 waltz step to open out.
A2	Repeat
B1	L.end r.arm-waist cw swing middle *while* r.end goes acw; l.arm-waist swing acw r.end *while* middle goes cw / reform circle and l.end t. ½ cw looping l.h.; wheel cw as sweet-heart trio.
B2	L.end unloop acw *while* cw looping up middle and guiding them across to their l.arm and then wheel acw / l.end unloops and draws to far right the middle *while* acw looping the r.end and guiding them to r.arm; rotate new sweet-heart trio cw then l.end release r.end and unwind.
All x n.	

A1	All forward in line with 3 waltz balances then, with a non-turning hambo step, all curve into basket with arms around neighbours shoulder—the dancer on the left and right doing a usual man-woman 1 hambo step of right-left-together and l-together-r respectively *while* the dancer in the middle does the less usual together-r-l Turn in basket hold with 3 hambo-steps – always trying to have each right foot go directly forward along l.o.d. then open out back into a line with 1 waltz step
A2	Repeat A1
B1	L. end release neighbours' hands and put right arm around the waist of the middle dancer and cw swing them 1¼ around with 2 waltz steps *while* the middle dancer raises their right hand and lassoos the right-end dancer acw 3/4 around the outside of those swinging; then the left-end releases the middle dancer and catches the right-end dancer on their left-arm and waltz-swings with them *while they* raise their left hand and lassoo the middle dancer cw around on the same joined hand as before the left-end dancer slides off the right-end dancer, catching their right hand in their left hand as they do so and taking hands also with middle dancer to reform the circle of 3 and straight away the left-end dancer raises both their hands and turns ½ cw over their right shoulder, looping own left hand over their own head, then wheel as a sweet-heart hold trio cw.
B2	The left-end dancer then unloops themselves acw *while* looping up cw under their raised right hand the middle dancer and guiding them across to their (the left-end's) left-arm and then wheel the new sweet-heart trio acw. The left-end dancer unloops and draws back to their right the middle dancer *while* acw looping the right-end dancer under their (the left-end's) left arm and guiding them across to their right arm; rotate this last sweet-heart trio cw and then, by left-end M releasing hand of right-end, all unwind back into starting line.
AABBx n Repeat a many times as will.	

Although a much more complicated dance than any of the Bordonian 2 person hambos presented in my *Lost Dances of Earthly Delights* Volume II: *Favourites for Four Settings* (Country 10: 'Handfasting Hambo', Town 7, 'Harmony Hambo', Court 9: 'Honeymoon Hambo') when broken down step by step, there is a certain logic to the figures of this dance. The A part is a basic 3 person Hambo danced twice and the B part is essentially two different waltzed figure. The first waltzed figure, the swing while someone is orbiting around the outside happens first on one end of the dance then on the other. The second figure, the twisting into a 3-person sweet-heart hold happens three times. Although the left end dancer (usually a man) leads all the twisting, all 3 dancers take a turn at being twisted into the middle of a sweetheart trio—first the left end leader themselves, then the middle dancer then the right end tail.

Although the direction of the wheeling might seem random at first, the direction you wheel on each occasion is the direction the left end dancer, the effective leader, is moving just before each trio has to wheel. The leaders twisting of themselves cw in the first sweetheart leads to a cw wheel, the leaders moving acw around the outside of the middle dancer as they are twisted in the second sweetheart onto the leaders' left arm leads to an acw wheel, and the leaders cw motion around the right end dancer as the latter is drawn into the third sweetheart on the leader's right leads to another cw wheel.

~ Holiday Holubiec ~

Form couples scattered around l.o.d. holding partner in back allemande hold—i.e. facing the same way while holding right-in-right behind her back and under that left-in-left behind his back.

Start man with left foot woman right foot free.

Dance as many times as will.

Play any mazurka structured AABB xn.

A1 Quickly slide into prom. f. on inside hs—W taking 4 *pas de basque polonaise* f. *while* M takes 4 sideways hop(click)-step-steps facing her / M drops to knee and w. his raised r.h. <u>lassoes W acw</u> about him, she w. 4 *pas de basque* and he rising on the last bar.

A2 w. 3 quick steps M 'throws' W onto l.arm (taking her l.h. behind her b. in his l., she putting her r.h. on his l.sh.) for acw holubiec wheel (M f. W. b.) w. 3 hop-step-steps /
retaining l.hs w. 3 quick steps W casts to his r. side where he puts his r.h. under her l.arm to take her r.h. behind her b. and they *holubiec* acw (M b. W f.)

Counterpart from proper side with gender role reversal:

B1 Slide into prom. f. but this time M takes 4 forward *pas de basque polonaise* W 4 sideways r. hop(click)-step-steps facing her /
W *pas de basque* b., to l., f. to r. *while* lassoing M once cw on her raised l.h.

B2 M 'throws himself' onto W' r.arm, taking her l.h. in his l.h. behind her b. and in his r.h. her r.h. behind his b. and they *holubiec* cw (M b. W f.) w. 3 hop-step-steps /
w. 3 quick steps M 'casts' to W's l.side (without letting go of hs) and cont. *holubiec* cw (M f. W. b.) w. 3 hop-step-steps

AABBxn Repeat.

A1	<u>Man releases his right hand and drops it to take with it the left hand of his partner</u> with whom he promenades forward, she taking <u>4 *pas de basque polonaise* he taking</u> takes sideways to the left while facing her hop(click)-step-steps, their joined hands held back as they do so. Retaining but raising inside hand with partner <u>M bends or drops to knee and lassoes the W once acw</u> about him, she travelling with 4 *pas de basque polonaise* and he rising on the last bar.
A2	<u>On 1st bar, with 3 steps, the man 'throws' woman across onto his left arm M taking W's left hand behind her back in his left hand and W placing her right hand on the man's left shoulder</u> *Holubiec* (wheel as a couple) acw (i.e. man forward woman back) with 3 hop-step-steps (rounding the outside leg) <u>On 5th bar, with 3 steps and without letting go of the joined left hands, the woman casts quickly out and goes behind the man to his right side where he puts his right hand under her left arm around her waist to there take her right hand.</u> *Holubiec* (wheel as a couple) again <u>acw (this time man back woman forward)</u> with 3 hop-step-steps, ending back on proper side.
B1	<u>On 1st bar with 3 quicksteps, the man releases his left hand and slides his right arm down to take with it the left hand of his partner and</u> they again promenade, but this time he with 4 forward *pas de basque* she with 4 sideways hop(click)-step-steps sideways while facing him. Retaining inside hand with partner <u>W lassoes the M once cw</u> about him, he travelling with 4 *pas de basque while* she (instead of falling to the knee as he did for her lasso) takes 1 forward, 1 to left, 1 back and 1 to right (to help shorten the man's route).
B2	<u>On 1st bar, with 3 steps, the woman 'throws' the man (or man 'throws' himself) across onto the right arm of the woman,</u> he taking her left hand in his left hand behind her back and in his right hand her right hand behind his b. and they *holubiec* cw (i.e. wheel as a couple M back W forward) w. 3 hop-step-steps

— John Gardiner-Garden, *Dance Delights*, 2020 —

On 5th bar, with 3 steps and <u>without letting go of the joined right hands, the man casts quickly out and goes behind the woman to her left side to reverse the hold </u>(holding her left in his left behind his back her right in his right behind hers) and they continue their <u>*holubiec*</u> (wheel as a couple) <u>cw (man forward woman back)</u> with 3 hop-step-steps.

AABBxn Repeat sequence as many times as will.

I devised this pattern to go at the beginning of a grand mazurka medley I was putting together in the Australian summer of 2017/18. That medley was featuring a dozen different 32 bar patterns, each themselves a medley of different fancy couple's mazurka ideas, starting with patterns inspired by early-19th century mazurkas that featured mostly an alternation between promenading and wheeling as a couple, and ones inspired by mid-19th century waltz and polka influence mazurkas. The medley as a whole was, however, missing three of the most common early mazurka figures—a promenade using *pas de basque polonaise*, the man dropping to the knee in order to lasso(o) his partner around him, and the throwing of the woman onto the man's arm and then wheeling side-by-side, switching sides and wheeling a fresh. I decided to put a form this sequence might take up right front in the grand medley. Out of possible ways to do the promenade, the *holubiec* and the switch (see my discussion in my *Dancing through the Ages,* Volume VIII, Part 1c), I chose the *holubiec* out of hop-step-steps and the switch using a technique I found hinted at in many sources—effectively a very quick ½ turn on the hand at the end of the arm onto which the partner was thrown which starts with the person thrown casting over their outside shoulder and ends them locking into beside their partner on the other side.

The first 16 bars of the above sequence present the pattern as you would normally expect it, with the man throwing the woman to his left arm and with the man going forward on the first wheel and back on the second. Although it involves a departure from early 19th century expectations, I then made the second 16 bars the counterpart of the first 16. Thus in the BB features roughly the same figures as in AA but there is a gender role reversal—the woman does the click-step-step promenade looking at the man, it is who lassoes her partner, it is she who guides her partner across her body into an *holubiec* hold, and she who goes forward on the first wheel and back on the second.

The second half of the dance is the most challenging part of the dance, as reversing of gender roles obliges the woman to do sideways steps while watching the man, the man to put his left hand up on his partner's right shoulder, to wheel with the man leaning back on the woman's arm, and for the woman to help the man switch from her right to her left side—all experiences to which a man and woman are not accustomed.

The sequence can be danced with a lot of dramatic accent. When promenading forward the one who is doing the side step should be looking directly at their partner as this helps suggest it is they who at the end of tha promenade are lassoing that partner (as opposed to the partner just going around them). When the man drops to his knee he can heighten the effect by stomping on the flat of his front foot as he drops, the knee of the rear leg shouldn't itself make a noise as it shouldn't actually hit the ground, just seem to. The transitions between the two halves of each *holubiec* wheel should be as smooth as possible and not interrupt the continuity of the acw wheel in the A2 or cw wheel in B2.

Though a challenging dance, once mastered, it can be a thrilling sequence to drop into any free (or planned) couple's mazurka.

~ Knot À Trois ~

Form columns with facing ranks of 3, 1 man between 2 women.

Start either foot

Dance as a progressive sequence as many times as will

Play any 32-bar waltz, intro. then AABB x n.

A1	W full r&l *while* M t. full r. and 1/2 l. to take opp. We's l.hs in his r.
A2	½ prom; M t.s. l. switching hs / counter orbit for W ptnrs to switch, finish M again holding We's l.hs in his r.
B1	½ prom; M t.s. l. switching hs / repeat knot, W finishing home
B2	½ prom. again; M l.h. t. ea. other to switch stars (all prog. but W have ch. sides) / W cross w. their same-side W by l.sh. and M go f;b. and t. about to collect ptnrs facing orig. direction in progressed pos.
All x n.	each time ending one placed progressed facing new opposites or, when at end of column, turning as individuals and waiting.

A1	With 2 waltz steps for each hand the 4 women <u>rights and lefts</u> with each other, starting right hand to opposite till all back in place *while* <u>men right hand turn each other</u> with 4 waltz steps then turn with 2 waltz steps and <u>come back</u> with <u>left hand</u> turn ½ way with 2 waltz steps <u>finishing</u> retaining left hand with opposite man and <u>taking hold of opposite two W's joined hands</u> (on their own base-line) all <u>with</u> free <u>right hand</u>
A2	With 4 waltz steps <u>promenade</u> thus ½ way around the set (women to opposite side, men to home side), towards the end <u>men turn</u> completely about <u>over left shoulder switching hands behind his back</u> so as to have lead women's left hand in his left hand and following woman's left hand in his right hand. With 4 waltz steps, the three <u>do a counter orbit knot</u>– the men raise both hands to guide the woman on his left in a wide acw orbit behind him while guiding woman on his right hand under his raised right hand and, with her turning over left shoulder as she does so, cw inside under arch with other woman, so as <u>to finish with women in exchanged place</u>, man's hands crossed left hand on top.
B1	Men slide into holding both women's left hands in his right hand <u>and they (the men) promenade women</u> with 4 waltz steps acw ½ way <u>back to own base-line</u>, turning, towards the end of the promenade, <u>over left shoulder</u> taking front woman's left hand in his right hand and rear woman's left hand in his right to form a kind of <u>triangle</u> <u>Repeat knot so W return to home</u> (M still on opposite side).
B2	All ½ <u>promenade again (M now home W on opposite side)</u>, but this time instead of the men turn single about they left hand turn each other to switch stars, so all are on opposite side with their original partners (but women have switched end of their rank). <u>women pass left shoulder</u> *while* <u>men go forward</u> with 2 waltz steps to greet opposite man <u>and back</u> with 2 waltz steps to collect own women who have now caught him up.
AABB xn	*Repeat sequence with different successive ranks of opposites.*

This dance uses a variant on a knot found in a dance I saw presented as a 'Doppelländer from Innviertel and Oberosterreich' but sets that knot in a sequence which allows the man to pass on with same original partners to do the knot with new woman each time. The knott doesn't come easily off the page, but once achieved, should henceforth flow easily. Make sure you have at least 4 ranks of 3 so you can dance twice before a rest at the end.

— John Gardiner-Garden, *Dance Delights*, 2020 —

~ The Lacework Mazurka ~

Form couples facing along l.o.d. holding l.hs over r.hs in low promenade hold.

Start weight on right foot, left foot free.

Dance as many times as will, alternate with 'The Zig-Zag' Mazurka, or put in a larger medley.

Play any mazurka set.

A1	Prom. f. w. 2 hop-drop-kicks; w. 5 steps M passes W to inside, point r.f. / Counterpart, point l.f.
A2	Wheel acw w. 2 hop-step-steps; w. 5 steps M acw rolls ('tumbles') W to inside free r.f. / Counterpart to free l.f.
B1	Swing cw on crossed hs w. 2 hop-drop-kicks; run 5 steps, swivelling on last to point r.f. / Counterpart, point l.f.
B2	R.h. t. w. 2 hop-drop-kicks; w. 5 steps M pass W behind, point r. / Cw 'neck' *tour* w. 2 click-step-steps; w. 5 steps M lassoos W in front to outside, point l.f.
All x n.	

A1	Promenade forward with 2 hop-drop-kicks, then with 5 steps M passes W across to inside, both finishing pointing right foot.
	Counterpart, M passing W back to outside and both finishing facing pointing left foot.
A2	Wheel acw (M back) with 2 hop-step-steps (i.e. hobbles – M with clicking) then with 5 steps M rolls W twirling once about across to inside finishing W on left of M, right hands crossed over left hands, both pointing right foot.
	Counterpart, wheeling cw (M improper & b) then M rolling W with cw twirl back to outside, finishing facing, left hands again crossed over right hands and left foot free.
B1	Swing cw on crossed hands with 2 hop-drop-kicks, then run with 5 steps, swivelling on the last to point right foot back in acw direction.
	Counterpart, finishing releasing each other's left hand and holding right hands while pointing left foot.
B2	Right hand turn with 2 hop-drop-kicks then with 5 steps M passes his right hand behind his own neck to guide the W behind his back to his left side and there catch her in a hold.
	Wheel cw in this 'neck' hold with 2 click-step-steps then with 5 steps M twirls W around in front back to his right side, finishing both pointing left foot ready for promenade.
AABB xn *Repeat sequence* as many times as will.	

This Mazurka offers a flashy 'relatively' simple (it is still a challenge) vehicle for enjoying two 'hop-first' steps— the 'hop-drop-kick' travelling step and the 'hop-step-step' wheeling step. The former is done whenever there is distance between partners and the later whenever partners are side-by-side. These steps constitute the first 2 bars of every 4-bar phrase. The second bars always consist of 5 gentle running steps which finish pointing the free outside foot. Put it all together and you have a dance that go well in a medley with the slightly more challenging **Zig-Zag Mazurka**. Where 'Zig-Zag' makes a feature of sharp angles, tight dizzy turns and dramatic triple heel-clicks, 'Lacework' makes a feature of gracefully interlacing of arms, smooth running and pointing that floats restfully in the air. To transition from 'Lacework' to 'Zig-Zag' just do the opening promenades of the 'Zig-Zag' with the left hands rather than right crossed on top and then release left hand to turn on right hand. The second time through 'Zig-Zag' you can do the promenades with right hands joined on top. To transition back to the 'Lacework' just offer right hand under left hands when taking the final cross hand hold.

— John Gardiner-Garden, *Dance Delights*, 2020 —

~ Lobster Quadrille ~

Form 4 couples in a square

Start right foot free

Dance as each of the 3 figures, then repeat with sides leading 1B.

Play intro. then ABC x 6 to do dance twice, 1s leading 1B first time, 2s leading second.

1)
A	R.sh. gyp. ptner / f. to neigh; b. to bump
B	Tops f&b x 2 *while* sides f&b x 1
C	Clap w. ptner r-own-l-own, r-own-l-own, both & bow /; same cnr

2)
A	All set / W's chain across
B	W chain b. past M who follow, catch and turn them to face in.
C	Alternate pulls: M-W-M-W, 2h t. ½ cw /; W-M-W-M, t. ½ cw.

3)
A	M lead into grand star ½ about /; wheel ½ cw
B	W r.h. grand star b. to place, wheel 3/4 acw and bow
C	Grand chain 2 steps each hand, bow on ea. side of set.

♩ = 120

A dance which satisfies the description of the dance which the Mock Turtle and Gryphon offer in word and song in of Lewis Carroll's 1865 *Alice Adventures in Wonderland,* and a tune which enables the song to be sung 'slowly and sadly', as described. Both dance and tune are by John Garden.

	The Mock Turtle's Song	*Turtle and Gryphon instructions in bold.*
	~ Part 1 ~	
A	**"Will you / walk a little faster?"** **said a whiting to a snail** **"There's a / porpoise close behind us,** **and he's treading on my tail.**	All r.sh. gypsy partner All 4 steps towards neighbour and 3 steps back to bottom bump your partner and then 1 count to bounce off into holding inside hands
B	**See how / eagerly the lobsters** **and the turtles all advance!** **They are / waiting on the shingle,** **–will you / come and join the dance?'**	Head couples take partner's inside hand and **advance** and retire **twice** towards each other, and *while* they retire the first time and advance the second side couples advance and retire once.
C	**Will you, won't you,** **will you, won't you,** **will you join the dance?**	All with partner clap right hand, own, left, own, Right, own, left, own, then take both hands and bow entreatingly as you about face

— John Gardiner-Garden, *Dance Delights*, 2020 —

	Will you, won't you, will you, won't you, won't you join the dance?	<u>With corner, clap right hands, own, left hands, own,</u> <u>Right hands, own, left hands, own,</u> <u>Take both hands and bow</u> as you turn back to partner
	~ Part 2 ~	
A	"You can / really have no notion how delightful it will be When they / take us up and throw us, with the lobsters, out to sea!"	All slow chassez **set to partners** right then left, finishing M holding W's left hand in his right With 8 steps all M **change lobsters and retire in same order** by assisting their W into <u>lady's chain across set</u> and courtesy turning oncoming opposite W.
B	But the / snail replied "Too far, too far!" And gave a look askance– Said he / thanked the whiting kindly, but he would not join the dance'	**Then** with 4 counts M **throw the lobster as far out to sea as you can** by <u>chaining the W back across the set</u>, but instead of immediately courtesy turning original back into set, **'Swim after them!'** – by <u>M</u> turning to <u>follow W</u> as they go past their l.side, <u>take them in skater's promenade hold</u> as you go. All **Turn a somersault in the sea!** by <u>courtesy turning/wheeling 1 1/4 acw</u> as a couple, and then <u>M, on the inside of set</u> *while* <u>W are on the outside, turning W under his raised left hand</u> and <u>switching to 2hs,</u> M **change lobsters again** by M (briefly on knee) taking W's hands and begging her (showing reluctance) to dance
C	Would not, could not, would not, could not, would not join the dance.	With 4 steps <u>M pulls</u> W back towards dance With 4 steps <u>W pulls</u> M back out of dance With 4 steps <u>2h turn</u> ½ cw
	Would not, could not, would not, could not, would not join the dance.	With 4 steps <u>M pushes</u> W back towards dance With 4 steps <u>W pushes</u> M back out of dance With 4 steps <u>2h turn</u> ½ cw
	~ Part 3 ~	
A	"What / matters it how far we go" his scaly friend replied. 'There / is another shore, you know upon the other side.	M release W's <u>right hand</u> from his left and with 4 steps <u>M leads W</u> by his right <u>back into set</u> With 4 steps <u>M take left hand and start grand star</u> acw With 4 steps grand star is <u>halfway around</u> set, With 4 counts M let go of left hands and <u>wheel</u> acw <u>½ about so W can take right hands</u> and all face back the way they came
B	The further off from England the nearer is to France– Then turn not pale, beloved snail,	With 8 steps all <u>grand star back</u> to home place With 8 steps W drop right and <u>couples wheel 3/4</u> cw

	but come and join the dance'	With 4 counts release hands and with 4 counts <u>bow</u> to partner – **back to land again**
C	**Will you, won't you, will you, won't you, will you join the dance?**	<u>Grand chain</u> round the set—<u>2 steps for each hand</u>: pull right hand past partner, left past next, pull right hand past next, left past next, giving right hand. to partner on other side of set, 4 count <u>bow</u>
	Will you, won't you, will you, won't you, won't you join the dance?	pull right hand past partner, left past next, pull right hand past next, left past next, giving right hand to partner in home place, <u>bow</u>
		'and that's all the first figure' repeat with new sides taking the role of 1s (preferably couple to right of last 1s)

In chapter 10 of Lewis Carroll's 1865 *Alice Adventures in Wonderland*, the Mock Turtle and Gryphon describe to Alice a dance called 'The Lobster Quadrille' and then demonstrate the dance while singing a song. I have 'reconstructed' a dance that might satisfy both the initial description (text in bold in the right-hand column) and the song (text in bold in the left-hand column). To set the scene here is the text leading up to the song:

The Mock Turtle sighed deeply, and drew the back of one flapper across his eyes. He looked at Alice, and tried to speak, but for a minute or two sobs choked his voice. "Same as if he had a bone in his throat," said the Gryphon: and it set to work shaking him and punching him in the back. At last the Mock Turtle recovered his voice, and, with tears running down his cheeks, he went on again:—

"You may not have lived much under the sea—" ('I haven't,' said Alice)—"and perhaps you were never even introduced to a lobster–"
(Alice began to say "I once tasted—" but checked herself hastily, and said 'No, never') "–so you can have no idea what a delightful thing a Lobster Quadrille is!"
"No, indeed," said Alice. "What sort of a dance is it?"
"Why," said the Gryphon, "you first form into a line along the sea-shore–"
"Two lines!" cried the Mock Turtle. "Seals, turtles, salmon, and so on;
then, when you've cleared all the jelly-fish out of the way–"
"That generally takes some time," interrupted the Gryphon.
"–you advance twice–"
"Each with a lobster as a partner!" cried the Gryphon.
"Of course," the Mock Turtle said: "advance twice, set to partners–"
"–change lobsters, and retire in same order," continued the Gryphon.
"Then, you know," the Mock Turtle went on, `you throw the–"
"The lobsters!" shouted the Gryphon, with a bound into the air.
"–as far out to sea as you can–"
"Swim after them!" screamed the Gryphon.
"Turn a somersault in the sea!" cried the Mock Turtle, capering wildly about.
"Change lobsters again!" yelled the Gryphon at the top of its voice.

"Back to land again, and that's all the first figure," said the Mock Turtle, suddenly dropping his voice; and the two creatures, who had been jumping about like mad things all this time, sat down again very sadly and quietly, and looked at Alice.
"It must be a very pretty dance," said Alice timidly.
"Would you like to see a little of it?" said the Mock Turtle.
"Very much indeed," said Alice.
"Come, let's try the first figure!" said the Mock Turtle to the Gryphon.
"We can do without lobsters, you know. Which shall sing?"
"Oh, you sing," said the Gryphon. "I've forgotten the words."

So they began solemnly dancing round and round Alice, every now and then treading on her toes when they passed too close, and waving their forepaws to mark the time, while the Mock Turtle sang the song given in the tabulation very slowly and sadly.

The reconstructed dance that keeps faith with the description, the song and contemporary dance expectations in all but two respects, and for those deviations there are good reasons.

Firstly, although the Gryphon and Mock Turtle say 'first form' 'two lines' and although the dance here plotted could well be done in two long 'Beckett formation' lines with all dancing all the time, I've favoured a 4 couple square formation with couples numbered cw 1s, 3s, 2s and 4s and opposites doing most of the dancing. This is more like a Quadrille as danced in 1860s England and more able to be danced around an Alice.

Secondly, although the first dance instruction which the Mock Turtle offers is 'Advance twice', to fit with the subsequent song and with the quadrille practise of acknowledging partner and corner I've proposed an opening 16 count introductory figure.

To help dancers remember which hand to clap when I would observe that whenever you sing 'Will' you clap right hands. The joke in our own dance scene was that 'Will (the name of one of our most capable and respected dancers and callers) is always right'.

It's possible that, indeed rather certain, that Lewis Carroll had a very different dance to that I have described above in mind when writing this scene. He probably had in mind standard quadrille figures he and his audience would have scene in the ballroom of the time, and it's also possible that he intended the three 'playings' of ABC, to reflect the same figures being led by different couples. If this this was the case, the exact nature of the original dance he is parodying eludes me. The one I offer above in its stead is hopefully a fitting fun substitute—a parody in its own right.

~ The Marathon Mazurka medley ~

Form as for 'Holiday Holubiec'.

Start man left foot free woman right foot.

Dance each of the 16 named dances each once.

Play the four selected strains from *Hart's First Set of Mazurkas* (transcribed by myself John Gardiner-Garden, with chords by Sally Taylor) each twice and then all that again (but that time no repeat of Tune 4).

	foot	*style*	*dance*	*source*
Tune 1	opp-osite	hop first	**Holiday Holubiec**	*Dance Delights*
"			**Barbarous Elegance**	Court 2
Tune 2	left		**Ad Absudam Sur Place**	Village 15
"			**Russian Tour**	Town 4
Tune 3			**Lacework Mazurka**	*Dance Delights*
"			**Zig Zag Mazurka**	*Dance Delights*
Tune 4	opp-osite	step first	**Vulgarian Salut.**	Village 2
			Conjuring L'Amour	Country 12
"			**Russian Gypsy Queen**	*Dance Delights*
Tune 1			**Boots and Blades**	Autumn 14
"			**Blackforest Mazurka**	Village 5
Tune 2			**Askance Romance**	Town 13
"			**Regatta Room Grapple**	Country 15
Tune 3			**The Washing Machine**	Court 14
"			**Footloose Gypsy**	Court 12
Tune 4			**The Cavalier's Mazurka**	Winter 14

Tune 1 = originals no.1

Tune 2 = originals no.5

Tune 3 = originals no.3

Tune 4 = originals no.2

— John Gardiner-Garden, *Dance Delights*, 2020 —

As with polkas, that featured in my **Grand Polka medley** above, I have enjoyed teaching couples mazurkas since the late 1980s, and in those 33-plus years have captured many historical and imagined step and figure variants inside many sequences. Mazurkas are meant to be improvised but I, like many teachers over the centuries, have found it useful to present students with possible improvisation ingredients in sequences. I developed 14 mazurka sequences that were 32 bars long, and 2 that were 16 bars long, and each sequence usually consisted of about 4 different step or figure ideas. I designed each sequence so that if the dancer didn't want to deconstruct it for their own purpose, they could repeat it over and over as a self-sufficient dance. I wrote tune sets for all the mazurka dances that appeared in my *Lost Dances* Volume I: *Pleasures for four seasons* and Volume II: *Favourites for four settings*, and between 2005 and 2008 I had a very active display team called the Bordonian Heritage Dancers which loved to include medleys of 3 or 4 of my couples mazurka dances in their performances (in between medleys of many other dances). We ended up with four different medleys, each set to a different *Lost Dances* set. Over the years the dancers in that display group, as in the Earthly Delight Historic Dance Academy dancers that succeeded them, changed but the mazurka medleys remained favourites, and in 2017 I had a group that wanted to try doing all 15 of my then published mazurkas in one long medley. I agreed to arrange it but conscious that most of those sequences were of the later mazurka-waltz turning variety, I decided to put at the beginning of the set a sequence that would showcase some more traditional promenade and *holubiec* wheel figures (that sequence became the 'Holiday Holubiec' published for the first time in this edition of my *Dance Delights*). I decided to set the grand 9-minute medley to the English social dance music composer Joseph Hart's 'The Original Mazurka' suite from late-1820s or 1830. Our pianists had four favourite tunes in that suite and a preferred order for playing them. By carefully arranging the dances I was able to group together those more old-style ones that started with a hop-first and those later-style ones that started with a step or glide first, and group those for which the man and woman start with the opposite foot and those for which they start both on the left foot—thus reducing the opportunities for transition confusions.

I'll not here write out the instructions for all 16 constituent dances, but the instructions for three can be found in this *Dance Delights* and for the other 13 in my *Lost Dances* Volume I and II. I'll not go into detail about particular transitions and progression substitutions which I recommended, but the performance we did of the medley at the National Multicultural Festival and at a ball at the Albert Hall, in Canberra, in April 2018 were videoed and hopefully one day I can include that video in an online library of some of our display videos (in the meantime I'm happy to share one with any interested dance group). I had hoped that we might have different couples in the display group start at different points in the medley, so at any one time onlookers saw lots of different variants, creating an illusion of spontaneity, but remembering where you are up to when others around you are doing different parts of the medley (and when you are getting progressively more and more tired!) was almost impossible, so we ended up on both occasions all dancing in unison.

Overleaf are facsimile of the four chosen tunes from the original Hart mazurka set piano score:

THE ORIGINAL MAZURKA.
1
No 1.
p
p
p

2
LADY CATHARINE GRIMSTONE.
No 2.
p
f

THE DUKE OF DEVONSHIRE'S FAVORITE.
3
No 3.
f
Ped
p
p
f
Ped

MISS ELPHINSTONE.
5
Coquette Figure.
No 5.
p
f
Ped
p

~ Mazurian Anglaise *or* Courland Fancy ~

Form proper duple minor longways set.

Start left foot free.

Dance as duple minor sequence.

Play a 32-bar mazurka intro. then AABB xn.

A1	1M2W dsd / swing in r.arm-across-stomach left-in-air hold
A2	1W2M same
B1	1s (above) cross by r.h.; ½ l.h. neigh. ending M pulling r.sh. b. and tucking r.arm under W's l. behind her back and facing same way / *holubiec* as cpl acw
B2	In b.-allemande hold go f. toward ptner; retire releasing hold / 1s (again, but this time from below) cross by r.h.; full l.h. t. same sex neigh.
All x n.	

A1	<u>1st man and 2nd woman do-si-do</u> with 4 *pas de basque polonaise* (starting left foot free so weight is on right at end for transition into hop first holubiec step…) <u>with 4 same-foot *holubiec* steps (hop right-step left-step right) swing once or twice cw around </u>in a dramatic 'Eastern European folkloric' hold: <u>right arm-across-stomach each other's stomach *while* own left arm is arced high in air and couple</u> (whose bodies are facing forward in the cw direction they are moving) <u>turn faces toward each other over own right shoulder</u>, separating at end back to starting place.
A2	<u>1st woman and 2nd woman do-si-do </u>with 4 *pas de basque polonoise* these same corners <u>swing</u> as other corners did in r.arm-across-stomach left-in-air hold
B1	with 4 *pas de basque polonoise* (this time in anticipation of the mirror foot holubiec man starts left foot free woman right) <u>1s</u> (above) <u>cross by right hand then ½ left hand turn neighbour ending M pulling right shoulder back and tucking right arm under woman's left arm behind her back and facing same way</u> <u>with 4 mirror-foot *holubiec steps*</u> (hop M on right W on left – step -step) *wheel* acw as a couple
B2	<u>retaining back-allemande hold go forward </u>with 4 *pas de basque polonoise* <u>toward partner then</u> with 4 backward *pas de basque polonoise* <u>retire releasing hold</u> with 4 *pas de basque polonoise* <u>1s</u> (again, but this time from below) <u>cross by right hand and full left hand turn same sex neighour.</u>
AABB xn Repeat as many times as will.	

In 1806 in Riga, then capital of the Russian Governorate of Livonia (next door to the Governorate of Courland—the two together covering much of modern day Latvia), Dietrich Alexander Ivensenn published *Terpsichore: ein Taschenbuch für Freunde und Freundinnen des Tanzes in Liv-, Kur- und Ehstland* ('Terpsichore: a pocket bock for friends of the dance in Livonia, Kurland and Ehstland'). This remarkable study included chapters on **den Angloisen** ('the English country dance'), **die Ekossoise oder den schottischen Tanz** ('the Ecossoise or the Scottisch dance') and **den masurischen Tanz** ('the Mazurian dance'). In the later he made the remarkable observation that there had developed a local hybrid between the mazurka and the English longways dance, where the footwork of the former was accommodated in the longways set of the later:

> **Der damalige Geschmack, das Masurische in einer Angloisen-Kolonne zu tanzen, ist eine hiesige Erfindung; denn, in allen Ländern, wo dieser Tanz einheimisch ist, habe ich ihn nie anders, also**

von vier Paaren als Quadrille vortragen gesehen. Einleuchtend wird es auch jedem kenner seyn, daß die mazurischen Schritte und Wendungen, in dem gedrängten Raum einer Angloisen-Kolonne nicht gut ausgeführt werden können. Das gracieuse Werfen des Körpers, das Anschlagen der Fersen, die abstoßenden Pas mit den Hacken—alles das, was diesen Tanz auszeichnet, erfordert einen weit größern Spielraum.

The recent fad to dance the Masurian [dance] in an *Anglois* [i.e. English country dance] column, is a local invention; because, in all countries where this dance is indigenous, I've never seen it danced other than in four couples as in a Quadrille. It will be obvious to every connoisseur that the Mazurian steps and turns can not be performed well in the crowded space of an *Anglois* a column. The gracious throwing of the body, the striking the heel, the 'stomp' step with the cutting—everything that distinguishes this dance, requires a far greater space.

In the absence of any surviving instructions for such hybrids (and alas there are also no surviving videos), I have here created my own duple minor longways proper 'Mazurian Anglais' and my own duple minor longways improper 'Mazurian Ecossaise'. In each I have endeavoured to show off both parent dance forms to the best advantage and as such believe you will not feel either your mazurka footwork cramped or your longways figuring impaired.

In the above 'Mazurian Anglais' I might suggest make two suggestions to do with steps. Firstly, if the man starts all his *pas de basques polonoise* left foot he will have his weight on right foot ready to hop on it to start his parallel *holubie* c in A part and mirror one in B1, even though the woman will need to change from left foot in A to right foot in B. Seconly, you substitute for a *pas de basques polonoise,* the mazurka step I call the 'soccer kick step'. For more on this step and for more on what Ivensen had to say about the Anglais, Ecossais and Mazurka see my section on 'The Country Dance' and 'Mazurka' in Part 1b of Volume VII and on 'Mazurka steps' in Part 1c of Volume VIII of my *Dancing through the Ages* (Canberra, 2020) series.

~ Mazurian Ecossaise or Livonian Lilt ~

Form <u>improper duple minor</u> longways set.

Start left foot free.

Dance as duple minor sequence.

Play a 32-bar mazurka intro. then AABBxn.

A1	Circle l. / Circle r.
A2	Mill r. / M release, t. about, drop to knee and hold up l.h. *while* W ¼ r.h. t. ea other then give l.h. to partner and go acw about them b. to place (retaining l.hs as M springs to his feet)
B1	Counterpart w. l.h. mill and lasso opp. r.h.
B2	bal. l. to take r.h., r. to take l.h.; repeat / l.h. t. opp. and pull thru by l.sh. (1s down 2s up) to take hs in a circle w. next couple
All x n.	

A1	<u>1s and 2s circle left</u> with 3 *pas de boîteux* ('hobble steps') then stomp-point
	<u>Counterpart</u>
A2	1s and 2s <u>mill</u> exactly once around <u>on right hand</u> w. 4 hobbles or *pas de basqe polonoise*
	<u>M</u> let go, <u>turn about, drop to knee</u> and hold up left hand *while* <u>W ¼ right hand turn each other then give left hand to partner and go in acw lasso about them</u> back to place (retaining left hands as M springs to his feet)
B1	Same 4 <u>mill on left hand</u>
	<u>Men</u> let go, <u>turn about, drop to knee</u> and hold up right hand *while* <u>women ¼ left hand turn</u> each other then give <u>right hand to partner and</u> go in <u>cw lasso about them</u> back to place (retaining right hands as M springs to his feet)
B2	<u>balance left</u> (possibly with a step-lift-lift) <u>to take right hand</u>, <u>balance right to take left</u>, <u>then the same balances and hand taking again</u> ending left hands joined
	with 4 *pas de basque polonoise* <u>left hand turn same opposite 1¼ and pass on</u> thru (1s down 2s up) to take hs in a circle w. next couple
AABB xn Repeat as many times as will.	

This dance, like the **Mazurian Anglaise *or* Courland Fancy** in the preceding entry, was inspired Dietrich Alexander Ivensenn's comment in *Terpsichore: ein Taschenbuch für Freunde und Freundinnen des Tanzes in Liv-, Kur- und Ehstland* ('Terpsichore: a pocket bock for friends of the dance in Livonia, Kurland and Ehstland'), Riga, 1806 . In the passage quoted in the previous entry, Ivensenn argued against the fad of dancing the 'Masurian dance' (i.e. mazurka) in an *Anglois*, arguing the steps of the former cannot be performed well in the crowded space of a column. Ivensenn did not say anything about including 'Mazurian' steps in an *Ecossoise*, another longways dance form on which he had a chapter, but here is my attempt to accommodate mazurka steps in the tight confines of an improper longways duple minor set, the most common formation for an *Ecossoise*. We don't know if Ivensenn's young compatriots were experimenting with putting mazurka steps into *Ecossoise* column, and it is possible they were not as it is harder to set a naturally 3/8 or 3/4 step to the 2/4 or 4/4 tune of an *Ecossaise* than it is to a slow 6/8 tune of an *Angloise* when 2 such steps can fit in a bar. In have gone possibly further than the young Riga enthusiasts in envisaging a **Mazurian Anglaise** and **Mazurian Ecossaise** that are set to 32 bars of mazurka music.

~ Mazurka country dance medley ~

Form longways set of 4 couples, couples 1&2 improper, 3&4 proper.

Start left foot free, facing on diagonal i.e. 1M facing 2W, 1W 2M, 3M 4W, 3W 4M.

Dance from inside of the column out (i.e. 2M starting with 1W, 3M w.4W) **Mazurian Anglaise** x 1, then 2 new inside couples dance and propagate into other half **Mazurian Ecossaise** x 3, then in both halves of set again dance **Mazurian Anglais** x ¾, end with a mazurka-ed circle left and right.

Play any 32-bar mazurka intro. then AABBxn, perhaps the 4 tunes from Hart's *First Set of Mazurkas* suite I proposed for **The Marathon Mazurka medley**, just x1 on each tune then back to the first tune x1.

Inside couples with neighbouring end couples (i.e. duple minor in each half of the set, starting 2M w. 1W, 3M w.4W) dance **Mazurian Anglaies x 1 thus**

A1 1M2W dsd / swing in r.arm-across-stomach left-in-air hold

A2 1W2M same

B1 1s (above) cross by r.h.; ½ l.h. neigh. ending M pulling r.sh. b. and tucking r.arm under W's l. behind her back and facing same way / *holubiec* as cpl acw

B2 In b.-allemande hold go f. toward ptner; retire releasing hold / 1s (again, but this time from below) cross by r.h.; full l.h. t. same sex neigh.

The new inside couples dance (original 1s and 4s) take hands in a circle in midle of column and dance and then propagate on into other half **Mazurian Ecossaise** x 3,

A1 Circle l. / Circle r.

A2 Mill r. / M release, t. about, drop to knee and hold up l.h. *while* W ¼ r.h. t. ea other then give l.h. to partner and go acw about them b. to place (retaining l.hs as M springs to his feet)

B1 Counterpart w. l.h. mill and lasso opp. r.h.

B2 bal. l. to take r.h., r. to take l.h.; repeat / l.h. t. opp. and pull thru by l.sh. (1s down 2s up) to take hs in a circle w. next couple

After waiting out 32 bars while the **Mazurian Ecossaise** is danced for the third time (on that time by the original 2s&3s in middle of set), the original 1s and 4s renter the dance from the opposite end of the column to their starting end doing the A1&2 and B1 of the **Mazurian Anglaise**, the 1s with the 2s, the 4s with the 3s.

For the final B2 of last played tune, all join hs and take 3 hop-step-steps to l. and stomp-point r.f. back to r., then 3 hop-step-steps to r. and a toestogether-toesapart *pas final* with joined hs in air, followed after music's end by a communal bow in 1st foot position.

This medley of the dances described in the two preceding entries, **Mazurian Anglaise** and **Mazurian Ecossaise,** was debuted by dancers and musicians of the Earthly Delights Historic Dance Academy at the National Multicultural Festival in Canberra in February 2020. The arrangement, alternating as it does between duple minor action in each half of the column and just in the middle of the column and between two different sequences each with different patterns offers a pretty and constantly changing kaleidoscope of diagonals, spins and circles and the fact that the **Mazurian Anglaise** pattern with which you opened to the first tune is returned to when the whole set is full inverted and you return to the first tune, produces an unconscious satisfaction for dancers and onlookers alike. Note, however, if you want to finish with the 8 bars of communal circling I suggest you have to all remember to cut the reprise dancing of the **Mazurian Anglaise** sequence short and anticipate sliding out of the side-by-side wheel with partner at the end of B1 into holding hands in a full 8-person circle.

I'll not here offer the full-worded instructions for the two constituent dances as they can be found in the dedicated entries on those dances and the summary box explanation of how those two dances are bound together should suffice. I'll also not offer the music score that worked so well for that debut display, as it is exactly the same as the 4 tune score derived from Joseph Hart's *First Set of Mazurkas* that I presented for 'The Marathon Mazurka medley', only here you need only play each of the 4 tunes once and then the first tune once again.

— John Gardiner-Garden, *Dance Delights*, 2020 —

~ The México Varsovienna medley ~

Form couples in ballroom hold, opposite feet, man left woman right foot free.

Dance this sequence as many times as will.

Play Luis Abadie's 'México. Varsoviana' which appeared in an *Album Filármonico* published in Paris 'Octobre de 1854' AABBx4 then 3-bar coda.

1AABB 'La Va ouvert' (Country 6) x 1—starting in waist-shoulder hold man left woman right foot free,
2AABB 'La Va melangée' (Court 9) x1—starting in front skater's hold, opposite foot free as above
3AABB 'La Va croisée' (Town 11) x1 - starting in high promenade hold, both left foot free
4AA: 1st half of **'La Va ouvert'** then
4BB: 1 (glide-cut-hop) hobble, 2 polka-redowas and 3-step pivot cw 1½ / cntrprt **3 bar coda** turn W out & bow.

— John Gardiner-Garden, *Dance Delights*, 2020 —

There have been many theories about the origin of the dance that is variously called 'La Varsovienne' (from the French), 'The Varsovienna' (an Anglicised version of the French) or 'Varsoviana' (from the Spanish). Anne Schley Duggan et. al. in *Folk dances of Scandinavia*, 1948, p.60 has noted that forms of this dance are common to many national groups, that in folk traditions everywhere it is danced in triple meter in either a two or three-part form, and that during the middle of the nineteenth century it was introduced by dancing masters in various countries to the ballrooms of the sophisticated. The two big question are, however, in which country might the dance have first originated, and did it originate as a folk or ballroom dance? I might briefly consider these questions together.

An Italian origin has been suggested by people noting the similarly between the name of the dance and that of Mount Versuvius and a Swedish origin has been suggested as the dance's place of origin as references to folk versions of the dance being enjoyed in Sweden go back to 1908, but neither of these theories have strong merits. More probable is a Polish origin, suggested by the fact that 'Varsovienne' means in French 'The one from Warsaw' and that much of the dance is very mazurka-like, but if the dance had been finalised in Warsaw it seems unlikely that the dancers would have given it the name 'From Warsaw'—this being the type of name that is given by people from outside a country to a dance that they believe in that countries style. Who were the most obvious candidates then for refining a Polish mazurka into a dance which usually carries a French name—the French. For a full discussion of the origin of this dance see my section on 'Varsovienne / Varsovienna / Varsoviana in Part 1b of my *Dancing through the Ages*, Volume IX: 1850-1875.

There is one other theory of origin, which though not as strong as the last one I posited above, is relevance to the setting I offer for my above dance medley. It is a Mexican origin. A Mexican origin has been suggested by the fact that there is such a strong tradition of the dance in Mexico and adjacent south west of the United States, and that the earliest extant music for the dance is Luis Abadie's 'México. Varsoviana' which appeared in an *Album Filármonico* published in Paris 'Octobre de 1854' (facsimile of cover right and of score below at end of this entry—source library uncertain, and for a chorded transcription of the suite see my entry on **Varovienne (1)** in *Dancing Though the Ages* Volume IX Part 2b) and if the dance wasn't born in Mexico, perhaps it was born in Spain and went to Mexico. This might explain why several early descriptions of the dance refer to it as a 'Varsoviana', the Spanish language equivalent for French 'Varsovienne' and that early Varsovienne scores bear names linked with Spain—such as the earliest Varsovienne scores published in America is Garbon's 'Souvenir de Barcelona' and L'Andalousie. Certainly in both Mexico and Spain 'La Varsoviana' is so entrenched as to have songs associated with the dance. These identifications are weakened, however, by several considerations. Firstly, Abadie's was a French composer, his score was published in Paris, and his score is no earlier than Dodworth's in New York. Secondly, the first dated appearance of Garbon's score is 1863. Thirdly, the spelling 'Varsoviana' might as often be the result of a corruption of 'Varsovienna', the Anglicised form of 'Varsovienne', as it was a consequence of Spanish-language influence. Fourthly, there are no pre-1853 reports of the dance in either Mexico or Spain. The fact that Abadie was French might actually strengthen the French origin theory.

Turning to the dance medley I have set to Abadie's score, it consists of three dances I published in my *Lost Dances of Earthly Delights* Volume 2: *Favourites for four settings*, Canberra, 2005. For many years both for displays and socially at balls we used to dance these in a medley to the Country 6 set, each twice than the first one once again. Here to this beautiful 1854 tune suite I have set a tighter medley of each of the three dances just once then back to the first and to a thrilling variation to end. If you perform this medley please be sure capture a romantic breezy feel by making all the holds, glide and turn as expansive as possible and hobbles, leaps and pauses as lightly and high as possible, with air in your lungs and under your feet.

ALBUM FILÁRMONICO

DEL

NUEVO ECO DE AMBOS MUNDOS

✠ MÉXICO

VARSOVIANA.

por L. ABADIE.

Octobre de 1854   1854

MÉXICO.

VARSOVIANA.

Por Luis ABADIE.

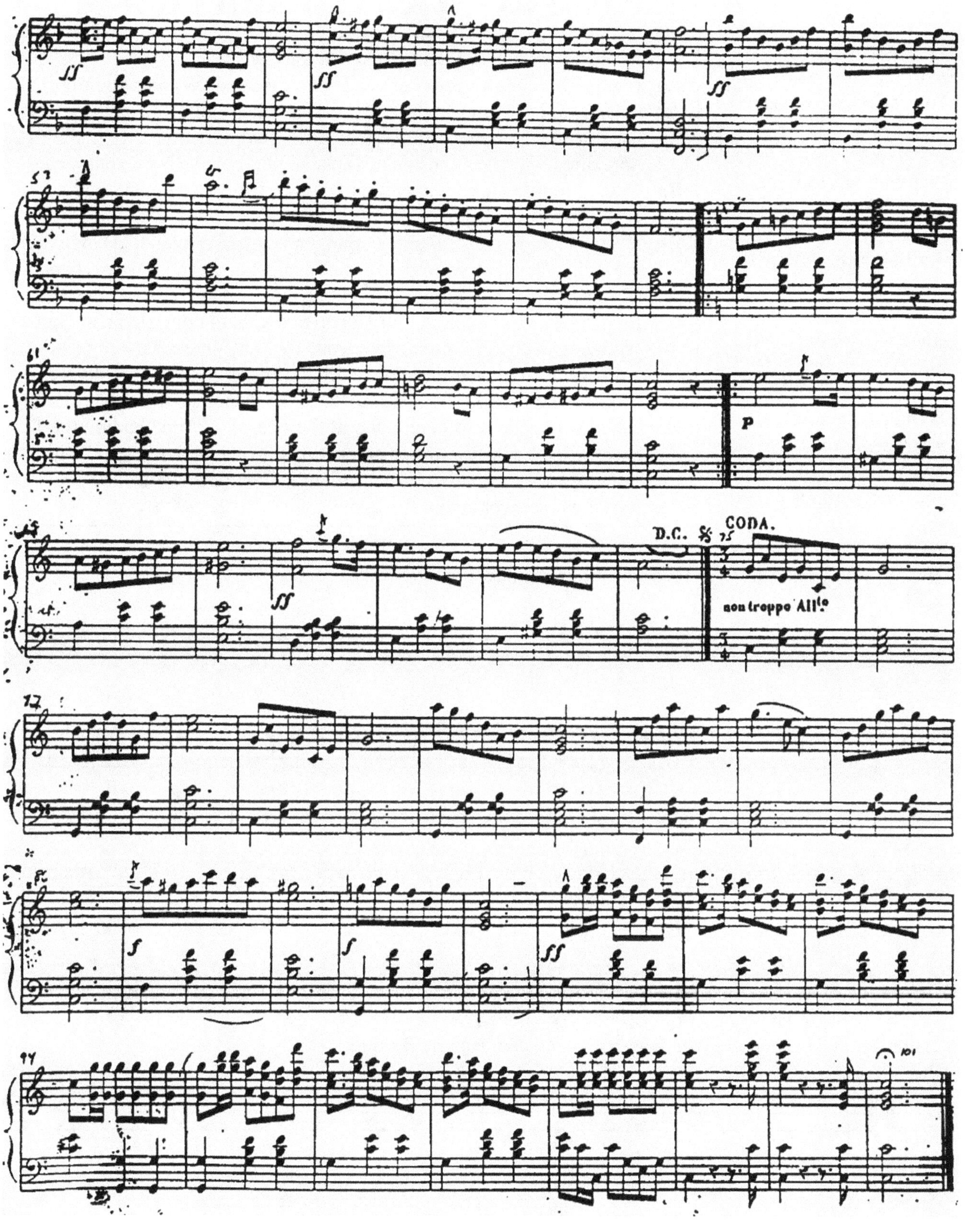
D.C.
CODA.
non troppo All.to

~ Mirror Measures—Heaven and Hell ~

Form facing pairs of W-M-W facing across dance space.

Start with left foot if on left side of hall (the 'heaven' sequence), or right foot if on right side of hall (the 'hell' sequence).

Dance whole combined sequence once or twice.

Play intro. then ABx4 (perhaps sequence 1 x 2 sequence 2 x 2) to return home then perhaps do all again.

If on left side of hall start doing 'heaven' variant:

Aa f. w. S l&r , D l.; C r&l, retire w. D r. to face end (W) on r. (ptnr no.1) /

Ab C l&r, t.s. l. w. D l. (middle 1/2 to face other end), sideways r&l., 3/4 t.s. r. w D r. to end ends (W) facing original direction but middle (M) opp. direction, taking inside hs (l.h.s w. ptnr no. 1, r.h.s w. ptnr no.2)

Ba C l&r (middle looking at end on l. then r.), all retire w. D l., all t.s. w. D r., all f. w. D l.

Bb all step b. on r. *while* taking hand in circle, all ½ circle w. 2D then open out w. 2C facing along opp. trio once again, but w. ends (W) exchanged.

AABB Repeat 'heaven variant' but set to a diff. end (W) first and instead of final 2C do 3ʳᵈ D to circle fully, open out w. b. to opp. trio facing out of set against orig. dir. w. r.f. free, ends (W) still in exchanged positions but because line faces other way orig. ptnr 1 is again on middle's r.

AABB x2 do 'hell' variant x 2 back to place: i.e. dance as before, but starting w. r.f. and setting first to l.end., and at the end of 2ⁿᵈ time ending the full circle w. 3D facing back towards other trio all in original order and with l.f. free. If on right side of hall, do hell variant x 2 then heaven variant x 2. Can repeat whole over again.

Version 1) With no sharps or flats added it is a modal but without tritones:

♩ = 130 [A]

G5 D5 G5 C5 G5 D5 G5 C5 D(add4) G5 C5 G5 Am

[B]

G5 C5 D5 C5 D(add4) D5 G5 D5 C5 Am D5

Version 2) The same notes with the Cs sharpened becomes modal with tritone:

♩ = 130 [A]

G5 D5 G5 Eb5 G5 D5 G5 C5 D(add4) G5 C5 G5 A5

[B]

G5 C5 D5 C5 D(add4) D5 G5 D5 C5 A5 D5

Version 3) The same notes with 2 sharps added can become B minor:

♩ = 130

Bm G A Bm F#m G A Bm G A

G D Em D G D Em Bm

Version 4) The chorded B minor tune can be rendered in C minor thus:

♩ = 130 [A]

Cm Ab Bb Cm Gm Ab Bb Cm Ab Bb

[B]

Ab Eb Fm Eb Ab Eb Fm Cm

— John Gardiner-Garden, *Dance Delights*, 2020 —

	The 'Heaven' sequence
Aa	<u>Forward with single left and right, and double left</u> then sideways step (a *continenze* or set) <u>right and left</u>, and <u>retire with a double right</u>, middle then turning to facing the end dancer on right (i.e. partner no.1)
Ab	The <u>middle and partner no.1 *continenze* left and right</u>, then both turn single left with a double left, partner 1 turning 3/4 to end facing in original direction *while* middle turns 1/2 to end facing other woman (the one originally on left= partner 2), middle and partner 2 sideways right and left, 3/4 turn single right with a right double (partner 2 ending facing in original direction, middle face against original direction (back to original direction) taking inside hands with neighbour (left hands with partner 1 right hands with partner 2)
Ba	*continenze* left and right (middle looking at left then right end), all push back and retire with a left double, all turn single right with a right double, all forward with a left double
Bb	all step back on right *while* taking hand in circle, all ½ circle w. 2D then open out w. 2C facing along l.o.d. once again, but with women in exchanged places.
AABB	Repeat 'heaven' sequence but this time partner no.1 will be the other person and instead of final 2 *continenze* do a 3rd double to complete a full circle, open out facing against in original direction with right foot free, W still in exchanged positions but still in exchanged positions but because line faces other way original end is again on middle's right.
	The 'Hell' counterpart:
AABB x2	Do 'hell' counterpart back to place: i.e. dance as before, but starting with right foot and setting first to woman on man's left (not M's original partner), and at the end of 2nd time ending the full circle w. 3D facing back back towards the opposite trio and with left foot free. If on right side of hall (if you were facing up, the woman's side in a longways proper dance), do hell sequence x 2 (with variation at end to change feet and direction) then heaven variant x 2, if on the left side of the hall (the man's side in a longways proper dance), do the heaven sequence first then the hell.
	Can repeat whole over again.

In 2014 Amelia Hamrick noticed and offered a tentative transcription of the tune that was written on the bottom of the man caught under the lute in the hell panel of Hieronymus Bosch's c. 1500 triptych *The Garden of Earthly Delights*. The tune seemed to stop 3½ bars short of a complete tune but at least two musician suggested endings for the tune and recorded it, one as a song and Jim Spalink as an instrumental piece on lute, harp and hurdy-gurdy—the three instruments in closest proximity to where the score is depicted in the painting.

In the painting notation the tunes starts on a 'b' and ends on a 'd' and there are no sharps or flats. This, with my own proposed final 3½ bars, produces a modal tune offered as version 1. If we add a sharp on the three 'c' notes we have the relevant bars present 'tritones' or 'devil's intervals'. If we add two sharps (on the 'f' and 'c' notes) we have a basic B minor tune that works on my G bagpipes. If we then transpose that tune up tone we have a basic C minor tune that works well on my C hurdy-gurdy. All four melodies sound strange upon first hearing, but can become infectious upon subsequent hearings. It is not entirely clear how Bosch or his musical informant intended the piece to be played with respect mode or tempo, but featuring as it does in a work of visual genius it seems likely that there was some ingenuity in the given notation and it was intended to be able to be interpreted flexibly. Perhaps he intended one rendering to be more 'heavenly' and another more 'hellish'. With thanks to my pianist friend Sally Taylor's chording, all four version can become conceivable harmonised pieces of music.

— John Gardiner-Garden, *Dance Delights*, 2020 —

I have taken the opportunity presented by the triptych's, and possibly also tune's, two-sided theme to write a dance that can be danced in both a 'heavenly' and 'hellish' manner. One way obeys all the rules of c.1500 courtly dance, in that dancers start left foot, the man (if the middle be a man) pays equal attention to both women, starting with his partner, and all step back at the start of the B strain bar 5 with their right foot, as if doing a bassedance, and on the second time through the sequence the man and his two women go forward again, but this time, because the women have swapped places, the man gets to greet the other woman first, making for a perfectly balanced dance. The other way is starting right foot, meaning nothing that follows feels natural—the man greets the woman on his left first, and everyone steps back at the strong point in the tune on the left not right foot. Some might imagine hell as being a really tedious or boring dance, but I have always imagined it as a dance where nothing follows as you would imagine, where everything is counter intuitive, and this small change to how you start does create an otherworldly experience. The frustration is all the more acute precisely because overtly nothing seems to have changed in the sequence—it's just that the unnatural starting foot has continual unnatural ramifications.

I have suggested making the default formation for the dance trio-facing-trio across the dance hall, with the trio on the left-side of the hall (as you face up) starting with the heaven sequence while those on the right-side start with the hell sequence. I have made that suggestion for three reasons. Firstly, having a trio opposite you gives you someone to look at, and if one half starts 'heaven' while the other starts 'hell' you will truly feel as if you are dancing in front of a mirror. Secondly, having the gap between facing trios run the length of the hall means the band at one end of the room or the audience at the other end can see both halves of the 2-trio set equally well and appreciate the mirror nature of their stepping. Thirdly, if you have multiple 2-trio set, they can be arranged above and below each other maintaining the same gap down the middle of the hall.

You can do the sequences offered above as a single trio set, and if you do I suggest you face up and do the 'heaven' sequence twice, then by adding the one extra weight change (i.e. changing the final *continenze* of the repeat sequence into a double) face down to do the 'hell' sequence twice. Indeed, when I first taught the dance I just had trios facing up. Seeing dance friends Katherine Tammaro and Katarina Teather experimenting with starting their trios back-to back made me realise formalising a trio-facing-trio start had the potential for instantly magnifying the mirror theme that is already there in the two sequences (so thank you Katherine and Katarina for the inspiration). Fourthly, the proposed arrangement, with heaven on the left facing hell on the right and all simultaneously active, mirrors the arrangement in the Bosch Triptych. In my dance you don't, however, have to frolic naked. Enjoy!

— John Gardiner-Garden, *Dance Delights*, 2020 —

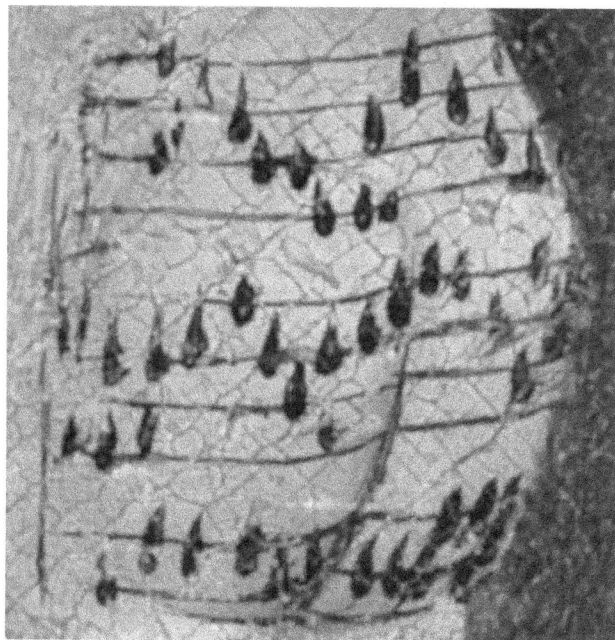

A part bars 1-4   A part bars 4-8 plus B part bar 1

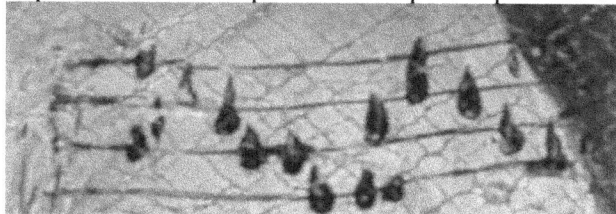

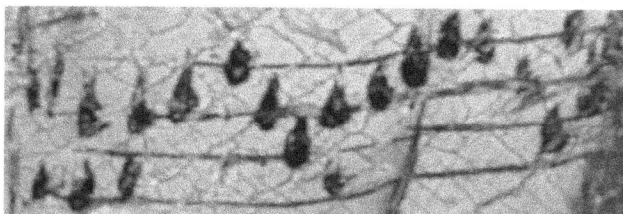

B part bars 2-4 plus first note? bar 5

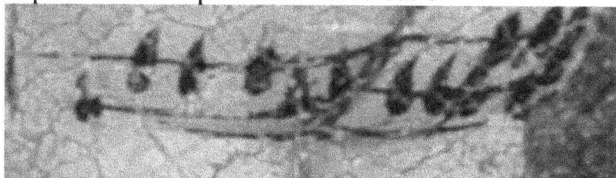

remaining 3½ bars have been supplied by myself.

— John Gardiner-Garden, *Dance Delights*, 2020 —

~ Missing the Neighbours ~

Form longways proper set for as many as will, but ideally for 4 couples

Start right foot.

Dance the triple minor sequence as many times as will, but if 4 couples in set, then each couple leads sequence twice before slipping to the bottom of set and the dance sequence is danced 8 times for all to return to places.

A1 1s set; cross r.h. / go down 1 place; cross by l.h. finish facing out between 2s&3s.
A2 1s do fig. 8 on own side (starting to r., i.e. 1M up 1W down) *while* others do full r&ls across then around minor set ending 2M and 3W facing out.
B1 1M2M 1W3W lead out on inside h.; lead b. on other h. *while* 3M1W ½ acw orbit inside set / 1M2M 1W3W f. & fall b *while* 3M1W complete acw orbit outside others
B2 All 6 circle l&r
All x n.

Play intro. then AABBxn (or if 4 couples, x8)

A1	1s set then cross the set pulling past each other by the right hand 1s go down the outside 1 place then cross set by left hand to finish facing out between 2s and 3s.
A2	1s turn to own right to do figure of 8 on own side (starting 1M up 1W down passing neighbour by right shoulder) *while* others (i.e. the 2s and 3s) do full rights and left around starting right hand with partner
B1	1M2M and 1W3W (i.e. 1s with neighbour on right hand) lead out then lead back, all *while* 3M1W ½ acw orbit inside set 1M2M 1W3W (i.e. 1s with same neighbour) forward and fall back *while* 3M1W complete an acw orbit outside others
B2	All 6 circle left and right

AABB xn 1s repeat from second place, and then (if 8 couple set) 1s slip to bottom and 2s commence sequences as new 1s from the top, and continue thus till all have had a turn leading and all have returned to place.

I wrote this dance in mid-2011 while staying with dance friends Linda and Gary Lieberman in Ames, Iowa, and enjoying Linda leading the Scottish Country dance 'Shake the bottle'. I can't now remember that dance, but remember there was some simultaneous action in it that was the inspiration for this dance. For nine years the dance was missing a debut. It was only in mid-2020, when preparing the material for this *Dance Delights* edition that I tried it out at my home with some novice and experienced dancers to some exciting Scottish reels. The dance worked better than I'd imagined it would and I was surprised how much of a thrill (and laugh) it was for all.

There are just two challenges. Firstly, beginners can get lost ('go missing') on some of the unaccompanied figures but the dance is forgiving enough for experienced dancers to sweep them back up into essential figures. Secondly, dancers can miss a smooth transition into the B1 lead out if the 2M and 3W, after their right&left chain in A2 start to turn either left or right to face into set, but a smooth transition is possible if those dancers make the final left hand of the chain a nice wide arc, let go early, keep their free left hand at waist-height as they travel to where they started and end facing out ready to drop the now free hand into the upturned right hand of the active dancer who comes from the inside of the set on an out-facing trajectory into the space between those chaining on the side.

I'll not be leaving it another 9 years before leading again!

— John Gardiner-Garden, *Dance Delights*, 2020 —

~ My Markowski mixup ~

Form couples.

Dance as arranged.

Play the St. Julien 'La Sicilienne' piano score at end of entry without going back at the *Dal segno* so just play 3 lots of 48 bars then go on to coda:

AA BB B'B'
AA CC C'C'
DD EE D'D'
(ignore the *D.C.*)
AA+8b. finale.

1A1	**Sicilienne var.:** 2 hops cutting free f. behind- in front, 2 hops pointing free toe in front- b. to shin; 3 glissades 1 *glissé*-½ cw t. / Repeat all in cntrpart
1A2	Repeat above.
1B1	**Anglicane/Impériale var.:** glide along l.o.d.-close rear foot freeing front foot, *assem . - sissone* w. cut back; glide-close-*assem.-siss.* w. leap ½ cw t / t. 2xcw as cpl. w. 4 x *assemblé-sissone*
1B2	Repeat in cntrpart. **2BB'** Repeat above **2AA** Repeat 1AA **Sicilienne var.**
1C1	**Hongroise var.:** Click hop-2-3(-&), repeat; 1 polka step to t. ½ cw, t. 1 x cw w. 2 pivots / 3 glissades 1 *glissé*-½ cw t.; counterpart
1C2	Repeat in counterpart **2CC'** Repeat above
1D1	**Schottische var.:** Open waist-shoulder hold 2 schottische (1-2-3-hop) step f. / 2 slow pivot steps; 4 quick pivot steps **1D2** Repeat above
E1	**L'Impériale var.:** hop-glide-cut-leap turning ½ cw; t. 1xcw as cpl. w. 2 x *assemblé-sissone* / Repeat in cnterpart. **E2** Repeat above
2DD	**Schottische var.:** As in 1DD but on 1st 4 bars travel zigzag in ballroom hold on l.diag. over hs then on r.diag. over sh.
3AA	Repeat the 1AA **Sicilienne var.** **Finale** 8 more pivots / turn W out; bow

1A1 b. 1-2 3-4 5-8	**Sicilienne variant:** <u>2 hops cutting free foot behind then in front, 2 hops pointing free toe in front then behind</u> <u>3 glissades 1 *glissé* (i.e. 4 quick slide, the first 3 closed the last unclosed) and ½ cw turn</u> <u>Repeat all in counterpart</u>
1A2	<u>Repeat above.</u>
1B1 b. 1-2 3&4 5-8	**Anglicane/Impérial variant:** <u>glide along l.o.d., close rear foot freeing front, *assemblé* and *sissone* with same and cut back</u> <u>glide-close-*assemblé* and make a quick *sissone* with leap ½ cw turn</u> Turn 2x cw as a couple w. 4 x *assemblé-sissone* (M wheeling cw backwards with his right leg rounding out each time)
1B2	<u>Repeat in counterpart </u>(this time M wheeling acw backwards with his left leg rounding out each time)
2BB'	<u>Repeat above</u>
2AA	Repeat 1AA **Sicilienne variant**
1C1 b. 1-2 3-4 5-6 7-8	**Hongroise variant:** <u>Click *while* making a hop then quick-2-3(-&) then repeat</u> <u>1 polka step to turn ½ cw then turn once cw with 2 pivots</u> <u>3 glissades and 1 *glissé* ending with ½ cw turn</u> <u>counterpart</u>
1C2	<u>Repeat in counterpart</u>
2CC'	<u>Repeat above</u>
1D1	**Schottische variant:**

— John Gardiner-Garden, Dance Delights, 2020 —

b. 1-4	Open waist-shoulder hold 2 schottische *chassé* steps forward (1-2, 3-hop lifting free foot; counterpart)
5-8	2 slow pivot steps and 4 quick pivot steps
1D2	Repeat above
E1 b. 1-2	**L'Impériale variant:** hop-glide-cut-leap turning ½ cw
3-4	turn once cw as a couple with 2 x *assemblé-sissone* (man wheeling back with right leg doing rounding)
5-8	Repeat in counterpart i.e. turning acw (man wheels backward with left leg doing rounding)
E2	Repeat above
2DD	**Schottische variant:** As in 1DD but on first 4 bars travel zigzag in ballroom hold on left diagonal over hands then on right diagonal over shoulder
N.B. The piano score calls for a return to the top, but I consider that optional. You might think dancing the whole sequence through a second time gives you a chance do it better, but you won't if exhausted!	
3AA	Repeat the 1AA **Sicilienne variant,** dancing the sequence right to the end of the musical phrase)
8b.Finale	8 pivots while traveling on along l.o.d. / turn W out; bow

Warning! The above dance, choreographed to the Alfred St. Julien 'La Sicilienne' piano score appended at the end of this entry to, is not for the faint hearted! It is the most challenging but also perhaps most rewarding of the three choreographies I was inspired to make out of 4 different 1850s Parisienne couples dance inventions that I have presented in my *Dancing through the Ages* Volume IX:1850-1875 (the other 2 choreographies are noted further below). The four dances are **La Sicilienne**, **L'Anglicane**, the **Hongroise** (in my work a version **(1)** and **(2)**) and **L'Impériale**. All these dances seem likely to have been composed by the enigmatic dance teacher and impresario whose real name may have been Maurice Nachmann or Maurice Mayer but who was usually known simply as *Maurice* or more commonly as *Markowski* (sometimes spelt *Markowsky*). Markowski was active in Paris between the late -840s and early- 1860s and his life swung erratically back and forth between fame and obscurity, fortune and poverty. The two pendulums were usually, but not always in tandem—there being times in his life when though famous, he was penniless, and though rich his authorship of many dances was going unrecognised. For a full discussion of Markowski life and work see my *Dancing through the Ages* Volume IX.

Because the above-named dances are not only challenging to perform but a challenge to remember, I decided to try to make an easy-to-remember sequence of them. I didn't manage to as easy to remember a sequence as I'd hoped, partly because I decided to shape the medley around the late-1850 St. Julien piano score entitled '*La Sicilienne, nouvelle danse de salon compose par Markowski*' (facsimile below from my personal collection). It is, however, a thrilling sequence if you can pull it off. To the A strain I set **La Sicilienne** but with a second half '4 slide' galop (as in **Hongroise (2)**) instead of the harder to time 3-slide galop. To the B strain I set **L'Anglicane** but rather than combine the balonné and leap to ½ t. each time, I made the first 2 bars end with an *assemblé-sissone* & cut (part way to a *balonné*) and the next 2 bars end with an *assemblé-sissone* & leap turn, and then made the 2nd part the 4 x *assemblé-sissone* 2nd part of *L'Impériale*. To the C strain I set **Hongroise (1)**, but added before you do the counterpart, a (4-slide galop&1/2 t.)x2. To the D strain I set a Schottische variant, the first time with the first half in open hold, the second time in a closed hold, and both times the 2nd part not 4 slow step hops, but 2 slow step hops and 4 quick pivots. To the E strain

I set **L'Impériale**, but instead of doing the first part twice then 4 *assemblé-sissones*, we do the first part just once and the 2 *assemblé-sissones* (as in the 2nd part of the original Anglican).

I initially gave the sequence a name that would help me remember the source dances: 'The Sicilian Anglican's scandalous dance with the Hungarian Emperor'. However, as there have never been many Sicilian Anglicans and as the King of Hungary was never an Emperor (the Austro-Hungarian Emperor was always Austrian—though the Empress of Austria in the late 1850s, Sissi, had a strong affections for Hungarian culture), I thought I'd better forgo trying to put the name of every inspiration source in the new dances' title, and had best chose something simpler. I arrived at the three-word suggested title for three reasons. Firstly, the dance is my own arrangement and adaptation of my own interpretation of period bits, and I freely acknowledge that those bits could be interpreted, adapted and arranged differently by someone else. Secondly, although the 1850s Parisian dancing master Markowski left no dance manual of his own and although his contribution to the development of couples dances in the 1850s are not widely recognised, he was the purported inventor of three of the above named dances (**La Sicilienne**, the **Hongroise** and **L'Impériale**) and may also have been the inventor of the **L'Anglicane**, and I believe his name deserves to be better known. Thirdly, although the combination pays homage to four different dances, it is not a medley of unchanged originals, but more of a mix-up of their bits.

If you haven't a pianist to play the St.Julien score there are other options for mixing up these same variant.

Option 1) Play any suite of 48 bar AABBCC jigs, such as my 'Ashby's Jig' & 'Bouncing Back' Spring 1 in my *Lost Dances of Earthly Delights* Volume I and don't try to fit in **L'Impériale**:

A1   **Sicilienne var.:** 2 hops cutting free f. behind- in front, 2 hops pointing free toe in front- b. to shin; glide-tog, glide -½ cw t. / Repeat all in counterpart   **A2**   Repeat above.

B1   **Anglicane var.:** glide along l.o.d.-close rear foot freeing front foot, bend *while* cutting free foot b. (or *assemblé*) starting to extend it for - leap *while* turning ½ cw; t. 1xcw as cpl. w. 2 x *assemblé-sissone* / Repeat in counterpart   **B2**   Repeat above

C1   **Hongroise var.:** Click hop-2-3(-&), repeat (step l.-tog.); 1 polka step to t. ½ cw, t. 1 x cw w. 2 pivots / repeat in counterpart (i.e. clicks and t. 1½ acw). **C2**   Repeat above

When doing the sequence for last time (e.g. returning to first tune in Ashby's Jig suite) instead of doing slow glide-tog.-glide-½ t. in AA do quick 4-slide galop & ½ t.

Option 2) play the 'Sicilienne' by [Jacques] Renausy in his *Méthode de danse,* Paris, 1861 (presented in my entry on that dance in *Dancing through the Ages* Volume IX, but to fit the musical pattern you will have to do some quick going back to earlier parts:

A1   **Sicilienne var.:** 2 hops cutting free f. behind- in front, 2 hops pointing free toe in front- b. to shin; glide-tog, glide -½ cw t. / Repeat all in counterpart   **A2**   Repeat A1

BA   **Anglicane var.:** glide along l.o.d.-close rear foot freeing front foot, bend *while* cutting free foot b. (or *assemblé*) starting to extend it for - leap *while* turning ½ cw; t. 1xcw as cpl. w. 2 x *assemblé-sissone* / Repeat in counterpart // As for A1 i.e. **Sicilienne var.**   **BA.** Repeat all

C1   **Hongroise var.:** Click hop-2-3(-&), repeat (*or* left-tog.); 1 polka step to t. ½ cw, t. 1 x cw w. 2 pivots / repeat in counterpart (i.e. clicks and t. 1½ acw)   **C2**   Repeat C1

DC   **L'Impériale var.** 4 walking steps f.; 4 pivots cw / 4 *assemblé-sissone* wheeling acw x 2 // As for C1 i.e. **Hongroise var.**   **DC** As above.

Reprise of AABABA As above, but during the As instead of glide-tog, glide do 4 glide galop.

Here below is the St. Julien score to which I have set the full 'mix-up' in my opening table.

LA SICILIENNE

Deuxieme Edition   Nouvelle Danse de Salon   a Mᵈˡˡᵉ Eugenie Meschyn

Composée par MARKOWSKI

Musique de

ALFRED DE Sᵀ JULIEN

2
LA SICILIENNE,
Nouvelle Danse de Salon.
Musique
d'Alfred de St. Julien.
à Mademoiselle Eugénie MESCHYN.
Andante.
INTRODUCTION
ff Ped.
p
rall.
a Tempo.
rall.
Allegro.
1A1
SICILIENNE.
f
p
f
1A2
8a
f
Ped.
A.G.1356.

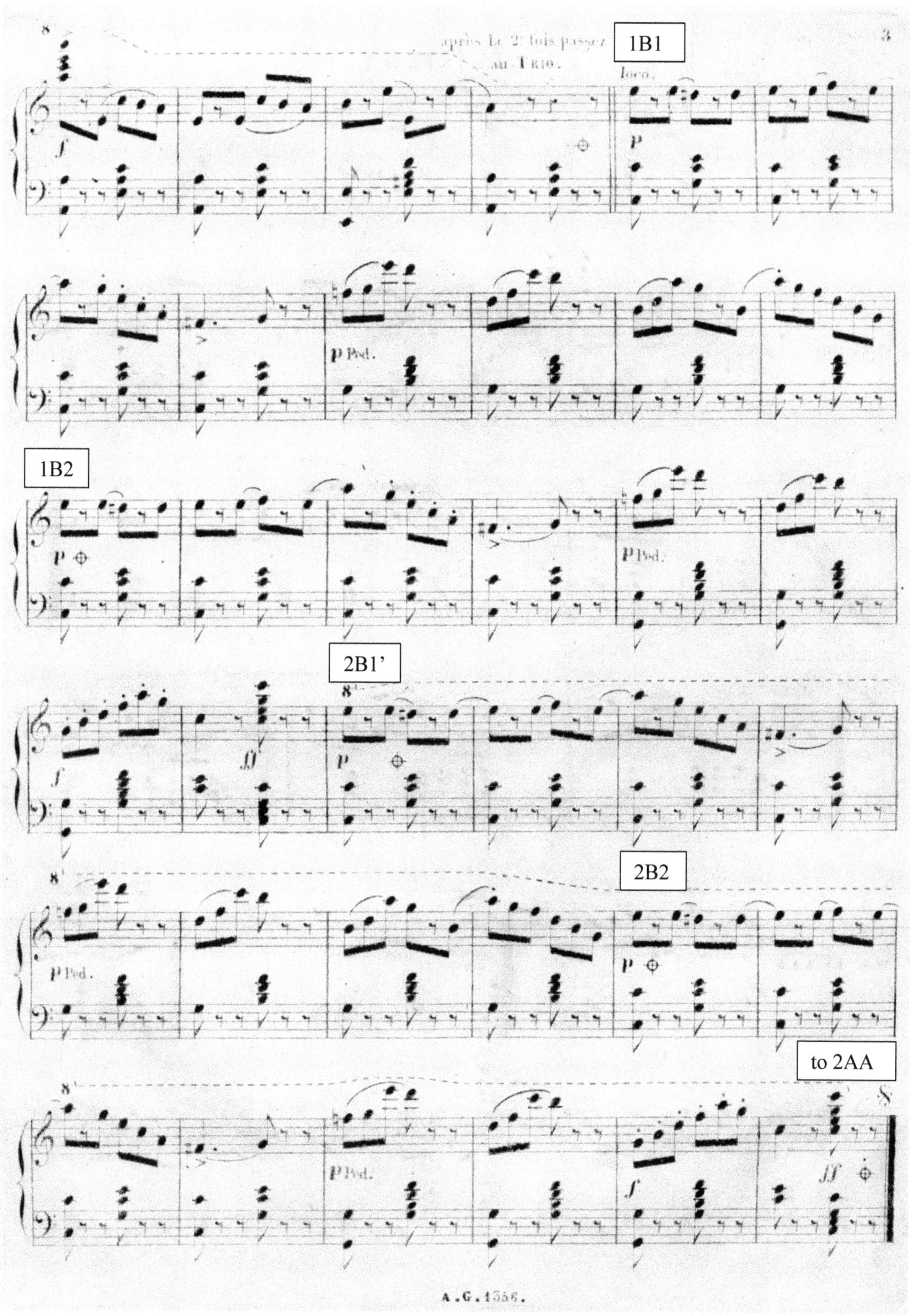
3
après la 2e fois passez au TRIO.
1B1
loco.
1B2
2B1’
2B2
to 2AA
A.G.1356.

1C1
2me Fois à l'8ve
TRIO.
1C2
1D1&2
Ped.
E1&2
1re
2e
8va
loco.
A.G.1356.

2D1&2
5
Ped
Optional *D.C.*
1ª
2ª
ff D.C. ad lib:
3AA
CODA
Ped.
8ª
loco.
Finale
A.G.1356.

~ The New Iolanthe Schottische medley ~

Form couples holding inside hand.

Start M right foot free W left foot free, outside hand raised in arc above.

Dance as arranged with schottische *chassés* (1-2-3-lift, counterpart) or step-hops (1&hop-2&hop, repeat).

Play the Popplewell Royle piano score appended at the end of this entry.

A1 **Chorus 1** (<u>starting on inside h.</u> w. inside f.) Prom. f. w. 2 *chassés*; wide outward t.s. (both hs in air) ending facing f. w. 4 step-hops / (hs on hips) cross sideways (M behind) &b.; (outside hs still on hip inside joined) prom. f. w. 4 step-hops

A2 **Chorus 2** (starting as before) Prom. f. w. 2 *chassés* f.; t.s. w. 3 step-hops & end w. point facing ptner and taking 2 hand open hold / 2 *chassé* along & against l.o.d.; on inside h. prom. f. w. 4 step-hops

B1 **Variation on** 2nd half of **Short Easy Shottiisi:** W turn cw out under near h. & acw b. under raised arm; prom. f. / same but M in cntrprt, <u>ending joining front hs.</u>

B2 W turn cw out under front raised h. & acw b. under raised arm into ballroom hold; t. as cpl. / same but M in counterpart.

A3 **Chorus 3** (<u>starting in open waist-sh.hold</u>, w. outside f.) prom. f. w. 2 *chassés*; t.s. w. M 4 W 3 step-hops to face / 1 *chassé* sideways to own l. (M along W against l.o.d. *while* taking ptnrs r.h.) & 1 *chassé* sideways r. (M against W along l.o.d. *while* taking ptners l.h. below); <u>in cross h. hold</u> w. 4 step-hops swing <u>ending in high prom. hold</u>

CC **Showdown Schottische**   **DD** **Southern Highland Schottische**
CC **Swish Switch and Swing**

A4 **Chorus 4** (<u>starting in high prom. hold</u> w. l.f.) Prom. f. w. 2 *chassés*; t.s. w.4/3 step-hops <u>into ballroom hold</u> / 2 *chassés* together along&against l.o.d.; t. as cpl.

B w. 4 *chassés* go face-to-face taking 2hs, b.-to-b. bringing rear h. f.;face-to-face, side-by-side taking waist-sh.hold / w. 2 more *chassé* M guide W in acw arc around him; w. 4 step-hops t. as cpl.

A5 **Chorus 5** (starting in ballroom hold) 2 *chassés* along l.o.d. (over hs, then ½ t. and over sh.); t. as cpl. w. 4 step-hops

Last 4 bars: 3 pivots (l-r-l) then hop on l., 3 pivots (r-l-r) then hop on r.; then with 3 last beats steps step M's l. W's r. while turning W out under raised l.arm to face, bow, and (on unplayed 4th beat or sometime after) rise.

	~ Chorus 1 ~
A1	<u>Starting on inside hand</u> with inside foot promenade <u>forward with 2 *chassés* then, with 4 step-hops, wide outward turn single (both hs in air) ending facing forward</u> With hands on hips <u>cross with sideways *chassé* (M behind) and back then with outside hand still on hip inside hands joined</u> promenade forward with 4 step-hops
	~ Chorus 2 ~
A2	Starting as before <u>promenade forward with 2 *chassés* then turn single with 3 step-hops & end with a point of free foot facing ptner and taking 2 hand open hold</u> <u>2 *chassé* along & against l.o.d. then on inside hand promenade forward with 4 step-hops</u>
	~ Variant on 2nd half of **Short Easy Shottiisi ~**
B1	<u>W turn cw out under near raised hand & acw back under raised arm then promenade forward</u> <u>Repeat same but M in counterpart, ending joining front hands.</u>
B2	<u>to W turn cw out under front raised hand & acw back under raised arm into ballroom hold then turn as a couple</u>

— John Gardiner-Garden, *Dance Delights*, 2020 —

	Repeat same but M in counterpart [this B2 action is [this part is identical 2nd half of 'Short Easy Shottiisi'—Village 1 in Lost Dances Vol.2]
	~ Chorus 3~
A3	Starting in open waist-shoulder hold, with outside foot promenade forward with 2 *chassés* then turn single, M with 4 W with 3 step-hops, to face 1 *chassé* sideways to own left (M along W against l.o.d. *while* taking ptnrs right hand) & 1 *chassé* sideways right (M against W along l.o.d. *while* taking partners left hand below) then in cross h. hold w. 4 step-hops swing ending in high prom. hold
	~ Showdown Schottische~
CC	[see 'Showdown Schottische' Town 10 in *Lost Dances* Volume 2]
	~ Southern Highland Schottische ~
DD	[See 'Southern Highland Schottische'—Country 4 in *Lost Dances* Volume 2]
	~ Swish Switch and Swing ~
CC	[see 'Swish Switch and Swing'—Court 13 in *Lost Dances* Volume 2]
	~ Chorus 4 ~
A4	Starting in high promenade hold with 1eft foot promenade forward with 2 *chassés* then turn single, man with 4 step-hops woman with 3, ending in ballroom hold 2 *chassés* together—one along and one against l.o.d— then turn as a couple.
B	With 4 *chassés* go face-to-face taking 2hs, back-to-back bringing rear hand forward, go face-to-face, go side-by-side taking waist-shoulder hold With 2 more *chassé* M guide W in acw arc around him then with 4 step-hops turn as a couple
	~ Chorus 5 ~
A5	Starting in ballroom hold take 2 *chassés* along l.o.d. (over hands then ½ t. and over shoulder), then turn as a couple with 4 step-hops
Last 4 b.	3 pivots (left-right-left) then hop on left, 3 pivots (right-left-right) then hop on right then with 3 last beats steps step M's left W's right *while* turning W out under raised left arm to face, bow and (on unplayed 4th beat or sometime after) rise.

Illustrating how just how popular Schottische-related dances were and how many variants were being created in the late 1890s is the story of the 'Iolanthe'. This was a dance invented by Robert Crompton and promoted by Crompton as a dance that was going to become as strong a ballroom staple as the polka. Despite Crompton's best efforts it wasn't to be, and although the music for it and an illustration of one attitude in it seem to have survived (see folio appended at the end of this section), the ten-figure schottische-related sequence itself does not seem to have. The tale reminds us both of the craze for schottisches in this period and of the ephemeral nature of dances in general so I might tell it more fully. Before relating the story of the dance I might make a few observations on my dance.

I choreographed my 'New Iolanthe' dance with a few parameters in mind. It had to start in the exact position depicted on the cover of the Royle sheet music, it had to fit and indeed complement that music score, it had to have lots of different figures, as Crompton's original 'Iolanthe' was said to have, and it had to be gain in physicality and flashy-ness—and all that without compromising memorability. As the sheet music's illustration shows an inside foot start, but I didn't want to be limited to that for dance variants, and as the music has an irregular but recurring chorus refrain, but I didn't want to be limited to do exactly the same chorus every time that was heard, I decided to use a chorus that would each time have the same overall character but each time be a little different so as to take the couple into and out of different starting feet and different holds, and to work the same development in physicality and flashy-ness that can be found in the 'verses' into these 'choruses' I have the chorus originally involve nothing more than forward facing promenading but each time it comes around to involve a bit more face-to-face and/or turning action.

In the middle of the sequence you will see I have included sequences I have already published in my *Lost Dances of Earthly Delights*, Volume 2, Favourites for four settings, Canberra, 2005. I hope you can put the whole dance together and find the pianist and dance company to bring it to life. I was very lucky and pleased to have the company of some wonderful keen dancers in our Earthly Delights Historical Dance Academy and some wonderful musicians who regularly play for us, led by the accomplished pianist Sally Tailor, and we the dance was debuted to much acclaim on Sunday 13 October when we had the dancers and musicians in the studio at our home in the Canberra suburb of Yarralumla, entertaining people who were visiting our garden as part of the Canberra Open Garden scheme… and we took it off the next week to a festival interstate and used it as a very well-received show opener.

Now back to the original Iolanthe! The story of the dance name starts in the early 1880's. The dance name 'Iolanthe' was doubtlessly intended to be an allusion to the same beloved ever-young fairy who is one of the main characters in the Gilbert and Sullivan 1882 opera, as the name Iolanthe seems not to have been used till Gilbert coined the name, possibly out of the Greek ιολη (*iole*) meaning 'violet' and ανθος (*anthos*) meaning 'flower'. Nothing beyond the name, however, links the Crompton dance with the opera. There is no couples schottische in the opera and the dance was not intended to be set to any music from that opera, Crompton explaining in the November 1892 edition of his *Dancing* journal, that his dance was initially set to the **Pas de Quatre music from Faust up to Date**, and Crompton indicates that his publisher even changed the name to 'Iola' in order to distinguish his dance from those (quadrilles and the like) based on that opera's music.

The story of the dance starts in the early 1890s. R.M. (Robert Morris) Crompton was an English dancing master who was active through the 1890s not only teaching, leading and composing dances, but also in promoting the organising of his profession, and went on to become the first president of the Imperial Society of Teachers of Dancing. As dance historian Susan de Guardiola put it in her Capering and Kickery blog, he was 'part of the early 20th-century movement to keep ballroom dance out of the hands of the "wrong" people, which primarily meant Americans, and especially African-American influences'. Crompton was very proud of this particular dance, and mentions it more than 30 times in *Dancing, a journal devoted to the terpsichorean art, physical culture and fashionable entertainments,* a magazine for which he was the main contributor. He appears to have created the dance in early 1891. Thus in that journal on 8 June 1891, under 'A new dance', it was reported that:

> **Mr. Crompton—to whose work on dancing we refer in another column—is recognised as a leading authority amongst professors of dancing, and ten minutes' conversation with him is sufficient to show that he is no mere surface student of the art. He approaches its study in the spirit of a high priest bound to uphold, protect, foster and preserve it in all its essential and not merely its superficial beauty and genuineness. A round dance emanating from the mind of such a representative of the art may be taken for granted as being distinctly original, pretty, musical and graceful. Such undoubtedly is "Iolanthe," the new dance. Mr. Crompton has been good enough to afford us a private view of "Iolanthe," danced by himself and one of his lady assistants. We may ourselves fairly claim to be experienced judges of dancing, and we have no hesitation in pronouncing the new dance to be altogether charming. It is *avant tout*, highly graceful and one feature in favour of its probable great success, is that the lady looks even far more graceful than the gentleman in performing the various pretty movements it embodies. We should hesitate to vouch that all ladies in executing the new dance would impart to their movements the same charmingly undulating grace of step and motion as did the accomplished lady who acted as Mr.**

Crompton's partner. Nevertheless, "Iolanthe" leaves open a wide field for the exercise of feminine gracefulness and for pleasing competition amongst dancers in the various degrees of grace and perfection with which the dance is executed. This, we repeat, is a feature sure to recommend it to the fair sex, who always have an eye, above all things, to graceful and beautiful effects. And what dance has a ghost of a chance if it does not recommend itself to them? There is more grace of movement and effect in "Iolanthe" than even in the waltz itself. It is a charming gift to the Terpsichorean art, and we both wish and predict for the new dance a great success. —*Civil Service Guardian*.

The new Society dance "Iolanthe," occupies the unique position of having achieved an immense success in the most aristocratic circles, almost before its existence has become known to the dancing profession generally. Unlike other dance novelties, it has required no extensive advertising, nor are its chances of becoming fashionable problematic. It is already popular, and has formed the leading feature at many country balls and private parties in Town during the last months ; in fact nothing, of the kind has elicited so much enthusiasm or acquired so rapid a popularity since the introduction of the Polka, which took the Town by storm and became a perfect mania in the fashionable world of 1844. There can be no doubt that what has received so marked an approval from the leaders of fashion will soon be in great request amongst all classes of dancers. The above indisputable facts are sufficient to induce every teacher of dancing in the kingdom to become acquainted with the latest addition to choric science. The prevailing taste evinced by the upper classes to learn fancy dancing, together with the introduction of this latest ball-room novelty, may be taken as a significant sign that there is really a desire for more variety in Terpsichorean pleasures. This is a most gratifying circumstance, and may be regarded as a very hopeful prospect for the future, as it cannot fail to be pecuniarily advantageous to the profession at large. A few leading teachers in London, who have just acquired the new dance, are unanimous in their praises of its animated and exhilarating movements. To see it performed is in itself enough to evoke a desire to learn it. The stereotyped question which has so often greeted other introductions, "Will it be danced or become fashionable?" need not be asked in this case. It is danced, most extensively, and by the very people of all others who can make it fashionable. It cannot, therefore, in any sense be considered an experiment. The music of "Iolanthe" consists of a specially arranged medley of airs, including the popular air "Pas de Quatre" from "Faust up to Date," the "Pas de Deux" from "Ruy Blas," &c., and is published by Messrs. Ascherberg & Co., of Berners Street, W

In September 1891:

The new Society dance, "Iolanthe," which created such a rage during the past London season, has excited the greatest interest among the leading teachers of dancing in this country. The eagerness evinced to acquire the novelty is only equalled by the expressions of delightful approval manifested on first beholding the dance. To avoid mistakes, however, Messrs. Ascherberg, the publishers of the music specially composed for the dance, have decided to call it "Iola, the Iolanthe Dance," in order to prevent it being confused with the dance music selected from the comic opera of "Iolanthe."

In October 1891:

The new dance "Iolanthe" promises to become quite as great a rage amongst teachers this winter as it was in fashionable circles during the past London season. No dance has ever been received with so much favour by the profession since the advent of the polka in 1844. Without a single exception, the large number of teachers who have recently acquired the dance, have experienced the utmost delight on first beholding the exceedingly graceful figures and steps which Mr. R. M. Crompton has arranged. There is, therefore, every indication that "Iolanthe" will be extensively taught during the approaching terms, and will, no doubt, be as eagerly welcomed by pupils, as it has been by the profession, who pronounce it to be the prettiest dance of its kind ever introduced into the ball room or academy.

In November 1891:

> At a very successful Society ball, held on the 29th ult., at Addison Hall, Kensington, the new dance "Iolanthe" created quite a furore. It was only down once in the programme, but the company-fully threefourths of whom danced it insisted on having it four times during the evening. One of the editorial staff of Dancing, who was present, says that he never before witnessed at a fashionable Society ball such vivacious enthusiasm exhibited in the rendering of a favourite dance. One maiden of high degree, with whom he danced it, almost-to use his own term" danced herself dead" in her enthusiastic liking for the prettily vivacious steps of this dance, and the scene as the ladies (in spite of the trains many of them wore), alternately skipped, glided and waltzed along the large ball-room floor, was particularly picturesque.

> The most favourable accounts continue to be received from teachers in all parts of the country, who are singularly unanimous in their praises of "Iolanthe," and state that wherever they have presented it, their pupils have manifested the most gratifying indications of approval. The phenomenal success "Iolanthe" has achieved is entirely due to its merits, and m no sense is it the result of extensive advertising.

> When "Iolanthe" was first introduced, it was performed to the "Pas de Quatre" music from Faust up to Date, owing to which the dance is known in some circles as the "Pas de Quatre." It is not surprising, therefore, that advantage has been taken of this to introduce an imitation of "Iolanthe," retaining the title of "Pas de Quatre." But as this production is only an imperfect copy of one of the ten figures arranged for "Iolanthe," teachers and others who have not yet acquired the dance, and who may desire to learn it, should be careful to obtain the original version, the music for which, "Iola," is published by Messrs. Ascherberg & Co., 46, Berners Street, W.

Other references appear in December 1891, under 'Provincial News' / Derby

> The new Society Dance, "Iolanthe."—Upwards of 250 patrons of the Derby Assembly Rooms on Saturday last were entertained by the introduction of a dance which has been the rage of the last London season, and is increasing in popularity. Mr. Taft and his daughter performed the delightfully fascinating figures of which "Iolanthe" is composed, and at the finish were greeted with tremendous applause, and vociferous demands for a repetition of the dance had to be complied with. We understand that "Iolanthe" will be introduced at several of the important balls which are to take place in Derby this season.

In Feb. 1892 it is reported that:

> The pupils of Mr. Cosmo Mitchell in Ashley Road School gave a dancing rehearsal in the gymnasium of the school. There was a large attendance of parents and friends. The manner in which the little folks went through the various dances was at once pleasing and remarkable. This part of the programme was commenced by the pupils dancing the Edinburgh Quadrilles, which they accomplished with ease and grace. "Iolanthe" was the next item, and probably the most important one on the list, as this is the first occasion on which the dance has been publicly performed in Aberdeen. "Iolanthe" was introduced into London only last season, and its reception there was so warm as to cause some apprehension that the new dance would eclipse the popularity of the waltz. It is, like the waltz, a round dance, and is performed to schottische time. The dance introduces ten different steps of movements, which display to the full the graceful action of which the body is capable, and imparts to the dancer a gentle undulating movement, which is decidedly charming. "Iolanthe," if danced in its entirety, will be a welcome acquisition to the list of ball-room dances. An infants' class showed wonderful training in their performance of the Lancers, followed by the polka and Circassian circle.

In an article on past New Year's Eve ball wrote: **A special feature of the program was the new society dance "Iolanthe," which was performed by Mr. Crompton and three of the lady assistants, and afterwards by a large proportion of the company. This charming dance gave the utmost delight.**

A month later, in March 1892, it was reported that:

> **Among the many pretty dances given at the Portman Rooms, Mr. Crompton's Grand Carnival Ball on the 2nd inst. will no doubt rank as the crowning event. "Iolanthe" was danced twice by the entire company, and vociferously encored each time; the grand Polonaise was also a great success. A crowd of costumes filled the beautiful rooms, and there were almost too many to make a special selection. Among the most striking characters was an imposing Britannia, accompanied by a lion, not a stuffed one, but a real, human being got up as a lion. There was a pretty Dorothy, Mrs. Peters as Sultana, all ablaze with diamonds, Miss Lotinga in blue velvet, as Duchess of Devonshire, her sister as Minnie Palmer, the Marquis de Leuville as Cabinet Minister, Mrs. Burroughs as Pierrette, Miss Hunting in green velvet, a black domino danced with Mary Queen of Scots, reminding the company of her executioner. Mr. Clarkson was also present as Bonnie Prince Charlie. Mr. Lotinga wearing "pink," and a great many more ladies and gentlemen, whom it would be quite impossible to mention separately or describe the costumes of all the Italians, Spaniards, romp clowns, &c. *Cela va sans dire* that Mr. Crompton with his usual assistant M.C.'s, Messrs. Knight, Wells, and Freshwater, looked admirable after the comfort and amusement of his patrons, and that the musical bill of fare, as well as the more substantial one referring to supper, satisfied the most exacting .anticipations. Dancing was kept up till far into the small hours of the morning, and the company dispersed with the generally expressed feeling that they would like "to have it all over again."**

In August 1892 it was reported that:

> **Considering that his immediate object in coming to this country was to visit his brother (who has resided in England for forty years, during which interval neither gentleman had seen each other), and that his stay in London only lasted one week, we esteem it as a great compliment to ourselves personally that Professor Zorn found sufficient time during his brief visit to give us daily a few hours of his most agreeable company. An opportunity was thus afforded for an interchange of ideas and for the discussion of many subjects calculated to advance the interests of our art and profession. Advantage was also taken of the occasion to acquire some of the most recent dances arranged by this eminent professor, who, at his own request, was also instructed in the Waltz-Minuet, and "Iolanthe," both of which dances elicited from him expressions of the highest approval. He became so interested in the system of instruction employed that he expressly requested permission—which was cheerfully given—to be present at lessons imparted to other pupils.**

December 1892 issue quoted the 'The pall Mall Budget', speaking of the Crompton academy: **"Iolanthe," the novelty of last season, however, is now quite the rage.** Crompton was still plugging his Iolanthe in January 1893 when he reported his correspondents reporting on a ball in Exeter that month as including:

> **March, Lancers, Valse, Scotch Reel, Varsoviana, Valse Cotillion, Iolanthe (*pas de quatre*), Minuet, Gavotte, Polka [...] Mazurka Quadrille, Minuet Valse, Quadrille, polka Mazurka, Hornpipe, New Valse-Minuet, Irish Reel, Highland Schottishe, Galop. "Iolanthe'," during its execution excited murmurs of admiration, which swelled into hearty applause at the close.**

and on a dance teacher's ball in Burton-on-Trent in February 1893 where **The "Iolanthe" was danced though all its ten figures, and the Misses Thompson may well feel proud and delighted with the ease, elegance and accuracy with which their eighty pupils performed it.**

I have not found a description of any part of Crompton's 'Iolanthe', let alone **all its ten figures.** The music folio which I have in my possession and have reproduced below, is almost certainly the music Crompton intended for his Iolanthe as it fits all the clues offered above—it was published by Ascherberg, was given the short title 'Iola', and was copyrighted in 1891. Inside that music folio, however, the dance description offered is not of Crompton's ten-figure dance 'Iolanthe', even though the cover announced the 'new dance 'Iolanthe', but Crompton's description (in English, French and English) of a pretty standard *Pas de Quatre* (see my Part 2 entry on **Military Schottische / Pas de Quatre / Barn dance**):

> **The 'Pas de Quatre'. Description of the dance by R.M. Crompton, Professor of Dancing, London.**
>
> **Lady and gentleman dance the first four bars (16 steps) side by side, the lady's left hand being placed in the right of her partner.**
> **Both advance three walking steps (beginning with the outside foot), then raising the inside foot in advance, both make a light hop on the outside leg. This movement is repeated by commencing with the inside foot, and hopping on the inside leg. The two movements are again repeated to complete the first four bars. The gentleman then taking his partner as in an ordinary round dance, the couple make four circular movements (i.e. eight half-turns executed with a light hopping or Waltz step), similar to the second part of the Schottische. Notwithstanding its title, the dance is performed in couples, any number participating simultaneously. The application of this title was due to the circumstance of the dance being almost invariably performed to the music of the enormously successful "Pas de Quatre" from the Burlesque "Faust up to Date."**

In Crompton book's *Theory and practice of modern dancing,* London, c.1890, p.87 there are entries on both 'The New Society Dance, Iolanthe' and on a dance called 'The Barn dance', 'Schottische Militaire' or 'Pas de Quatre', as if the two are distinct from one another. With respect the former Crompton writes:

> **This exceedingly attractive and popular dance, since its introduction by Mr. Cromptom, has achieved an almost phenomenal success. It has been pronounced by both profession and press, to be the prettiest dance ever arranged for the ball-room; but as no written explanation of the ten figures of which it is composed can adequately describe the dance to enable a person to acquire it without a master, it would be of no service to the reader to give a technical explanation here.**

I suspect Crompton's mind was made up and he never publicly issued any instructions for the dance.

Why was Crompton reluctant to describe the ten figures of his 'Iolanthe' when he seems so keen for the dance to spread all around the world and must have realised that the dissemination of written notes could facilitate this? Was it just because he didn't think written explanation would do it justice or was it because he wanted people to take lessons with him (for both pecuniary and artistic reasons) or because for all his keenness to write on dance (witness his *Dancing* journal) and his preparedness to write a small dance guide, he was unsure how to describe in print a complicated gesture-filled

IOLANTHE AND BARN DANCE.   87

The New Society Dance, "Iolanthe."

THIS exceedingly attractive and popular dance, since its introduction by Mr. Crompton, has achieved an almost phenomenal success. It has been pronounced by both profession and press, to be the prettiest dance ever arranged for the ball-room; but as no written explanation of the ten figures of which it is composed can adequately describe the dance to enable a person to acquire it without a master, it would be of no service to the reader to give a technical explanation here.

THE BARN DANCE.

PROPERLY speaking, this dance should be called the "Schottische Militaire," the name by which it was first known. Owing, however, to its being so frequently danced in America to a popular melody entitled "Dancing in the Barn," its name eventually became abbreviated to that which is now more generally applied to it. With ridiculous inappropriateness, it is also, like "Iolanthe," frequently miscalled the "Pas de Quatre." The step of the "Schottische Militaire" is exceedingly simple, and is performed as follows:—

Lady and Gentleman dance the first four bars (16 steps), side by side, the lady's left hand being placed in the right of her partner.
Both advance three walking steps, (beginning with the outside foot), then raising the inside foot in advance, both make a light hop on the outside leg.
This movement is repeated by commencing with the inside foot, and hopping on the outside leg.
The two movements are again repeated to complete the first four bars.
The gentleman then, taking his partner, as in an ordinary round dance, the Couple make four circular movements—(i.e., eight half turns executed with a light hopping step), similar to the second part of the Schottische.

dance? The dance guide he published c.1890 was a relatively straightforward project as it was consisted of descriptions of dances that were well-known and had been described elsewhere. When it came to his own dances he may have become increasingly fussy about how they were described. His c.1890's **New Lancers** and **Greensleeves** are described without too much fuss, but the description of his dance **The Tantivy**, that appeared with credit to Crompton in Lamb's c.1900 *Everybody's Guide to Ball Room Dancing*, is very long (4 pages) considering how short and simple the dance is. So perhaps Crompton could not imagine how he would manage describing the ten figure of his Iolanthe or perhaps publishers had indicated his instructions were going to be far too long for anyone to bother with.

IOLA

The New Dance "Iolanthe"

POPPLEWELL ROYLE.

Tempo di Schottische.

PIANO.

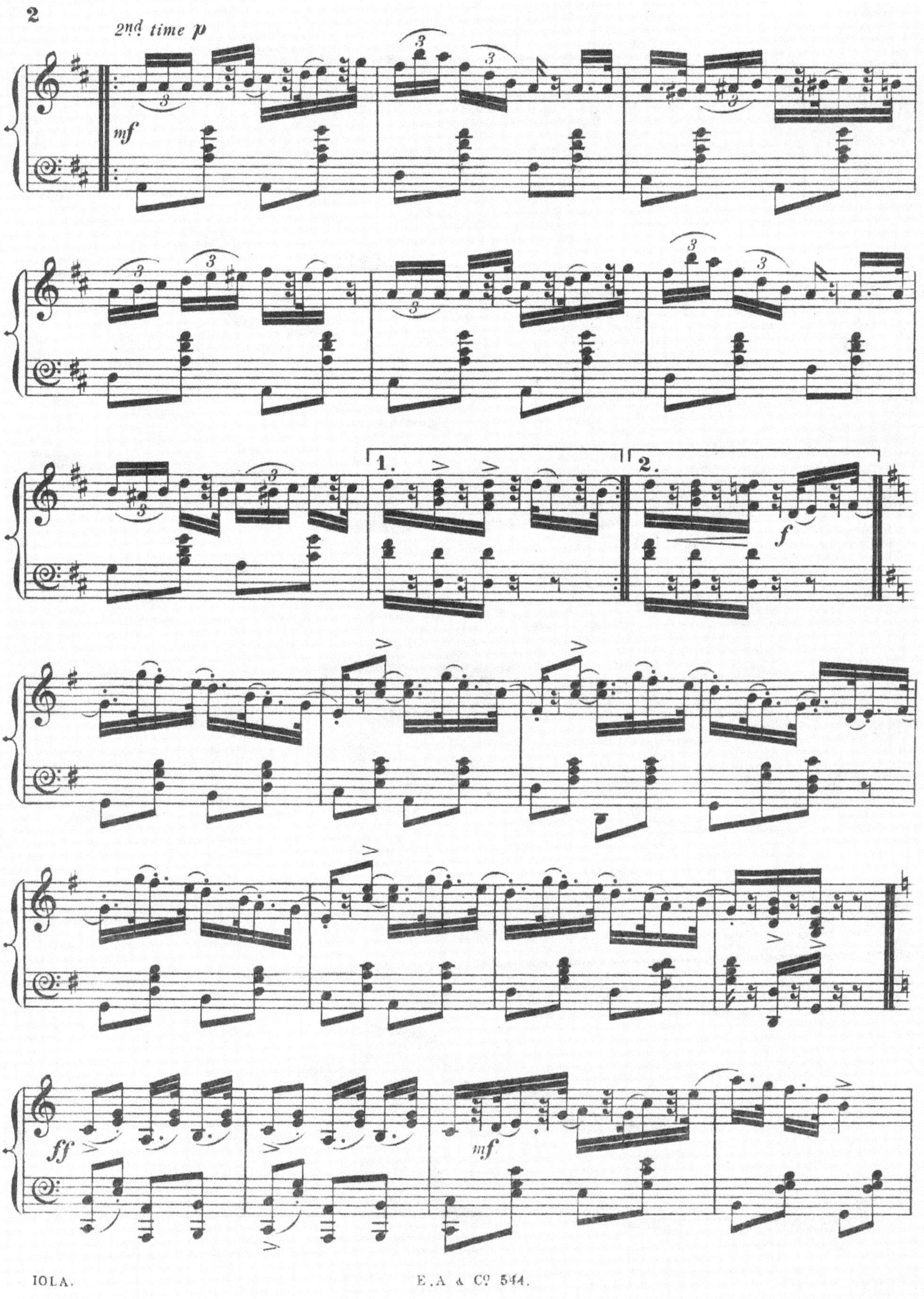
2
2nd time p
mf
1.
2.
f
ff
mf
IOLA.
E.A & Co 544.

2nd time 8va higher.

4

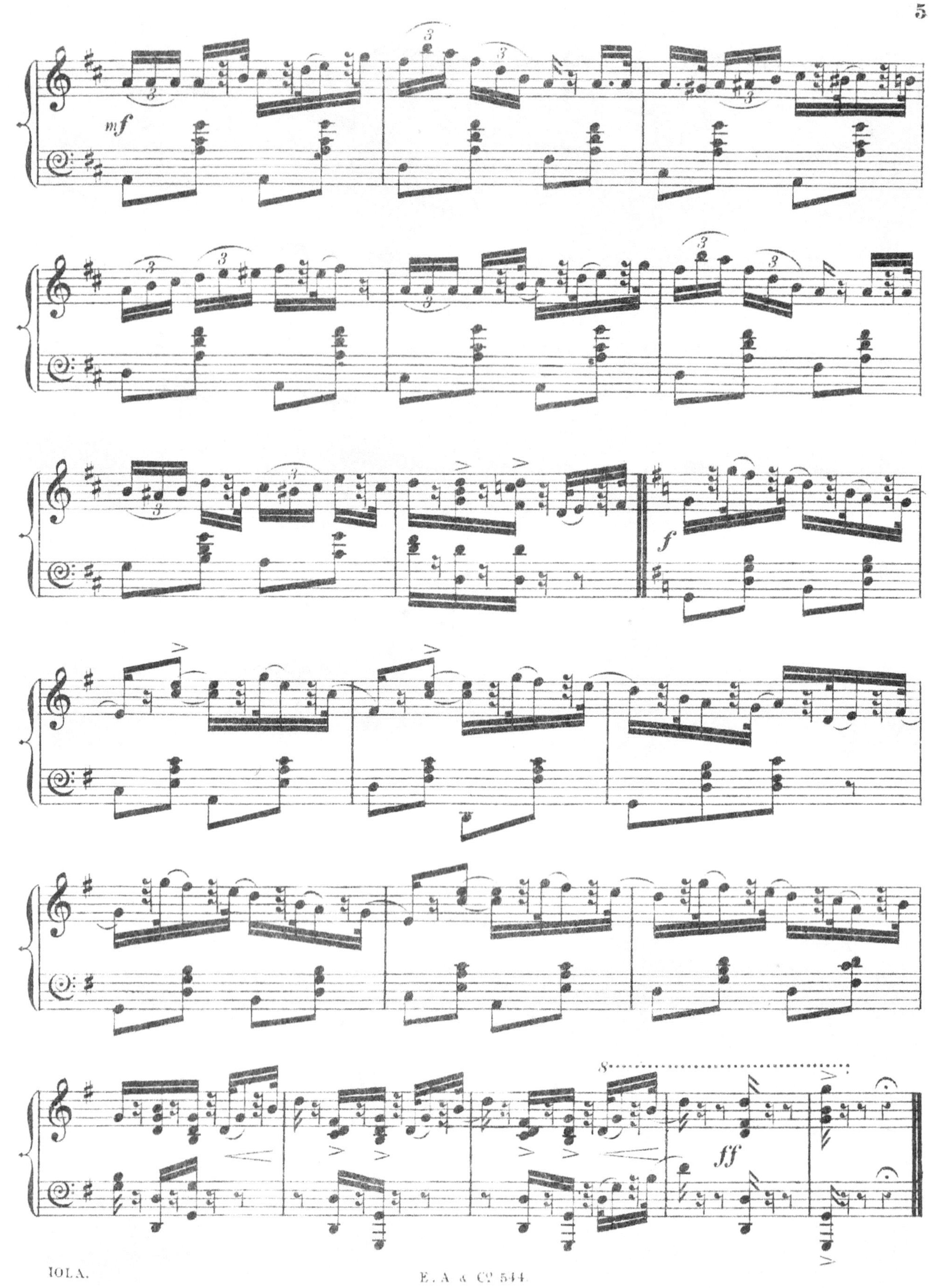
5
mf
f
ff
8
IOLA.
E. A. & Cº 544.

The "Pas de Quatre."

DESCRIPTION OF THE DANCE
BY
R. M. CROMPTON, Professor of Dancing, London.

LADY and Gentleman dance the first four bars (16 steps) side by side, the lady's left hand being placed in the right of her partner.

Both advance three walking steps (beginning with the outside foot), then raising the inside foot in advance, both make a light hop on the outside leg.

This movement is repeated by commencing with the inside foot, and hopping on the inside leg.

The two movements are again repeated to complete the first four bars.

The gentleman then taking his partner as in an ordinary round dance, the couple make four circular movements (i.e. eight half-turns executed with a light hopping or Waltz step), similar to the second part of the Schottische.

———

Notwithstanding its title, the dance is performed in couples, any number participating simultaneously. The application of this title was due to the circumstance of the dance being almost invariably performed to the music of the enormously successful "Pas de Quatre" from the Burlesque "Faust up to Date."

Le "Pas de Quatre."

DESCRIPTION DE LA DANSE
PAR
R. M. CROMPTON, Maître de Danse à Londres.

LE Cavalier et la Dame dansent les quatre premières mesures (16 pas) côte à côte, la main gauche de la dame mise dans celle de son cavalier.

Les deux avancent trois pas (et par exemple la dame commence avec le pied droit et le cavalier avec le pied gauche); en levant l'autre pied un peu sur le devant tous deux font un petit saut sur le pied posé.

Ce mouvement est répété une fois, et par exemple la dame commence cette fois avec le pied gauche et le cavalier avec le pied droit, alors tous deux sautillent sur le pied posé.

Après ceci les deux tours sont répétés pour compléter les quatre premières mesures.

Après cela tous deux dansent une simple danse en ronde en quatre cercles (c'est-à-dire à exécuter huit demi-cercles avec un pas léger de Valse) pareil à la deuxième partie d'une danse écossaise.

———

Malgré son titre la danse est exécutée par un couple ou plusieurs couples. La circonstance que ce titre a été donné à cette danse est que la musique du "Pas de Quatre" dans le Burlesque "Faust up to Date" (d'un succès extraordinaire) est choisie généralement pour cette danse.

Der "Pas de Quatre."

BESCHREIBUNG DES TANZES
VON
R. M. CROMPTON, Tanzmeister in London.

HERR und Dame tanzen die ersten 4 Tacte (16 Schritte) nebeneinander, die linke Hand der Dame in die rechte ihres Partner gelegt.

Beide gehen drei Schritte vorwärts (und zwar beginnt die Dame mit dem rechten und der Herr mit dem linken Fusse), während sie hierauf den anderen Fuss etwas nach vorne heben, machen beide einen leichten Sprung auf dem stehenden Fusse.

Diese Bewegung wird einmal wiederholt, und zwar beginnt die Dame diesesmal mit dem linken Fusse, der Herr mit dem rechten, dann hüpfen beide auf dem stehenden Fusse.

Hierauf werden beide Touren wiederholt, um die ersten vier Tacte auszufüllen.

Danach tanzen beide einen gewöhnlichen Rundtanz vier Umdrehungen (d. h. 8 halbe Drehungen mit einem leichten Walzer-Schritt ausgeführt) ähnlich dem zweiten Theile eines Schottisch.

———

Obgleich der Tanz "Pas de Quatre" heisst, wird derselbe paarweise in beliebiger Anzahl ausgeführt. Die Benennung "Pas de Quatre" geht daraus hervor, dass die Musik des ausserordentlich erfolgreichen "Pas de Quatre" aus der Burleske "Faust up to Date" fast ausschliesslich für diesen Tanz benutzt wird.

~ Parlour Games ~

Form square sets of 4 couples, identifying tops and sides.

Start right foot free.

Dance twice through the sequence, 2nd time with sides dancing heads role (option of repeating all in counterpart).

Play intro. then the following transcription of the jig from the end of the first Sonata of the mid-18th century 'Il Pastor Fido' ('The faithful shepherd): ABCDEFGHIJ x 2 (for option 1 or 3) or x 4 (for option 2) *either* in the key of G thus:

A	Opening (16 counts): walked circle l. / r., sides face out
B	*Chorus*: (8 counts) lead f & b. *while* sides lead out & b.
CD	1/4 chases (12 counts each): heads thru by r.sh. & cw chase *while* sides cw chase & thru x 2 **E** *Chorus*
FG	1/2 chases (16 counts each) heads thru by r.sh. & cw chase *while* sides cw chase & thru x 2 **H** *Chorus*
IJ	1/4 chases as before (12 counts each) x 2. **then**

Option 1) Repeat above w. heads & sides switching roles.
Option 2) After both heads and sides have 'lead' sequence w. cw chases & r.sh passes, dance whole again in cntrprt, i.e. w. opening circle r&l. and w. chasing acw and passes by l.sh.
Option 3) After heads lead cw-sequence, sides lead acw-one.

— John Gardiner-Garden, *Dance Delights*, 2020 —

or, if you need the tune in the key of C in order to play on a hurdy-gurdy which cannot play below 'g', then you might try this:

	~ The Basic ~
A	*Opening:* With 8 steps <u>circle left</u> / with 8 steps circle <u>right</u>, finishing with <u>side couples</u> doing 'California <u>twirl</u>' with partner (i.e. woman going under man's raised right hand to <u>change places and face other way</u>) and sides thus facing out of set while heads face in.
B	*Chorus:* With 8 counts, <u>tops lead in a double and back</u> *while* sides lead out a double <u>and</u> <u>back</u>

C	*1/4 chases* (12 steps each): <u>Tops</u> with <u>4 steps go in</u> to form a right shoulder line, with <u>4 steps</u> continue on <u>to other side passing incoming sides by r.sh.</u>, and with <u>4 steps</u> top M chase partner <u>1/4</u> way <u>cw</u> around the set, *while* sides chase partner <u>1/4 cw</u> around set, with <u>4 steps</u> go <u>in</u>, passing the tops as they come out, and with <u>4 steps</u> pass opposites by right shoulder <u>to</u> emerge on <u>opposite side</u>
D	with 12 counts <u>same again</u> with W chasing M cw, all finishing on opposite side of set.
E	*Chorus* (8 steps): - as before -
F	*1/2 chases* (16 steps each): <u>With 8 counts tops</u> pass opposite by r.sh. to go through the centre <u>to the other side and with 8 counts</u> M chase 1/2 way <u>cw</u> around the set, *while* sides with 8 counts <u>chase</u> cw ½ way, and with 8 counts <u>pass through the</u> centre
G	<u>same again</u> with W chasing M cw to finish back on same opposite side to where ½ chases started.
H	<u>*Chorus*</u> (8 steps): - as before -
IJ	<u>*1/4 chases*</u> (12 steps each): <u>as before</u> to arrive back in home position, <u>but finishing with</u> side couples taking inside hands after their last pass thru and California twirl to face into <u>the set.</u>

	~ Options to follow the basic ~	Means 'A-J' ends up played
Option 1— Changing the lead	After doing the 'Basic' to 1 playing of the tune repeat A-J with tops and sides changing roles but with the opening circle still left and right, with the chases still cw and all the passing still by the right shoulder.	x 2
Option 2— changing the lead then the direction	After doing the 'Basic' plus Option 1 to 2 playings of the tune, repeat the tune another 2 times (i.e. another A-J x2) to do the whole dance ('Basic' + 'Option 1') in reverse direction with all the opening circle being to right and then left, all the chases being acw and all the passing being by the left shoulder.	x 4
Option 3— changing lead and direction	After doing the 'Basic' to 1 playing of the tune repeat A-J not only with tops and sides changing roles but the direction/side of all the action changing, i.e. opening circle goes right and left, all the chases being acw and all the passing being by the left shoulder.	x 2

This is one of the first dances I choreographed, writing it to go to a tune played by the band called 'Dancerye', for whom I was calling in the early 1990s. Gillian Alcock, the hammered dulcimer player with that band, introduced the tune and it was a great tune for that band as the band also featured Heloise Mariath playing hurdy-gurdy and the music is from a collection of six Sonatas for musette (a type of bagpipe), hurdy gurdy, flute, oboe or violin and basso continuo. The hurdy-gurdy and bagpipe (my own two main instruments) though rarely used in art music today (and rarely used in renderings of this suite these days), were much used in art music at the time, especially when wanting to bring out a pastoral or Arcadian theme. As different hurdy-gurdies and bagpipes can be set up to play best in different keys, and as they all tend to have a narrow range (especially pipes which would be hard pressed to play the whole tune), to give you choice I've provided the tune in the key of both G and C.

With respect the music, the sonatas were long believed to have been by the Italian composer Antonio Vivaldi (1678-1741), but are nowadays believed to have been by Frenchman Nicolas Chédeville (1705-1782) somewhat in imitation of Vivaldi, whose music was very popular in Paris at the time. For my dance the jig suite needs to be played twice through.

With respect the dance, my composition is relatively simple, needs no fancy period steps and is not as complicated as it can look from the outside, or seem from the inside. It can, however, be unforgiving if you lose concentration—and the hypnotic music and dance patterning can make that all too possible. Knowing the following can help preventing a set implosion. Firstly, you always use 4 steps to go from the edge to the centre or ¼ of the way around the outside— and, as a corollary, always take 8 steps to go all from one side to the other, whether directly through the centre or curving around the outside in a ½ round, so always take slightly small steps when going straight through the centre, and slightly longer ones around the outside. Secondly, you always do the chorus either on original or opposite side. Thirdly, the pattern is somewhat palindromic—after the opening circles and chorus, do the ¼ chases to get to the other side, the chorus, ½ chases to go once around, the chorus and ¼ chases to get back to home side.

As in the Chédeville sonata the jig offered above as A-J is played twice, and as it could conceivably be played another two times if removed from the context of the sonata and put in a dance context, in my summary box and reconstruction table above I have described three options to what might follow dancing the basic version of the dance to one playing through of the tune suite.

The first option is the one debuted nearly 30 years ago. It requires just 2 playings of the tune, with the second time the heads California twirl to face out and the sides do the chorus going in while the heads go out, and thus all the subsequence action is done in reverse head/side roles to the first time through. The chases, however, all remain cw (i.e. turn right) and the passing through remains always by the right shoulder.

The second option I offer is possible if you want a challenge and have musicians who don't mind playing the tune a 3rd and 4th time (a recording you have manipulated to provide a 3rd and 4th playing). It involves doing Option 1 and then repeating the whole dance in reverse direction, i.e. playing A-J another 2 times and redancing with all the chases being acw and all the passing by the left shoulder.

The third option is more challenging again, as it requires in the 2nd playing of the tune overlapping both Option 1's change of lead to the side couple with Option 2's change of direction, and thus you don't have to go past 2 playings of the tune to treat onlookers to the spectacle of everything being done both ways. A big thanks to the 8 dancers who at a get-together at my place in August 2020 just before this book was completed prove this 3rd most-challenging option possible!

~ Pastime in Good Company ~

Form a circle of dancers, either coupled or .
individuals, either seated or standing, around the perimeter of dance floor, with a nominated starting man or woman standing inside circle.

Start left foot free.

Dance steps as seek&greet random mixer till all who will are on floor then, with couples forming a circle (M facing acw W cw) dance same steps as a grand chain & greet regular mixer as many times as will.

Play intro. then AABx n.

Snowball seek & greet random mixer figure till all on dance floor:
AA **Seek:** Lead seeks a partner w. 4 slow ornamented doubles (i.e. in every 2 bars take 2 plain steps and 3 quick ones)
B **Greet:** *continenze* l. to take and make a small bow on r.hs, *continenze* r. to take l.hs under right, then w. a fleuret (3 quick steps in 1 bar) M t. W cw under raised hs / cntrpart turning M acw under raised hs ending letting l.h. that is under joined r.hs. drop
AABxn Repeat the above sequence, each time starting pulling r.sh past the one just greeted and tumbled and seeking & greeting someone new.

Transition:
AABB When all are on the dance floor, upon a signal, find a new ptner w. just 1 ornamented double and use the remaining 3 to swing them in a r.h. t. into a single circle, M facing along l.o.d. W against, and there do greet figure with tumbles. Then upon another signal…

Grand chain & greet regular mixer figure as many times as will:
AA **Grand chain:** w. 1 ornamented double per hand, and starting right hand and left foot chain past 4 people
B **Greet:** w. 5th person met do the earlier B-strain greeting figure.
AABxn Repeat as many times as will.

		Seek & greet random mixer to snowball onto dance floor
A1	**Pastime with good company** **I love & shall until I die**	Lead dancer seeks a partner w. 2 ornamented doubles (i.e. in every 2 bars take 2 plain steps and 3 quick ones)
A2	**grudge who lust but none deny** **so god be pleased thus live will I**	Another 2 ornamented doubles to continue the search for a prospective partner, or if found to start to gypsy them/
B1	**for my pastance hunt sing & dance my heart is set**	Facing found partner *continenza* (a slow unclosed bar-long step) left to take and briefly bow on right hands, *continenza* right to join left hands under right *while* again bowing slightly, then with 3rd bar both do a *fleuret* starting left (3 quick steps in one bar) man tumbles the woman cw under his raised hands

— John Gardiner-Garden, *Dance Delights*, 2020 —

B2	all goodly sport for my comfort who shall me let	*Counterpart*: Facing *continenze* right (releasing right hs which are underneath and retaining left hands as left arms stretch out, *continenza* left to join right hands under left, then with *fleuret* woman tumbles man acw under raised right hands (or if man is too tall, man tumbles woman acw)
AA BB xn		*Repeat* this part by pulling past this partner by the right shoulder and seeking and bring out a new partner, until the transition into a circle is signalled
		Transition into a circle
AA BB		When all are on the dance floor upon a signal (or call of 'last time') dancers, <u>find a new partner with just 1 ornamented double and use the remaining 3 to swing them in a right hand turn out to periphery of floor to form a single circle</u>, men facing acw along l.o.d. woman cw against it, <u>then greet and tumble</u> on right hand and greet and tumble on left hand. Then upon signal:
		Grand chain & greet regular mixer as many times as will
A1	youth must have some dalliance of good or ill some pastance	<u>With 1 ornamented double per hand and starting right hand and left foot grand chain past 4 people</u>
A2	Company me thinks then best all thoughts & fancies to digest.	
B1	for Idleness is chief mistress of vices all	Facing *continenza* left to take right hands, *continenza* right to join left hands under right, then with 3 quick steps (a *fleuret)* man tumbles woman cw under raised hands
B2	then who can say. but mirth and play is best of all.	Counterpart: Facing *continenza* right, releasing right but retaining left hands, *continenza* left to join right hands under left, then with *fleuret* man tumbles acw under woman's raised right hands (or man tumbles woman)
		Repeat as directed.

This dance is a simplified version of one I created in January 2010 when a couple asked me to compose a dance to this song for their wedding. The steps and figures needed to be simple and have a 16th century flavour but I couldn't decide between several figure ideas so suggested a suite in 3 parts. In revisiting this dance 5 years later and then 5 years later again, I've simplified the steps and figures further, and settled on just one sequence that will work for either dancers moving randomly alone or dancers formed in a circle or in transition between the two. The ideal, I suggest, is to dance the sequence as a snowballing random mixer till all are on the floor dancing, then, upon a signal encourage couples to move to the periphery of the dance floor (replacing seeking with right and left hand turn) and form a single circle while doing the transition form of the sequence, then, perhaps upon another signal, go onto the regular mixing mode by bringing in the grand chain in lieu of the seeking figure.

This song *Pastime with Good Company* is believed have been written by King Henry VIII in early 16th century for Catherine of Aragon. It became a very popular tune and the tune was recorded in many 16 century tune books. In the 1548 work the anonymous *Complaynt of Scotland* refers to *Passetyme with gude companye* as among the popular songs within the kingdom of Scotland. The oldest known version is part of the c.1513 *Henry VIII Manuscript* (BM Addl. MSS. 31,922; Addl. MSS. 5,665; MSS. Reg. Appendix 58) signed 'by the King's hand' and held by the British library (see facsimile at the end of entry). Here is my transcription of the lyric, together with a modern rendering:

My transcription (with expansions)	Modern English
The Kynges Balade	The King's Ballad
Passetyme with good companye,	Pastime with good company
I love, and shall untyll I dye.	I love & shall until I die
Gruche who wyll, but none deny,	grudge who lust but none deny
So God be plesyd, thus lyfe wyll I.	so god be pleased thus live will I
For my pastaunce:	for my pastance
Hunt, syng, and daunce,	hunt sing & dance
My hart is sett	my heart is set
All goodly sport,	all goodly sport
Fore my comfort,	for my comfort
Who shall me lett?	who shall me let
Youth must have some daliance,	youth must have some dalliance
Of good or yll some pastance,	of good or ill some pastance
Companye me thynketh them best,	Company me thinks then best
All thouts and fansyes to dygest.	all thoughts & fancies to digest.
For ydleness,	for Idleness
Ys chef mastres	is chief mistress
Of vyces all:	of vices all
Than who can say,	then who can say.
But myrth and play	but mirth and play
Ys best of all?	is best of all.
Companye with honeste,	Company with honesty
Ys vertu, vyce to flee.	is vertue vices to flee.
Company ys good or yll,	Company is good & ill
But ev'ry man hath hys frewyll.	but ev'ry man hath his free will.
The best ensyue,	the best ensue
The worst eschew,	the worst eschew
My mynd shall be:	my mind shall be.
Vertue to use,	vertue to use
Vyce to refuse,	vice to refuse
Thus shall I use me.	thus shall I use me.

If you are using a recording and the arrangements has a pause or a held note at the end of each playing or singing of the tune I suggest you use it to bow to the person you have just tumbled with. This can, indeed, be such a pleasant addition to the dance, that even if enjoying live music you may want to introduce a pause for such a bow at the end of each playing.

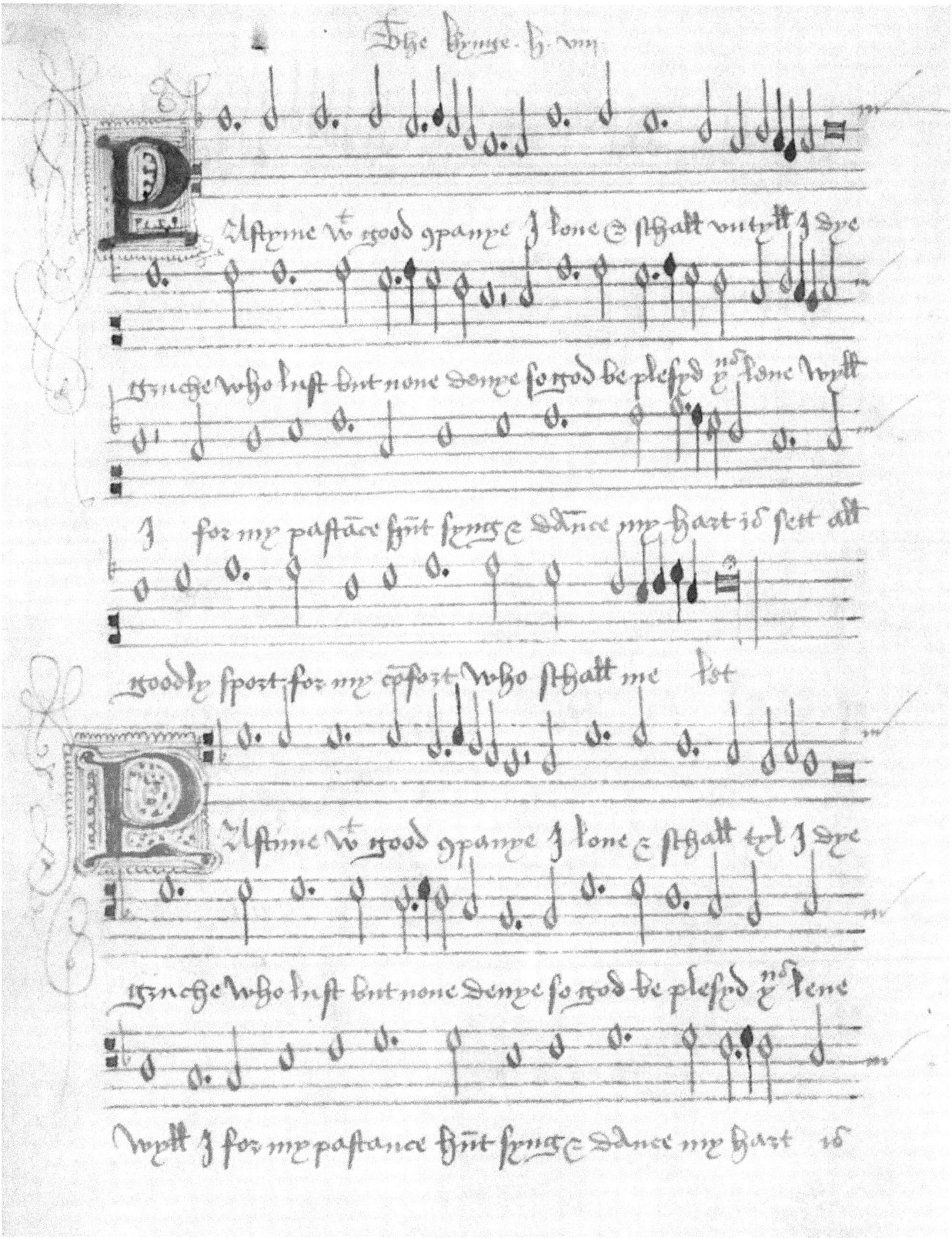

sett all goodly sport for my gfort who shall me let.

Pastime wt good gpany I love e shall do tyl I dye

grucche who lust but none deny so god be plesed thus leve I

Wytt I for my pastance hunt syng e dance my hart

is sett all goodly sport for my gfort who shall me let.

youthe must have sū daliance off good or yll sū pastance.
Company me thynks then best all thoughte e fansye to dygest.
ffor Idillnes is cheff mastres of vices all then who can say.
but myrth and play is best of all.

Company wt honeste is vertu vices to flee.
Company is good e ill but evy man hath hys fre wyll.
the best ensew the worst eschew my mynd shalbe.
vertu to use vice to refuse thus shall I use me.

~ The Philosopher's Stone ~

Form a square set of four couples numbered cw

Start with left foot.

Dance the sequence 8 times. If doing the 'Half-power version' have each M lead in turn with small circle, triangle, square and final big circle going cw, then each W lead with key actions going acw. If doing the 'Full-power' version 1M, 1W, 2M, 2W, 3M, 3W, 4M & 4W lead in turn, i.e. alternate between M and W leading and key actions going cw and acw.

Play any double time tunes 32 bar x 8. I recommend 'The Emperor of the Moon' (17th cent. for when a man is leading and 'The Earth maidens' ruse' which I wrote with

When 1M leads:

A1 1M stamps l.,r.; advances toward 3M l,r / as 1M beckons w. l.h. 3W f. l, r; as 1M beckons w. r.h. 2W f. l, r. / this 1st trio circle l.

A2 1st trio quick 12 glissades cw around triangle (4 facing in to 1st cnr, 4 facing out to 2nd, 4 facing in to 3rd) then 4 step 2/3 t.s. l., *while* 3M 4&1W meet and circle l. *while* 2&4M start slow cw square w. 2 slow in-facing glissades to 1st cnr, 4 facing out to 2nd, 2 facing in ½ way to 3rd.

B1 1st trio chase skipping acw circle *while* 2nd trio slip triangle *while* spare men complete square w. 2 slow glissades facing in to 3rd cnr, 4 facing out to 4th cnr, 2 facing in to home place

B2 All circle l.

When 1W leads:
Repeat all in cnterpart w. 1W stamping r. and l. and w. small triangle, triangle, square and final big circle all being traced acw (i.e. to r.),

For 'half-power' version follow 1M leading with 2M, 3M and 4M leading (all starting l.f. and key actions cw, i.e. to l.) then have 4 woman successively leading (i.e. starting r.f. and key actions cw).

For 'full-power' version alternate lead between M and W leading with leadership passing acw around set (1M, 1W, 2M, 2W, 3M, 3W, 4M then 4W) and with starting foot and key actions direction alternating.

improvements and chords by Sally Taylor (who has also chorded the Emperor tunes below) for when a woman is leading. If doing the 'Half-power' version play each tune 4 times. If doing 'Full-power' version, alternate between the tunes.

The Emperor of the Moon

♩ = 110 [A]

Gm — D⁷ — Gm — F — B♭ — E♭ F — Gm Cm — D Gm

[B]

Gm — Cm — B♭ — E♭ — B♭ — Dm — Cm — Gm — D Gm

The Earth maiden's ruse

♩ = 110

Gm — Cm — Gm — Cm — Gm Fm⁷ — D° — Cm — Fm Cm — D

Gm — A⁵ Dm — B♭ E♭ — F Gm Cm — F Gm — E♭ — F — Gm — D — Gm D Gm

[1.] [2.]

~ 1st playing, 1M leading with cw action ~			
1st trio: 1M, 2W & 3W		2nd trio: 3M, 1W & 4W	Left over pair: 2M & 4M

— John Gardiner-Garden, *Dance Delights*, 2020 —

1A1	**The meeting:** On counts 1&2 <u>1M stamps left and right in place</u> then on counts 3&4 1M <u>goes forward toward 3M (opposite) with a step left and right</u> On counts 5&6 <u>M beckons with left hand to 3W who steps left and right forward</u> to take 1M's left in his right <u>then</u> on counts 7&8 <u>M beckons with left hand to 2W who steps left and right forward</u> to complete the hand-holding trio		
	The small circle: With <u>8 steps</u> (starting left) <u>1M 2W 3W circle cw in the middle once around, release hands and fall back home</u>		
1A2	**Trace the triangle:** <u>Trio trace the triangle in a cw circuit between each other's home places with 4 inward facing slip steps</u> leading with left foot and left shoulder <u>then</u> after turning single acw 60^0 go with <u>4 outward facing slip steps</u> with right foot & shoulder leading	**The meeting**	**Trace the square:** go in a cw circuit between imagined corners of the set taking <u>2 slow inward-facing slide-together steps to 1st corner</u> then after turning single acw 90^0 take <u>2 outward-facing slide-together steps</u> halfway <u>to 2nd corner</u>
	and after turning single acw 60^0 go with <u>4 inward facing slip steps</u> to home place <u>then</u> with 4 walking steps do a 240^0 acw <u>turn single left to end facing acw around the circle</u>	**The small circle**	continue with <u>2 out-facing slide-togethers into 2nd corner</u> then after turning single acw 90^0 take <u>2 in-facing ones towards 3rd corner</u>
1B1	**Chase the circle:** Same trio take <u>16 skip-steps acw around the outside of the set and back to place</u> (8 skips for each ½ of wide circuit)	**Trace the triangle:**	Continue with <u>2 in-facing slide-togethers into 3rd corner</u> and after turning single acw 90^0 <u>take 2 out-facing ones towards 4th corner,</u>
			Continue with <u>2 out-facing slide-togethers into 4th corner</u> then after turning single acw 90^0 go take <u>2 inward facing slips</u> back to <u>home</u> place.
1B2	<u>**Grand circle left:**</u> all 8 dancers take hands in and walk cw with <u>15 steps an inward facing circle and then close</u> feet back in place.		
	~ 1W lead version with acw action ~		
	1st trio: 1W, 4M & 3M	2nd trio: 3W, 1M & 2M	Left over pair: 2W & 4W
2A1	**The meeting:** 1W stamps right and left in place, then steps forward towards 3W (opposite) with 2 steps. Then 1W beckons with right hand 3M to step		

	right and left forward and with left hand 4M to step forward. **The small circle:** With 8 steps same 3 circle acw		
2A2	**Trace the triangle:** Trio slip acw (i.e. to right) around triangle alternately facing inward, outward inward and turn single r. to end facing cw around the circle	**The meeting** **The small circle**	**Trace the square:** go in an acw circuit between imagined corners of the set taking 2 slow inward-facing slide-togethers to 1st corner then 2 outward-facing halfway to 2nd corner, 2 out-facing into 2nd corner, 2 in-facing ones towards 3rd corner
2B1	**Trace the circle:** take 16 skip steps cw around the outside of the set and back to place	**Trace the triangle:**	2 in-facing slide-togethers into 3rd corner, 4 out-facing ones to 4th corner then 2 inward-facing slips back to home place.
2B2	**Grand circle right:** all 8 dancers take hands in and 16 steps acw around an inward facing circle.		
	~ Pattern ~		
	For 'half-power' version follow 1M leading with 2M, 3M and 4M leading (all starting l.f. and key actions cw, i.e. to l.) then have 4 women successively leading (i.e. starting r.f. and key actions cw). **For 'full-power' version** pass leadership between M and W acw around set (1M, 1W, 2M, 2W, 3M, 3W, 4M then 4W) with starting foot and key actions direction alternating.		

I was inspired to write this dance by the survival of the following diagram and name in dance text of c.1610. The diagram is the twelfth and last dance formation presented in a record of the *Ballet de Monseigneur le duc de Vandosme* (also known as the *Ballet d'Alcine*), and it is given the name 'Pouvoir supresme' ('Supreme power') shown on left. As I have discussed at length in my section on France in *Dancing through the Ages* Volume III: 1600-1650, the Vandosme dance formation catalogue overlaps significantly with another dance formation catalogue from the same period, the Kungliga Biblioteket Cod. Holm S 253 (or 'Stockholm manuscript'). Jennifer Nevile in her "Dance Patterns of the Early Seventeenth Century: The Stockholm Manuscript and 'Le Ballet De Monseigneur De Vendosme.'" *Dance Research: The Journal of the Society for Dance Research*, vol. 18, no. 2, 2000, pp. 186–203, found 12 figures in common. As I discuss in my *Dancing through the Ages* Volume III, although I find only about 6 figures clearly analogous, I agree with Nevile's thesis that there was a theatrical dance vocabulary that was largely shared between early 17th century French dancing masters working in Paris and the near abroad. Although I am not convinced by Nevile's equating of the Vandosme 'Pouvoir supresme' with the Stockholm manuscript's 11th figure, a 10-dancer figure, I do find the Vandosme 'Pouvoir supresme' image analogous with the 12-dancer 1st figure on Stockholm manuscript's f.17v shown on right:

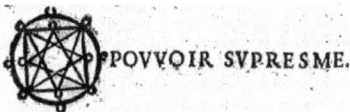

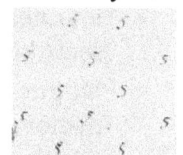

Both the Vandosme and Stockholm ms formation catalogues seem to reflect c.1610 French court practice and seem to make use of alchemical imagery. As I discuss at greater length in my *Dancing through the Ages* Volume III: 1600-1650, from its probable birthplace in Alexandria, Egypt around 300 B.C. alchemy was brought into eastern and southern Europe by Arab practitioners in the last quarter of the 1st millennium, and started to gain influence in Western European in the 12th century. In the 14th century it was forced underground by Papal condemnation, but by the early 16th century alchemical practice was gaining respectability and a pseudo-chemical-based medical system advanced by the Swiss alchemist Paracelsus started displacing traditional Galenic herbalism. In the late 16th and 17th century works on the subject multiplied—see for example Gerhard Dorn's 1584 *Dictionarium Theoprasti Paracelsi,*; Simon Forman's

1597, *Principles of Philosphi*, Martin Ruland's 1612 *Lexicon alchemiae*, and 1650 *A Chymicall Dictionary* (an abbreviated translation of Dorn's work), William Johnson's 1652 *Lexicon Chymicum*, Elias Ashole's 1652 *Theatrum chemicum Britannicum*, an annotated a collection of several alchemical works, including John Gower's 14th century *Concerning the Philosopher's stone* (a translation of a still earlier *Secreta secretorum*), and William Salmon's 1695 *Dictionaire Hermetique*. The audience for such books was very wide and the books often included images that represented stages in the *opus*. The *opus* was the cycle of distillations and coagulation that an alchemist might engage in in pursuit of the magical 'fifth element' that harmonises all, or 'philosopher's stone' that had the power to perfect imperfection in all things, transform base metals into gold and transform an earthly man into an illuminated philosopher. The production of this element or stone was regarded as the ultimate goal of the alchemists' work, or *opus*.

There were many distinguished men of the time interested in alchemy. In the English-speaking world these included Sir Walter Raleigh, George Villiers ('the Duke of Buckingham', King Charles I's trusted advisor), King Charles II, and Isaac Newton, the latter exploring the subject in his unpublished 1680s *Index chemicus*. Writers such as Shakespeare, John Dryden and John Milton all made alchemical allusions in their writing, the latter writing in his *Paradise Lost* (Book 3 lines 606–9) of the **arch-chemic sun** whose fields **Breathe forth elixir pure** and whose **rivers run potable gold**. Writers such as Thomas Nashe, John Donne and Ben Jonson wrote satirically on the subject, the latter offering in his 1610 comedy *The Alchemist* (Act 2 scene 3) an exchange between the sceptical Surly, who points out that alchemists can't even agree with each other, and the alchemist Subtle, who suggests that symbols, parables and allegories are par-for-the course in rare fine arts.

That many of the Stockholm manuscript figures were intended to represent things which may have had meaning in the alchemical image lexicon is also clear. As Jennifer Nevile notes in her "Dance Patterns of the Early Seventeenth Century: The Stockholm Manuscript and 'Le Ballet De Monseigneur De Vendosme.'" *Dance Research: The Journal of the Society for Dance Research*, vol. 18, no. 2, 2000,p.194) a dozen of the names given to figures in the Stockholm ms are names of images which Lyndy Abraham in *A dictionary of alchemical imagery* (Cambridge University, 1998) has found associated in centuries of texts and illustrations with the alchemical *opus*. For example:

- **carriaue** ('a square') is associated variously with the physical earth, the four seasons, and the four elements (earth, air, fire and water) which the alchemist was trying to integrated and harmonised with a circle, the representation of unending perfection—see Abraham's entry on 'Square and circle';
- **coue** ('neck') is associated with the neck of the alchemical vessel—see Abraham's entry on 'Crow's beak';
- **croi** ('cross') is associated with the fixation of the volatile spirit, or the meeting point of the four elements, which alchemists try to combine to produces the sought-after fifth element or philosopher's stone—see Abraham entry on 'Cross';
- **dare/dair** ('dart'), or Cupid's arrow, is associated with the secret fire that destroys the old metal, or the old spiritual state—see Abraham's entry on 'Cupid';
- **estoille** ('star') is associated with the transforming medium, Mercury, that has the power to resolve and unite opposites, and to create harmony and balance (see Abraham's entry on 'Star (six-pointed)'— see Abraham's entry on 'Star (six-pointed)';
- **leunnes** ('moon') is associated with silver, as well as representing the female principle of the opus— see Abraham's entry on 'Luna';
- **langue de sacpon** ('serpent's tongue') or the 'serpent' itself, is associated with the dark, dangerous matter (Mercury at the first stage of the opus) with which the alchemist begins his work—see Abraham's entry on 'Serpent"
- **salleman** ('salamander') is associated with the masculine seed of the metals, the hot, dry, active principle of the alchemical opus—see Abraham's entry on 'Salamander';
- **solleille/soller** ('sun') The sun was one of the major alchemical symbols. It represented gold, the masculine principle of the opus, and also philosophical gold, which is gold created by the art of alchemy—see Abraham's entry on 'Sol' and 'Sun';
- **tourteau** ('tortoise') is associated with the alchemical basin—see Abraham's entry on 'Tortoise'.

The alchemical implications of the Vandosme catalogue is less immediately apparent but all 12 of the images in that catalogue seem to have equivalents in the Stockholm manuscript catalogue and the Vandosme catalogue's last dance formation, the *Pouvoir suprême* or 'Supreme power', is the well-known alchemical symbol for 'fifth element' or 'philosopher's stone', involving as it does the unification of the circle, triangle and square. The 'philosopher's stone' was often depicted in late 16th and 17th literature as unifying, in various ways, the circle, triangle and square. For example, left below is the image of the philosopher's stone in the German alchemist Michael Maier's *Atalanta Fugiens, hoc est, Emblemata Nova de Secretis Naturae Chymica* (rough translation: 'Atalanta Fleeing, that is, New chemical emblems of the secrets of nature'), published by Johannn Theodor in Oppenheim in 1617, and below right is one of several images with the same structure in the *Mutus liber* ('Wordless book'), an alchemical work by a certain 'Altus' (his identity subject to debate) published by Pierre Savouret in La Rochelle in 1677:

If you overlay these images you can see that Altus's image alludes to the same small circle, square, triangle and large circle that Maier's image makes explicit:

Although some modern day commentators are inclined keen to prescribe exact formulas for deriving a 'philosopher's stone' image in the proportions suggested by Maier's and 'Altus'' work, see the lower half of

— John Gardiner-Garden, *Dance Delights*, 2020 —

the figure as always representing the earthly or material world and the upper part the heavenly or spiritual world, and are prepared to ascribe colours and detail meaning to the various segments, I do not think there was consistency of proportions and meaning across the 17th century. As Ben Jonson has his sceptical character Surly observe in his 1610 comedy *The Alchemist* (Act 2 scene 3) **Alchemy is a pretty kind of game, / Somewhat like tricks o' the cards, to cheat a man / With charming. […] What else are all your terms, / Whereon no one of your writers 'grees with other?** to which the Alchemist named Subtle can only plead that alchemists do no more or less than others in making their art obscure:

> **Was not all the knowledge / Of the Aegyptians writ in mystic symbols?**
> **Speak not the scriptures oft in parables?**
> **Are not the choicest fables of the poets,**
> **That were the fountains and first springs of wisdom,**
> **Wrapp'd in perplexed allegories?**

The way the great circle is divided in Vandosme image 12 and the seemingly cognate Stockholm manuscript's image 1 on f.17v is different from the way Maier and Altus divide it. Here they are again to the left and right. The difference between these and the pictures above is not surprising, for although c.1610 was the height of the alchemical fad in western Europe, there were many ways of representing most alchemical ideas and the dancing masters behind these designs were not necessarily ascribing to the alchemical philosophy or trying to conjure any alchemical effect. They were more likely simply having fun with a widely understood contemporary image language, trying to meet expectations and trying to equip choreographers with ways to add *gravitas* to a ballet.

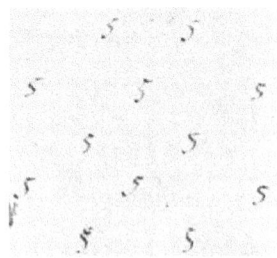

It is to have fun with this image language and to answer the following question that I decided to make my own 'Philosopher's stone' dance. How in the course of a dance can you not only create the potential overlapping shapes of a circle, triangle and square but have dancers trace all three overlapping shapes at the same time?

Both the Vansdome and the Stockholm manuscript image involve 12 dancers, and in January 2020 I devised in my mind's eye a way of having 12 dancers do such tracing. It never felt, however, an entirely natural social dance so I never wrote down those ideas and subsequently lost them. I returned to the problem in August 2020. I decided that in order to make the dance instantly more social I'd try to achieve the simultaneous triangle, square and circle (large and small) inside a 4-couple square set, a very common social dance formation. The triangle and square I decided on were going to be the large perimeter-touching ones we have in the Vandosme and Stockholm manuscripts rather than the small ones we have in the Maeier and Altus images. The above dance sequence is the result. It can work at several levels. It works as a social dance as it starts with some sparse action lead by just one dancer in a common social dance formation during which everyone gains their orientation, it builds up the overlapping shapes and then finish with a reassuring communal circle. It works as a representation of the Vandosme image 12, because although it uses only 8 dancers not 12, in the second half of A2 the dancers are simultaneously tracing a small circle, a triangle and a square and in the B1 they are simultaneous tracing of a large circle, square and a triangle. It should prove both socially, physically and intellectually satisfying. Upon successive repeats of the sequence different dancers will get to lead and the triangles and squares are made on different axes (somewhat as in the Vandosme image). If done accurately, the dancers will come close to but never actually collide. The highest risk for collision is when the second trio start their meeting though the first trio's triangle, but if the 1st dancer in a trio always take two stamp in place (if a man left and right, and if a woman right and left) and then as they take 2 steps beckon with the hand that corresponds to their step the opposite on diagonal that corresponds with their step, and those opposites step in the order they are beckoned (thus if a man beckons the woman on his left diagonal as he arrives in the middle takes 2 steps in ahead of the woman on the right diagonal; if a woman leads and beckons, the man on her right diagonal as she arrives to make the trio circle takes 2 steps in ahead of the man on the left diagonal). By doing this when the second trio meet to take hands in the middle they will do so, if instigated by a man, in a cw order—first the man, than the woman one removed on his left diagonal then woman next on her left (i.e. in an cw order) and the 1st trio dancers will be slipping the triangle just in front of the lead man, just behind the woman who enters next and just in front of the last woman. Conversely, if it is a turn when action is being initiated by a woman, they 2nd trio will enter the middle in an acw order—first the woman, than the man one removed on her right diagonal then man next on her right and the 1st trio dancers will be slipping the triangle just in front of the lead woman, just behind the man who enters next and just in front of the last man.

I recommend two ways of doing the dance to 8 lots of 32 bars. The 'Half-power' way is for all the men to each take turn leading (with key action always starting left and going to the left—even the acw skip around the outside goes to the left if you think of it as starting facing out) then women to each take turn leading (with key action always starting right foot and going to the right). The 'Full-power way is to alternate the man-led versions with a woman led-version (so the axis of the dance pattern shifts 1/8th each time around the set. Either way the dancer's experience the forces of the choreography working upon their bodies from every direction, and the spectators get to see the three overlapping shapes kaleidoscope before their eyes on every possible axis. If you dance the half-power version and you sweep the dance floor afterwards you may find some specks of gold dust. If you dance perfectly accurately the 'full-power' version you may find both the floor and your cloths sprinkled with gold dust. If you dance the 'full-power' version perfectly accurately around a base metal object resting the whole time undisturbed on a pedestal in the exact middle of the set, you may succeed in turning it to solid gold!

The ideal musical setting for this dance, if you are going to alternate men and women leading, is a pair of alternating 32 bars double time AABB tunes that are somewhat minor and mysterious and have a 16th or 17th century feel. I recommend two.

For whenever a man is leading I recommend a tune found in *The dancing master*, London, volume 1, from edition 8, 1690, to 18, 1728 as '(The) Emperor of the Moon' and in Dezais, *Recueil de nouvelles contredances*, Paris, 1712 (with virtually the same diagrams in Ernst August Jayme's *Recueil de contre danse*, Wolfenbüttel, 1717, p.85) as 'L'Empereur dans la lune'. My reasons for the recommendation are several. Firstly, the tune has an appropriate structure, rhythm and feel. Secondly, the moon was very important in alchemy, a crescent moon being the symbol for the silver. Thirdly, the tune title refers to a play that was possibly one of the first works of science fiction in the English language and was written by arguably the first professional female playwright in the English language, Aphra Behn. In this play the moon-obsessed philosopher Dr Baliardo doesn't want his daughter Elaria or niece Bellemante to marry anyone other than someone from the more superior moon-civilisation, so the young ladies' lovers, Don Cinthio and Don Charmante, impersonate the 'Emperor of the Moon' and his brother. The story goes back to Nolant de Fatouville 1684 *Arlequin empereur dans la lune* but the tune, even if part of the 1687 production of Behn's play, was unlikely to have been part of any production of de Fatouville play, as the original tune, in a longer form, seems to have been composed by Englishman Richard Motley (first appearing in an appendix to the second volume of *Vinculum societatis* in 1688, then in a keyboard arrangement by Henry Purcell for *The second part of musick's hand-maid,* 1689). For more on the 'Emperor of the Moon' dance and Behn's play see my entry on **Emperor of the Moon** in my *Dancing through the Ages*, Volume IV: 1650-1700, Part 2a.

Whenever a woman is leading I recommend a tune I wrote (with very welcome amendments offered by Sally Taylor who has offered the chords) to go with 'Emperor of the Moon'. For several reasons I call it 'The Earth Maidens' ruse'. Firstly, it was intended to match go with the 'Emperor of the moon' tune, and in Aphra Behn's play by that name two Earth maidens help their lovers impersonate the Emperor of the Moon and his brother. Secondly, in alchemical thought the Earth was one of the four most important elements, and is represented by an upside down triangle dissected by a horizontal line—and although not on exactly the same relative axes as in the dance, in this dance a solo dancer is often tracing a line directly into an inverted triangle that is being traced by others. Thirdly, if the upper part of the Altus/Maier type 'Philosopher's Stone' image is thought of as representing the heavens, the lower part can be thought of as representing earth.

~ Polka Nationale ~

Form couples holding inside hand.

Start opposite feet, M left W right.

Dance any figure as many times as will.

Play 'The National or Celebrated Opera Polka dance by Mad.lle Carlotta Grisi and Monsr Perrot at Her Majesty's Theatre' as here transcribed or as in piano score at the end of entry.

A1	Prom. along l.o.d. swinging inside hs f&b / reverse along l.o.d.
A2	cw waltz / reverse
B1 Ch. of arms; cnterprt / repeat	**B2** cw waltz / reverse

With heel&toe:

A1 H&t , prom.; cnterprt / repeat	**A1** Bohemian waltz / reverse
C1 H&t, ch. of arm; same b. / repeat	**C2** Bohemian waltz / reverse

With crossed hands:

A1 Moulinet r / l	**A2** Cross-h. cw waltz / reverse
D1 Lassoo on r.h. / cnterprt on l.h.	**D2** Cross-h. cw waltz / reverse
A1 Lassoo on r.h. with twirl	**A2** Cross-h. cw waltz / reverse

Then <u>either</u> go back through figures (will match score and transcription):

E1 H&t, ch. of arm; same b. / repeat	**E2** Bohemian waltz / reverse
A1 H&t , prom.; cnterprt / repeat	**A2** Bohemian waltz / reverse
B1 Ch. of arms; cnterprt / repeat	**B2** cw waltz / reverse
A1 Prom. on swinging inside h.	**A2 final** cw waltz / reverse
8 bar finale cw waltz	**2 bar** t. out & bow

<u>or go direct from E1 to A2 final</u> (to match abbreviated Polka Nationale):

E Bohemian waltz / reverse	**A2 final** cw waltz / reverse
8 bar finale cw waltz	**2 bar** t. out & bow

♩ = 110

A · G D G D D⁷ G — or hold d' — then AA

B · D A D D A D — then AA

C · d G D G D G D G — then AA

D · C G C G — then AA

E · D G D G D A D G D G D A D — then AABB then final AA and finale as follows

final As · G D G D D⁷ G G D⁷ — 1. 2.

finale · G D⁷ G D⁷ G D⁷ G

A1	*La promenade:* <u>Promenade with polka steps forward along l.o.d. swinging inside hands forward and back</u> **(1)** <u>reverse along l.o.d.</u>

A2	*La valse:* cw waltz **(2)**
	reverse **(3)**
B1	*Changement de bras:* Change arms (i.e. 'throw' partner from right arm across to left arm) **(6)** then counterpart
	repeat
B2	*La valse:* cw waltz **(2)**
	reverse **(3)**
	With heel&toe:
A1	Straight *Pas Bohémien* ('Bohemian step') Heel & toe, promenade then counterpart **(5)**
	repeat
A1	Turning *Pas Bohémien* or Bohemian waltz: heel and toe, ½ cw turn with 1 polka step, then heel and toe with new front foot, ½ cw turn with 1 polka step **(5)**
	reverse
C1	Heel & toe, change arm (i.e. 'throw' partner from right arm across to left arm) **(7)** then counterpart (heel & toe with other foot and 'throw' partner from left to right arm)
	repeat
C2	Turning *Pas Bohémien* or Bohemian waltz **(5)**
	reverse
	With crossed hands:
A1	*Moulinet d'une main* ('Mill on one hand'): Mill on right and left hand **(8)**
A2	*Valse tortillée* ('Twisted waltz'): Cross-hand cw waltz **(4)**
	reverse
D1	*Moulinet en suivant* ('Mill following'): Lassoo on right hand **(9)**
	counterpart on left hand
D2	*Valse tortillée*: Cross-hand cw waltz **(4)**
	reverse
A1	*Pass double* ('Double pass'): Lassoo on right hand with twirl **(10)**
A2	*Valse tortillée*: Cross-hand cw waltz **(4)**
	reverse
N.B.	[Then *either* go back through figures (will match my transcription) *or* directly from E1 to a final A2]

E1	<u>Heel & toe, change of arm</u> (7) <u>then same back</u> <u>repeat</u>	
E2	<u>Bohemian waltz</u> (5) <u>reverse</u>	[Skip these if wanting to match an abbreviated playing of the 'Polka Nationale']
A1	Straight *Pas Bohémien:* <u>Heel & toe, promenade then counterpart</u> (5) <u>repeat</u>	
A2	Turning *Pas Bohémien:* <u>Bohemian</u> (5) <u>waltz</u> <u>reverse</u>	
B1	*Changement de bras:* <u>Change arms then counterpart</u> (6) <u>repeat</u>	
B2	*La valse:* <u>cw waltz</u> (2) <u>reverse</u> (3)	
A1	*La promenade:* <u>Promenade forward swinging inside hand</u> forward and back (1)	
A2	*La valse:* cw waltz (2) reverse (3)	
8b. finale	*La valse:* _cw waltz (2)	
2b.	turn out & bow	

At the height of the Polka craze in Europe in the mid-1840s many choreographies were shaped to display thrilling variants on stage, and many piece of music composed as a setting for such displays. One such musical suite was 'The National or Celebrated Opera Polka', and it was used a setting for a polka display by Madamoiselle Carlotta Grisi and Monsieur Perrot at Her Majesty's Theatre'. I don't know the composer, and one is not named on the c.1844 London sheet music in my collection which I have appended to this entry. We do, however, know some of the figures commonly used. As I discuss in Part 1 and 2 of my *Dancing through the Ages,* Volume VIII: 1825-1850 they were:

1) *La promenade:* Polka swinging joined inside hands f; b
2) *La valse:* Polka turning cw
3) *Valse à rebours*: Reverse polka
4) *Valse tortillée*: Cross-hand cw polka
5) *Pas Bohémien:* Heel and toe, polka; counterpart.
6) *Changement de bras:* forward, 'throw' partner across; repeat in counterpart
7) Doing 5) w. 6)
8) *Moulinet d'une main:* right then left hand
9) *Moulinet en suivant:* M raises joined right hand and 'lassoes' W around
10) *Pass double*: As above but cw twirl her at end of first lasso and do counterpart back on left hand and acw twirl her.

In the absence of any record of the actual sequence that Grisi and Perrot danced to this above tune, I have put together a choreography that uses all of the above figures in a pattern that I have found satisfying to teach, lead and dance in a social setting. I've offered the variation name and number in my table.

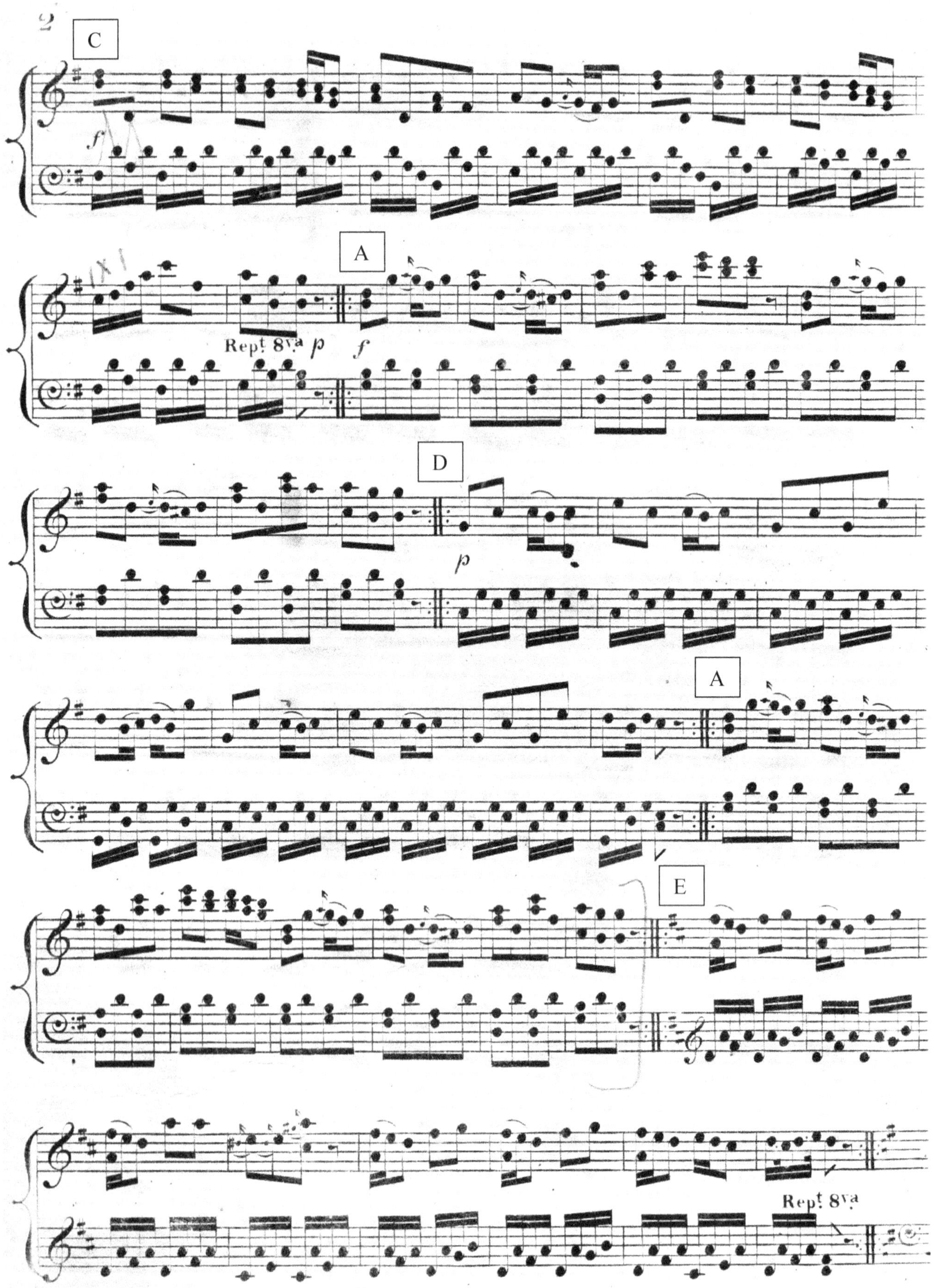
2
C
f
A
Rep.t 8va p
f
D
p
A
E
Rep.t 8va

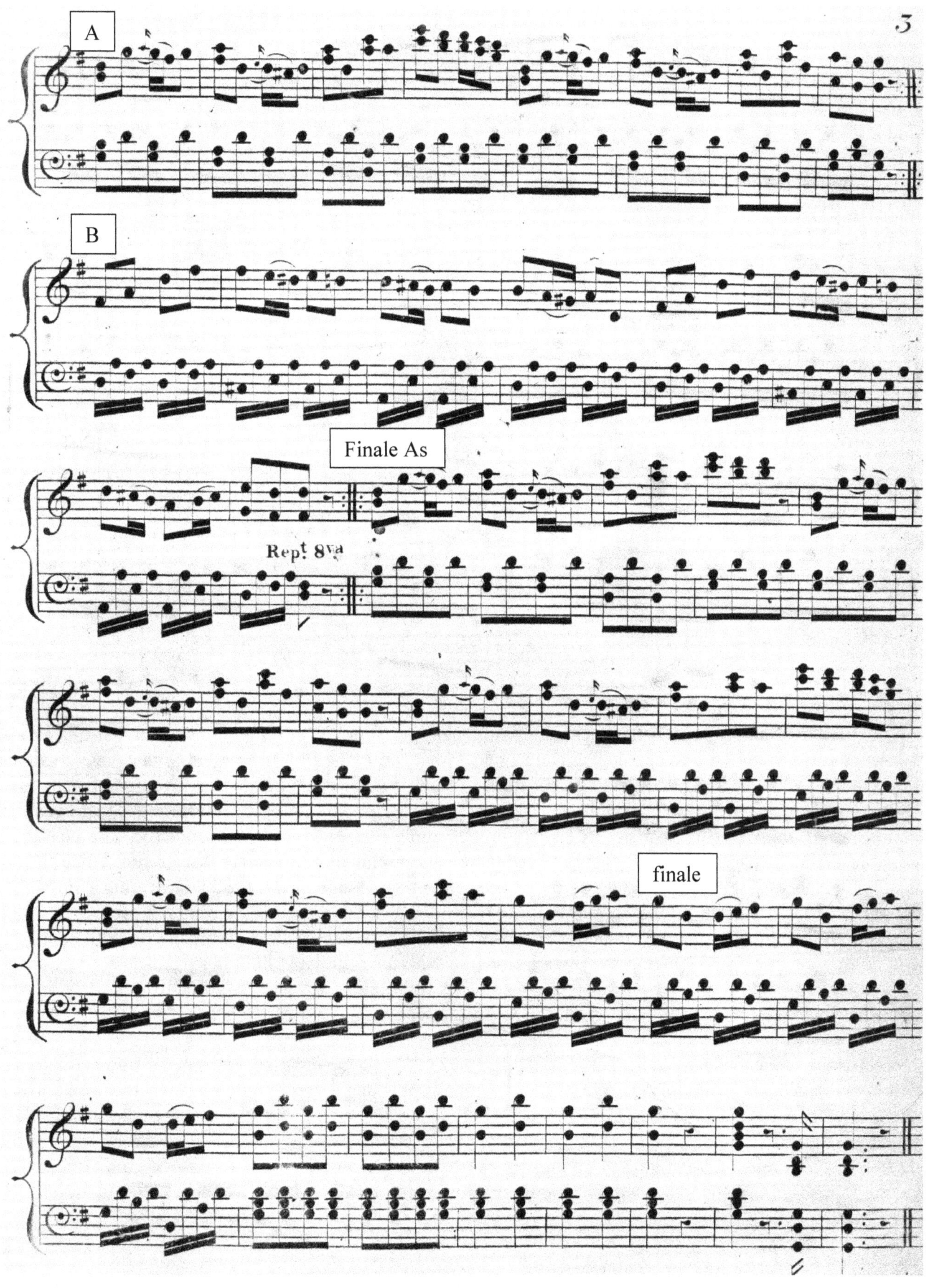
3
A
B
Finale As
Rep.t 8va
finale

~ The Recurring Dilemma ~

(an improper contradance)

Form longways duple minor improper set

Start either foot (but preference right)

A1 F&b. to opp..; r.sh. dsd same	**A2** F&b. to ptner; l.sh. dsd same
B1 r.sh. gyp. opp; ½ cw 2h t. / ½ *chassé croisé* ptner ; f&b. to opp.; ½ r&l	
B2 l.sh. gyp. ptner; ½ acw t. / ½ *chassé* opp. / f&b to ptner; ½ ptner, t.s. l. (Mx1 Wx1½)	

Dance as duple minor improper sequence as many times as will.

Play Bourrée no.2 from Bach's suite for solo cello no.4 movement 5 AABB x n

The tune for Bourrée no.2 in Bach's suite for solo cello no.4 movement 5 is so beautiful that it is almost impossible to not wish to hear it again and again. However, in the fifth movement of that suite, to which I have set my dance **The Conundrum (a cotillion to Bach's cello suite 4 bourrées)** we hear this tune but once. Here I offer a variation of the choreography set to Bourrée no.2 in **The Conundrum**, that tweaks it into being a longways for as many as will improper duple-minor contradance sequence. The change is possible musically as Bourrée no.2 does not need to transition immediately back to Bourrée no.1. The change is possible dance-wise, as all you need to do is replace the final ½ right and left of **The Conundrum** with 4 counts to ½ right hand turn your partner (ending man facing in the direction he wants to progress woman opposite to that direction) and 4 counts to turn oneself single (man once about, woman once and a half). If you do this the man arrives facing in original direction with his right hand held out palm-up slightly ahead of woman, who then drops her left hand into the man's right ready for the forward and back towards new opposites at the beginning of the reprise of the A1 of the sequence.

As this dance sequence features just one of the dilemmas that make up the giant cluster of different dilemmas that is my dance **The Conundrum**, but as the dilemma in this dance (seemingly over whether you want to dance with the opposite or your partner) recurs not only in the course of the sequence, but recurs afresh every time the sequence is repeated with a new opposite, 'The Recurring Dilemma' seemed a fitting title for the dance. If you want more rhyme/symphony in these titles you might want to call the big dance 'The Conundrum Cotillon' and this small on 'The Recurring Dilemma contredance'.

~ The Rewind Waltz ~

Form a Sicilian circle of couples facing couples, 1s starting facing acw, 2s cw.

Start either foot.

Dance as many times as will

Play any 32-bar waltz set, intro. then AABB x n.

A1	Mirror 2h t. opp. (1s start between) / holding inside hs with ptner waves with opp. (1s start under)
A2	M ½ poussette ptner acw to open out facing orig. direction / With new opp. circle ¾ and pull r.sh. past ptner into wave around double circle
B1	Push back out of wave & circle same ¾ r. / pouss. back on prev. track
B2	waves w. orig. opp. (2s start under) / mirror 2h turn orig. opp. 1½ (2s start between) ready to flow on to new opp.
All x n.	

A1	With 4 travelling waltz steps <u>mirror 2 hand turn opposite</u> (starting 1s between - 1M and 2W acw, 1W and 2M cw) Releasing hands with opposite and taking inside hands with partner, do with 4 travelling waltz steps <u>arching waves on same route </u>with same opposites – starting 1s going between as 2s arch over, then 1s retire arching as 2s retire under to finish all back in place.
A2	Turning in to take <u>2 hands with partner and </u>with men pushing then pulling their partners, <u>poussette</u> with 4 travelling waltz steps <u>acw ½ way around this couple</u> so as to finish one place progressed and to open out facing original direction. <u>Taking hands with new opposite couple circle</u> with 3 travelling waltz steps cw <u>3/4</u> around to face in or out of set <u>then</u> release hands from circle, pull past opposite by r.sh., to momentarily take hands in a wave (r.h. with original opposite gender opposite, l.h. with same gender dancer) and <u>balance</u> forward with 1 waltz step.
B1	With 1 waltz step <u>push back from wave</u> into former circle, <u>and</u> with 3 travelling waltz steps <u>circle 3/4 back to the right</u>, then with 2 waltz steps circle back to the right (acw). With 4 travelling waltz steps <u>poussette back on previous</u> zig zag <u>track</u> (start M push again) around original opposites to finish back in original place above.
B2	<u>With original opposites</u> and with next 4 waltz steps, <u>do arching waves in exchanged roles</u>, so 2 go between/under and arch back, *while* 1 arch over and retire under. Releasing partner's hand, with 4 waltz steps <u>mirror 2h turn same opposites on same route</u> (1M and 2W cw, 1W and 2M acw)—the opposite direction to in A1 and this time once and a half around to progress.

The above dance is the result of playing with different ideas over a long period. In earlier, now discarded versions of the dance (under working titles 'Trompe d'Oeil' and 'Poussetting Palindrome') I tried to create a palindrome in which there was never a moment you are not holding at least one of your partners hands, but that deprived you of the opportunity to fully engage opposites and neighbours so led me on to the more socially satisfying form the dance takes above. In this final version you are usually, but not always, holding one hand with your partner.

Along the way to this final form, I tried to shape the ideas into satisfying a challenge from US Dance historian Alison Thompson to write a dance which satisfied the fabulously profound mixed-metaphor: 'The Sieve of Time will Winnow the Wheat from the Chaff and Press the Vintage of Emperors from the Vintage of

Peasants', but although this challenge took me away from earlier forms of the dance, I was seeming to be led more in the direction of an hour glass than sieve – and indeed, I might subtitle this dance 'The Hour Glass Waltz'.

In A1 you have the flowing of grains through a narrow aperture. In the first part of A2 you have the zigzag tracks the larger final grains might make as they rattle on their way and in the second part of A2 you have the circle action of picking the timepiece up to tip it over. B1 opens with the timepiece being activated in reverse direction and for the rest of B2 the grains run back on themselves.

An image for the modern day, and one reflected in the alternate title, is of film of people waltzing which reaches a certain point and is then rewound.

This dance attempts to rise to all the main challenges posed by a palindrome (and there are conceivably several different sorts when it comes to dances). In a dance palindrome you have to make sure all the transitions work well (as the same limited figures need to come into and out of different figures in the first and second half of the dance), to make sure you are consistent in your palindromic imagery (so that if you decide to reverse not just figure order, but also direction with respect partner and direction with respect the set, then you do so throughout), to make sure the dance still works as a social dance (a mixture of partner and neighbour interactions, couple and group interactions etc) and to make sure it has a nice half-way moment of 'reverse' and to make sure its end flows neatly into a new beginning without repeating itself exactly. This dance would score well. It is a 'rewind' sort of palindrome where at the end of A2, if you were to press rewind on the video, you would get the tracks traced in B1&B2—without dancers needing to feel in the second part that they are going backwards (as all the figures are legitimate forward figures), and the fudge that is necessary to give the dance a development and the dancing couple new opposites is very discrete – you just do your final 2 hand turn a little quicker to go around a bit more than once so that 1s can 'funnel through' and meet a new couple.

Although it's possible that the same figures can be set to a non-waltz tune, among a waltz's advantage is that at the A2 end all balancing forward into a interlinked giant single wave around the room and the B1 starts all balancing back out of that wave, so the moment of reversal sits (with a foot in the air) midway through a figure that we normally think of as a single figure, namely, balance forward and back.

Although it is easy now and again to forget the appropriate up-coming figure, as you are nearly always holding at least one of your partner's hands, so long as you don't both have a mental block at the same time, all should be well. Indeed, it may prove a relatively easy dance for an experienced dancer to lead an inexperienced dancer through.

~ Rough Seas ~

Form duple minor proper longways set.

Start right foot free.

Dance as duple minor progressive sequence.

Play any 32-bar hornpipe set, intro. then AABB x

A1	1M2W set; ½ r.h. t. / 1W&2M ½ l.h. t.; set
A2	1&2W set; ½ l.h. t. / 1st cnr axis ½ r.h. t.; set
B1	Circle l. / 1s assisted mirror cast into line across
B2	starting r.sh. to neigh. 3/4 hey for 4 then w. l.h. 1s 1½ down, 2s ½ up.
All x n.	

perhaps 'The Sailor's Hornpipe' (also known as 'College Hornpipe') in the key of D

together with 'Soldier's Joy' in D:

A1	<u>1M and 2W</u> (1st corners) <u>set (possibly with a back-skipping) and ½ right hand turn</u> into each other's place, <u>1M and 2M ½ left hand turn</u> (into each other's place) <u>and set (possibly with back-skipping)</u>
A2	1W and 2W (at top of set) set and ½ left hand turn 1W and 2W (on 1st corner axis) <u>½ right hand turn</u> into each other's place <u>then set</u> to each other
B1	<u>Circle left</u> then using 2s (who let go of their partner) as a pivot 1s lead up through their neighbours, release their own partner's hand and enjoy a wide <u>mirror assisted cast</u> ¼ of the way around <u>till</u> neighbours too can release hands and all four dancers are <u>in a line</u>, 2s facing out back-to-back with partner in middle, 1s on opposite ends facing in.
B2	Starting right shoulder to neighbour do a nearly complete <u>hey for 4</u>, but <u>when 1s face each other in the middle a second time</u> (from improper side *while* on way back to own side) <u>they left hand turn</u>

— John Gardiner-Garden, *Dance Delights*, 2020 —

	each other 1½ *while* <u>moving down</u> the set, <u>and when the 2s</u> shortly after this <u>face each in the middle for the second time</u> (having completed their penultimate end loop by imagining giving right hand to a phantom opposite), <u>they left hand turn each other ½ way</u> to proper side, with 1M swinging in towards new 2W ready to start sequence again.

AABBxn Repeat for each couple to have turn leading from the top, and possibly all the way back to place.

Although this dance can be set to any sort of music and danced with any sort of steps, I wrote it imagining that it would be set to hornpipes, that the pulling past on different angles in A1 and A2 was like sailors pulling on rigging ropes and would be done with folkie 1-2-3-hop 'schottische' steps, that the setting in the corners would be done with maritime-like back-skipping, that the B1 circle into casts would be like the billowing out of sails, and that the B2 weaving and swinging up or down would be as if the result of the deck sloping this way and that in rough seas.

At the same time as playing with these images, I was keen to explore ways dancers could avoid the bumping into each other that is so common when everyone swings in the same line, as is often the case in dances in the bushdance and ceilidh dance traditions. Such collisions are usually avoided in modern contra compositions, by having couples swing on the side of the set. It occurred to me that another way to avoid collisions was to have couples swing out of phase with each other, so even if they are at some point swinging in the same spot as each other couple it is not a spot the other couple are presently swinging in. So it is, in this dance I contrived to have dancers enjoy a satisfying swinging left-hand turn with their partner that starts in the same spot in the middle of the set, having the 1s do their out-of-phase with the 2s. The 1s start their turn earlier than the 2s, and do a 1½ left hand turn moving down *while* the 2s come into the centre place slightly later and do a ½ left hand turn moving up. The 2s need to resist the temptation to give each other right hand, having missed out on giving right hand to their opposite on the way back, for it is better for their trajectory at the beginning of the next sequence if they end this sequence on their partner's left hand.

~ The Russian Gypsy Queen ~

Form couples facing along l.o.d. holding inside hand

Start opposite feet, M left W right.

Dance as many times as will.

Play any slow waltz, redowa or mazurka.

A1	Prom. w. 1 glide-cut-leap, 3 kicks; 3 walking steps, and change side with 2 stamps / counterpart
A2	T. ½ cw w. 1 redowa, then prom. w. 3 kicks; 3 walking steps and face w. 2 stamps / counterpart.
B1	T. cw x 2 w. 4 glide-hop-hops / polka mazurka; wheel cw w.2 hobbles
B2	Counterpart, starting turning in along l.o.d.
All x n	

A1	Promenade with <u>1 redowa</u> (glide-cut-leap), <u>3 kicks, 3 walking steps then 2 steps to change sides /</u> same on other foot on other side and change back into ballroom hold
A2	In ballroom hold <u>1 redowa to turn cw ½ about and open out a little looking over shoulder along l.o.d., 3 kicks</u> continuing along l.o.d. over shoulder, <u>3 walking steps then 2 stamps to face / counterpart</u>
B1	With <u>4 glide-hop-hops turn partner</u> cw twice around / hobble along l.o.d. w. <u>glide-cut-hop, turn ½ cw with a glide-cut-leap</u> redowa; <u>wheel as a couple</u> cw <u>with 2 hobbles</u>. Finish releasing the waist-shoulder side of the ballroom hold to open out improper, i.e. M on outside W on side.
B2	<u>Counterpart of B1</u>— M always takes W in natural ballroom hold (so in counterpart dancers will be lead with shoulder rather than hand when turning or hobbling along l.o.d.) and always turn/wheel cw in the last 3 bars. Finish sliding back out into proper open inside hand hold.
AABBxn Repeat as many times as will or put into a medley with other mazurka sequences.	

The title of this dance is not so much a homage to Valentina Ponomareva, the diva with the 4 octave range who bills herself on albums etc as 'The Russian Gypsy Queen', as to several late 19th century mazurka sequences, the essences of which I thought might be more easily remembered for social dance use and thus more widely enjoyed if they could be crafted together into a single 32 bars sequence. Thus, A1 is the same as Gilbert's 1890 'The Russia' (see entry in Volume X)—except I have used the final 2 stamps to change sides rather than about face and dropped Gilbert's against l.o.d. dance counterpart as it doesn't make for a useful free style around the room variant. In A2 I have echoed the opening sequence with a turning sequence using the same footwork, but in A2 (as opposed to in A1) the change of sides happens on the first bar not the last bar. The middle 4 bars of B1 are the same as the pre-counterpart half of the popular 'Gitana (i.e. Gypsy) Waltz' (see entry in *Dancing through the Ages* Volume IX) and the last 4 bars of B1 are the same as the pre-counterpart half of the 'Czarina' (Russian for 'Queen', see entry in *Dancing through the Ages* Volume IX)—i.e. the 3rd bar of B1 serving as both the end of the 'Gitana waltz' sequence and beginning of the Czarina sequence). The counterpart halves of the Gitana and the Czarina are danced when you dance the counterpart of the B1 sequence in B2.

— John Gardiner-Garden, *Dance Delights*, 2020 —

~ Schiarazula's Hey ~

Form a single circle of couples, facing partner.

Start left foot.

Dance as a progressive mixer.

Play intro. then
Giorgio Mainero's 'Schiarazula Marazula' (published in Venice in 1578) AABB x n.

A1	Side on l.diag. w. l-r & *while* looking at ptner over r.sh. 3 claps over own l.sh.; back w. l-r and w. hs on hips turn ¼ cw w. 3 stamps
A2	Counterpart on other side starting other f.
B1	Chain w. 2 steps & 3 stomps for every hand, starting r.h. to partner, left to next.
B2	Continue past 3rd and 4th but end w. 1 instead of 3 stamps
All x n.	

in Am

♩ = 110

or in Cm

♩ = 110

A1	Side on slight left diagonal (i.e. to right shoulder) with 2 steps (l-r) and *while* looking at partner over r.sh. make 3 claps of own hands over own left shoulder fall back with 2 steps (l-r) and with hands on hips turn 1/8 cw with 3 stamps to face and then on upbeat turn further 1/8 cw to face on new slight right diagonal and start raising hands
A2	Side on slight left diagonal (i.e. to left shoulder) with 2 steps (r-l) and *while* looking at partner over r.sh. make 3 claps of own hands over own r.sh.; fall back with 2 steps (r-l) and with hands on hips turn 1/8 acw with 3 stamps to face and then on upbeat turn further 1/8 acw to return to facing on original left diagonal and start raising right hand
B1	Chain in series of ½ hand turns around the circle with 2 steps & 3 stomps for every hand, starting right hand to partner, left to next—being sure not to release one hand till you've taken the next so at end of every 2 bars you are momentarily holding hands on both side.
B2	Continue past 3rd and 4th but as you approach 5th opposite (new partner) make 1 stamp instead of 3 stamps and don't take hands.
AABBxn	Repeat as many times as will.

— John Gardiner-Garden, *Dance Delights*, 2020 —

This great tune was by Giorgio Mainerio (1530s–1589). He was an Italian born musician, composer, ecclesiast and occasional wizard who mostly wrote sacred music but who also wrote a collection of songs and dance tunes entitled , *Il primo libro de balli accomodati per cantar et sonar d'ogni sorte de instromenti di Giorgio Mainerio Parmeggiano Maestro di Capella della S. Chiesa d'Aquilegia,* Venice, 1578. It is in this collection that we find his 'Schiarazula Marazula'. The meaning of the tune's title has defied attempts at explanation, but a simple and catchy tune deserved a simple and catchy dance. I first wrote a one to match round 1990. It appeared in the first dance books I ever book wrote, *A Country Dance Companion*, Canberra 1991, and I, Ian Blake, Peter Coombe and Michael Stenning, members of my first ever band, Peasant Wedding, recorded the tune on an album called *Off the Wall* (Volume 2). Ian did a fabulous job with an arrangement that brought out the tune's hypnotic drone nature. I wasn't so happy with that original dance, but have tweaked it on and off while retaining (hopefully improving) its utility for occasions when a simple social big circle mixer is need that doesn't need to be historical but needs to go to exciting music that is historically Renaissance.

~ Sechs Deutsche *or* Crossed Conversations ~

Form a cross of 8 couples (16 dancers) with 2 couples facing in, one behind the other, from each side (2 facing down from top, 2 facing up from bottom, 2 in from left side of room, 2 in from right side of room, woman always starting on the right of man, and all middle 4 couples ready to start, those facing up or down with vertical axis sequence, those facing in from sides with horizontal axis same sequence off-set by 8 bars.

Start outside foot and ready to go sideways with a 2-bar long slide-together-slide *chassé* and later to travel forward with brisk waltz steps, and turn as a couple using either waltz steps or step-hop-hops.

Play-ing		Vertical axis	Horizontal axis
		Starting cpls facing in middle every cpl. dance this Variant 1 x 3	
1	**A1**	*Chassé ouvert*	
	A2	Mill r.h. / mill l.h.	*Chassé ouvert*
	B1	*Chassé croisé*	Mill r.h. / mill l.h.
	B2	F & b. / f & arch through	*Chassé croisé*
			F & b. / f & pass through
2-4		Variant 1 propagates through set, and as each couple arrives at end they change sides with their partner to reenter with the W on right by doing a free allemande (see notes)	
5		Starting original middle cpls from exchange sides (while others continue with Variant 1) every couple do this Variant 2 x 3.	
	A1	*Chassé ouvert*	
	A2	R&l.	*Chassé ouvert*
	B1	*Chassé croisé*	R&l.
	B2	Full circle l. and arch thru	*Chassé croisé*
			Full circle l. and pull thru
6-8		Variant 1 propagates through set till middles arrive home	
9		When finished doing circle & pull thru (vertic. axis dancers will have finished this at end of 8)B2 but horiz. axis dancers needing to take 9)A1 to do this) they start waltzing around own end cpl	
10		When finished waltz around own end, waltz the hall.	
Option in Playing 10 instead of rest or allemande, all the men from where			

Dance as until all return to place in set, and then couples waltz around neighbours and waltz hall.

Play intro. then Beethoven's *Sechs Deutsche* for piano and violin, WoO 42 (composed c.1796) with all strains repeated and only repeating a tune when it is followed by a trio that ends with D.C. (i.e. 10 lots of 32 bars).

Play-ing		The four couples in the vertical column	Horizontal column— same but 8 bars delayed
		Starting cpls facing in middle every cpl. dance this Variant 1 x 3	
1	**A1**	*Chassé ouvert:* go sideways with step-together-step across 2 bars of ¾ away from partner <u>then</u> in next 2 bars <u>balance sideways towards and away from partner</u> <u>Same back home</u>	
	A2	<u>mill on right hand</u> mill <u>on left hand</u> and as dancers arrive home they should momentarily take partners left hand so that the man can use it to guide his woman across into…	*Chassé ouvert*
	B1	*Chassé croisé* (man behind partner, lady in front of her man) <u>with 2 slow sideways step-togethers then</u> in exchanged places <u>balance toward and away from partner.</u>	Mill r.h. / l.h.

— John Gardiner-Garden, *Dance Delights*, 2020 —

		Same back home (man again behind woman), ending as you take the waltz balance back changing from holding partners inside hand to holding two hands with facing opposite.	
	B2	Holding inside hand with partner go forward towards opposite with 2 step-step-step-hop sequences and retire backward with step-hops / then go forward and arch through (with the nominated end making arch)	*Chassé croisé*
			Forward, back and arch
2-4	Variant 1 propagates through set, and as each couple arrives at end they wait out 32 bars, and while they wait they enjoy a free allemande with partner (see notes) and changing sides with them so as to reenter with the woman on right of the man		
5	Starting with the original middle couples from exchange sides (while others continue with Variant 1) every couple do this Variant 2 x 3.		
	A1	*Chassé ouvert* as before	
	A2	Full rights and left, starting right to opposite and ending with left to partner, and as dancers pull back into home place monetarily retain partner's left hand so that the man can use it to guide his woman across into…	*Chassé ouvert*
	B1	*Chassé croisé* as before	R&l.
	B2	Full circle left with opposite couple and arch through (with the nominated end again making arch)	*Chassé croisé*
			Circle and arch
6-8	Variant 2 propagates through set till middles arrive home		
9	When finished doing circle & pull thru (vertical axis dancers will have finished this at end of 8B2 but horizontal dancers needing to take 9A1 to do this) they start waltzing around own end couple		
10	When finished waltz around own end, all waltz the hall with partner.		

The *Deutsche* ('German'), like the *Écossaise,* was one of the great dance crazes in Europe in the first decades of the 19th century. Just as the *Écossaise*, though usually a longways dance (with similarities to the English Country dances) could occasionally be a couples dance (and in this form was perhaps one of the ancestors of the mid-19th century ballroom Schottische), the *Deutsche*, though usually a free couples dance (one of the ancestors of the early 19th century ballroom waltz), could occasionally be part of a longways set dance (see for example, my entries on **Magri's contradanza XXXVIIII** and **Der Prager-Student** in Volume VIII of my *Dancing through the Ages*, dances which end respectively with a 'Taice' (Italian for 'Teutsche') and a 'Teutsche' (a variant on word 'Deutsche').

The 'Deutsche' tunes which Beethoven composed around 1796 for his *Sechs Deutsche* for piano and violin (WoO 42) may have been intended for free dancing, but just six years later Johann Heinrich Kattfuß included in his *Taschenbuch für Freunde und Freundinnen des Tanzes*, Leipzig, 1802 a longways dance called the 'Conversation' which was effectively a **Contre-Ecossaise** set entirely to 'Deutsche' or 'Waltz' music (see my entries under **Conversation 1&2** in Volume VII of my *Dancing through the Ages*). Kattfuß's 1802 'Conversation' seems to have been more of an idea than a particular choreography as twenty years another dance by the same name and mechanism but slightly different figures was published later by Christian Länger and the idea may also have influenced the development in England of a cross between the English country dance, quadrille and the waltz called **The Spanish Dance** or **Spanish Waltz** (see entries in Volume VII and VIII of my *Dancing through the Ages*). While the two-above Conversation variants, like many Spanish Waltz variants, were set to a 3-part triple time tune played AABBCC, and while many waltzes in that structure were published in Germany in the last years of the 18th and first two decades of the 19th century (including Beethoven's 1819 *Elf Wiener Tänze*), this is not the structure of the Beethoven's *Sechs Deutsche*. If we want to dance to Beethoven c.1796 *Sechs Deutsche* played straight through, repeating a tune only when it is followed by a trio that ends with D.C. (that is as 10 lots of 32 bars) and we want it to be a longways dance using the figures Kattfuß and Länger use in their Conversation dances, we have to completely rearrange Kattfuß and Länger. It is this I have done, using every one of their figures in choreography, but in a choreography that has lots of twists. The first twist is that formation. Instead of just one middle-starting column, I have two columns crossed with each other. The second twist is the mechanism, instead of all the middles starting at the same time, I have those on the vertical column starting first, and those in the horizontal column starting exactly the same sequence 8 bars later. The third twist is transitioning midway from one sequence to a different one (2 of the 8 bar dance phrases remaining the same while 2 change to that are slightly more daring and unforgiving than the ones in the first pattern). The fourth twist is that in the ninth playing I have couples break out of the previous progression pattern and waltz around the couple next to them on their starting segment of the cross. The fifth twist is that in the tenth playing have the couples break further still from the normal mechanism to waltz around periphery of the space occupied by their set.

For my choreography I chose to keep the figures simple and close to ones provided for in the Conversation— to start with the mill and sideway action of Kattfuß's dance and end with the allemande in Länger dance. I chose, to have the mill go on right hand then back on left hand, as a left-hand mill flows very nicely into the man going behind on the *chassé-croisé* that follows. I also chose to have all the sideways action performed as 2 slow bar-long sideways slide-together '*chassé*' (or glissade) followed by a quick balance toward and away from partner. I chose not to include an allemande of one's opposite in the body of the dance as there might not be sufficient room in the centre of the set for two couples to allemande without bumping into each other, but to invite dancers to allemande their partner when they are on the end of their column and needing to change sides. When couples have their 32 bars of free allemande/Deutsche they might want to vary their turning.

In AA they might like to do:
- 2 bars of a 'pretzel-hold' right-arm-back-allemande
- 2 bars with left hand free (as in allemande illustrated on p.34 of Julio Severin Pantezze, *Methodo, ou explicac, am para aprender com perfeiçaó a dançar as contradanças, dado à luz, e offerecido aos dignissimos senhores assignantes da casa da assemblea do bairro alto* [Method or explanation, on how to learn to dance contradances to perfection, bringing to light and offered to the most dignified gentlemen of the assembly rooms of the higher order], Lisbon, 1761 (on right)
- 2 bars join left hands in an arbour overhead
- 2 bars of the AA both twirl about under under the raised left hand
- 8 bars doing the same in a left-arm-pretzel-back allemande hold

In BB they may like to take a ballroom-like hold and do:
- 4 bars of 1-2-3 waltzing cw on the spot
- 4 bars of step-hop-hop waltzing cw on the spot
- 8 bars wheel as a couple acw while the man period-ically lifts partner 'La Volta'-like into the air (as in illustration on right—provenance unknown to me).
- For the finale in playing 9 and 10, I recommend you take partner in any early waltz hold of your choosing, and waltz using either quick 1-2-3s or step-hop-hops, or a mixture of both patterns.

— John Gardiner-Garden, *Dance Delights*, 2020 —

(369) 1

SECHS DEUTSCHE

für Clavier und Violine

Beethoven's Werke.

componirt von

Serie 25. No 308.

L. van BEETHOVEN.

No 1.

Comp. 1795.

No 2.

Stich und Druck von Breitkopf & Härtel in Leipzig.

B. 308.

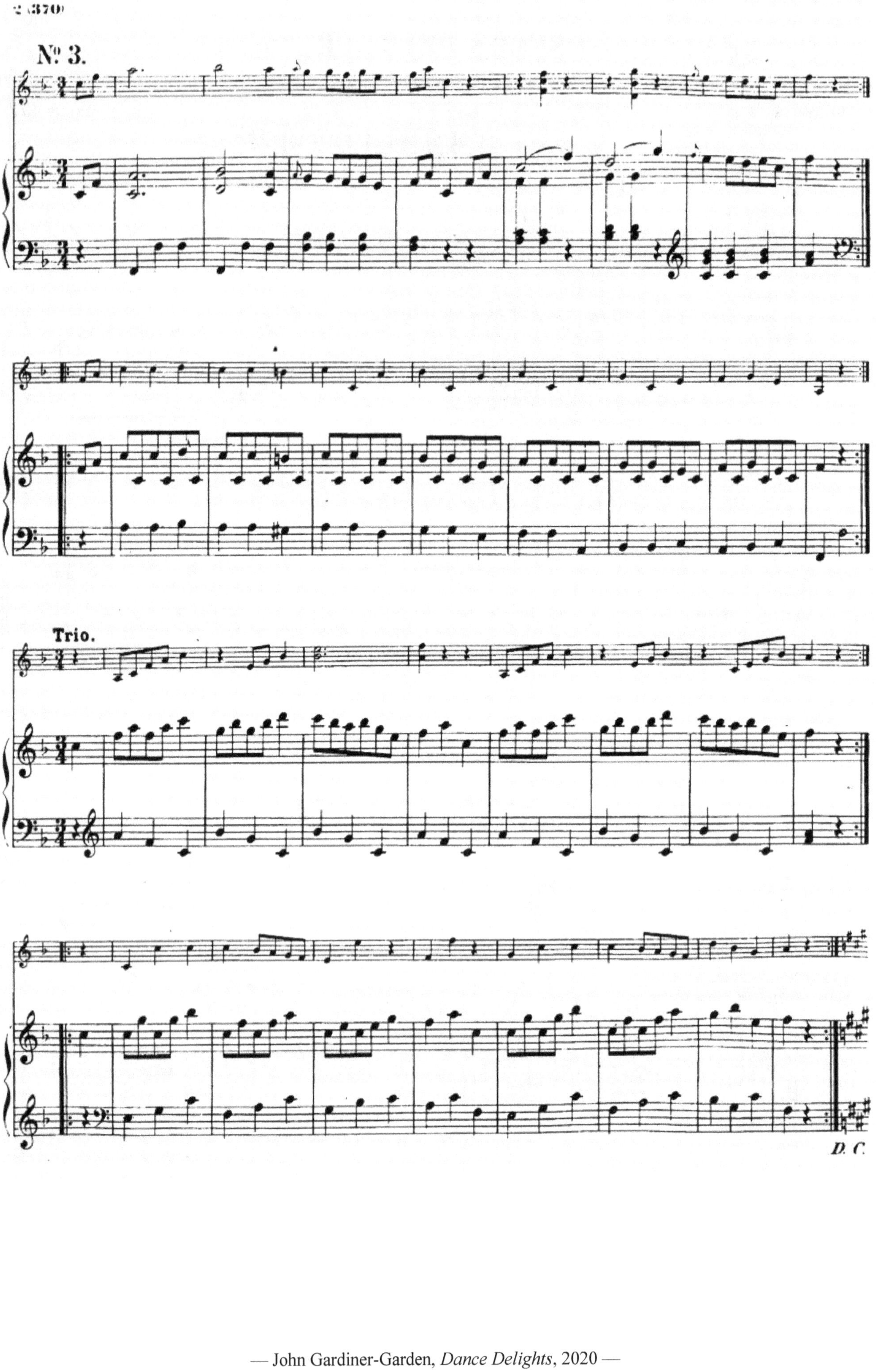
2 (370)
Nº 3.
Trio.
D. C.

Nº 4.

Nº 5.

B. 308.

1872

No 6.

Trio.

D. C.

B. 308.

~ Sechs Ecossaisen or Perpetual motion ~

Form 2 facing couples (W on right of M).

Start left foot and ready to use a 'schottische sequence' throughout: l-r, l-hop; r-l, r-hop / l-hop, r-hop; l-hop, r-hop

Dance the 6 consecutive progressive sequences.

Play intro. then Beethoven's c.1806 *Sechs Ecossaisen* for piano, WoO 83 as published in Leipzig by Breitkopf and Härtel, 1862-90: *Ludwig van Beethovens Werke, Serie 25:*

I) – led by 1s from above
A1 ½ circle l. / full 2 h. cw t. opp. **A2** ½ circle l. / full 2 h. cw t. ptnr
B1 1s prom. down / wheel about as a cpl (*while* 2s go up outside, veer in to take inside hs, and wheel about
B2 1s return into 2ⁿᵈ place and 2s come down to meet them / all push back 2. 4 step-hops
II) – led by original 2s who are now facing down from above
A1 ½ circle r. / acw t. opp. **A2** ½ circle r. / acw t. ptnr **BB** As before.
III) – led by 1s from above
A1 ½ r.h. mill / r.h. t. opp. **A2** ½ r.h. mill / r.h. t. ptnr **BB** As before.
IV) – lead by original 2s who are now facing down from above
A1 ½ l.h. mill / l.h. t. opp. **A2** ½ l.h. mill / l.h. t. ptnr **BB** As before.
V) – led by 1s from above
A1 W chain r.h. over / l.h. t. opp. **A2** W r.h. b. / l.h. t. ptnr **BB** As before.
VI) – led by original 2s who are now facing down from above
A1 M chain l.h. over / r.h. t. opp. **A2** M l.h. b. / r.h. t. ptnr **BB** As before.

Supplement—Instrumental-Musik, Nr.302 (reproduced at end of entry), with each tune play just once.

		~ Écossaise I—1s with 2s below ~
A1		1s and 2s ½ circle left with 2 'schottische' steps (i.e. left-right, left-hop; right-left, right-hop) 2 hand cw turn opposite with 4 step-hops and retake hands in a circle
A2		1s and 2s circle ½ left again and then 2 hand cw turn partner back into place
B1		1s promenade with 2 'schottische' steps down the middle on inside hand and then with 4 step-hops wheel ½ acw about as a couple with 4 step-hops *while* 'inactive' 2s promenade individually up outside, veer in to take inside hands and wheel 1/2 about
B2		1s and 2s promenade towards each other (woman on right of man) with 2 'schottische' steps till pressing raised outside hands, then push back and retire a little with 4 step-hops
		~ Écossaise II—2s with 1s below ~
AA		As for **Ecossaise I** except circle right and 2-hand acw, make sure that once again you 2-hand turn opposite before you 2-hand turn partner.
BB		As before
		~ Écossaise III—1s with 2s below ~
AA BB		As for **Ecossaise I** except instead of circles and 2 hand turns, ½ right hand mill then full right-hand turn opposite, ½ right hand mill then right-hand turn partner
		~ Écossaise IV—2s with 1s below ~
AA		As for **Ecossaise III** except ½ left hand mill and left hand turn each time.
BB		As before
		~ Écossaise V—1s with 2s below ~

— John Gardiner-Garden, *Dance Delights*, 2020 —

AA BB	As above but instead of circling or milling <u>chain the ladies across and back</u> (ladies step-hopping when left hand turning opposite and again when left hand turning partner)
	~ Écossaise VI—2s with 1s below ~
AA BB	As above but <u>men chain across left hand</u>, right-hand turn opposite, chain back left- and right-hand turn partner.

In the above dance I offer a twist on the historical *Écossaise* (also called *Écossoise*). This dance form was a great craze in northern Europe in the first decades of the 19th century. It was similar to the contemporary longways English country dance or *contredanse Anglaise* in that the formation tended to be for as many couples as will, but the sequences tended to be shorter, the mechanism duple rather triple minor, the tempo quicker, the steps involving more 'schottische-like' quick-2-3-hops and step-hops, the figures were more-likely to end with the 1s promenading down and back into 2nd position, and the starting position for the 1s though usually as in your average *Anglaise* was perhaps more likely to be improper. Any suitable figures could be set to any suitable tune, and indeed it is possible that dancers felt free to change the figure part way through the dance and musicians felt free to change the tune as well. The twists I offer are of two kinds.

Firstly, I have the tune and dance figure change every 32 bars. Although it is possible that the figures were most commonly changed only when a new couple took the lead at the top of the set, and that the musicians only changed the tune after several playings of any given tune, there is no reason why a lead couple might not change the figure part way through their leadership turn and that musicians might not change the tune, or part thereof, with every playing. With this in mind, although I cannot be sure how close Breitkopf and Härtel presentation of Beethoven's *Sechs Écossaisen* is to Beethoven's original, I decided to follow the Breitkopf and Härtel presentation in calling for the six dance tunes (with the common BB) to be played one immediately after the other, and decided to match them with six relatively simple but interesting progressive dance sequences (with a common BB) to be danced one immediately after the other.

Secondly, although an historical Ecossaise set was usually for as many couples as will, and although it is possible to do this dance in that form (if, as couples emerge at the top of the set, wait out and rejoin as improper 1s, they are prepared to take their lead from the 2s as to which pattern they are up to), the form in which I first tested this dance during the 2020 pandemic when only allowed a few visitors in my studio, is a set of just 2 couples and this is my preferred form. In that form no-one has to rest out, the ones from above lead the figure with the circle left, mill right and woman's chain, and the 2s from above lead the counterparts, i.e. leading the figure with where the circle right, the mill left or the chain of men. The only challenge is ensuring each iteration starts with the woman on the right. The couple promenading down can arrange this by wheeling ½ about after their promenade down but not wheeling after their promenade up. The couple who is 'waiting' while the actives promenade down can meet their partner, go individually up, veer in to take inside hands and wheel ½ about to face down. The 'inactive couple' can then advance towards the upcoming couple and then both couples fall back with 4 step-hops. So with just 2 couples not only does no one miss out a turn but the 'actives' and 'inactives' are both dancing all the time.

In the above table I have presented the dance as if the tunes are written out in 2/4 as indeed they are in the Breitkopf and Härtel score, and thus in both my table and summary box one 'schottische' step falls across 2 bars and if bars are separated by a ',' ';' or '/' the action for one whole strain is represented l-r, l-hop; r-l, r-hop / l-hop, r-hop; l-hop, r-hop. Personally, however, I prefer to think of the tune as in 4/4 with one 'schottische' step contained within 1 bar, so the first half of each strain consists of 2 bars of l-r-l-hop, r-l-r-hop, and the second half of each strain consists of 2 bars doing l-hop, r-hop; l-hop, r-hop. The dance's relationship with the music is the same, however you choose to think of it.

For more on the nature and evolution of the 'Écossaise', on Écossaise steps according to contemporary testimonies, and on Écossaise choreographies (such as **Contre-Ecossaise, Ecossaise mit 2 Colonnen, Katfuß's Ecossoise no.1, Kreuz-Ecossaisen, Länger's Ecossaise no.1** and **Lauchery's Ecossaise for 1823**, published in Germany, and **The Alexander, The Attempt, The Czar, The Fair Circassian, The Volga**, and

Russian Dance (1), 2) and (3) published in England) see Part 1b, 1c and 2 respectively of my *Dancing through the Ages* Volume VII: 1800-1825.

2 (362)

SECHS ECOSSAISEN
für Clavier
von
L. VAN BEETHOVEN.

Beethoven's Werke.

Serie 25. № 302.

um 1823.

Stich und Druck von Breitkopf & Härtel in Leipzig.

B. 302.

— John Gardiner-Garden, *Dance Delights*, 2020 —

~ The Short Country Bumpkin ~

Form 3 trios of W-M-W facing up for long original long version, facing in for my short version, middle-man wearing a hat.

Dance original figures, or, the short 1 figure version of my devising.

A1	The 'Bumpkin' dances in middle *while* others circle left around him—ending bumpkin facing cnr on up l. diag. *while* other M face own near l. diag.
A2	Bumpkin set to & r.h. t. 1st l. diag. W / set to & l.h. t. W at other end of long diag. *while* end M set to & r.h. t. l. diag. W (middle side) / set to & l.h. t. W in cner
B1	Same three reels on same route, starting r.sh. to 1st W set to
B2	Outside ranks toward centre; all set *while* Midde M surrenders hat (or crown) to facing (top) M (or the latter takes hat from middle M) / middle and top ranks pass by r.sh. *while* other rank falls b.; all set *while* 8 take hs ready for circle.

Repeat with hat passing down and bottom ranks switching, and continue with alternate ranks switching so after 6 times through all return to original place.

Play an AABB tune reel or jig x 6, perhaps x3 first 2 parts of the jig Campbell offers for long version of dance:

then x 3 a reel like 'Highland Laddie' in G:

A1	The man in the middle (the 'Bumpkin') <u>dances on the spot</u> *while* others 2 men and 6 women <u>circle left around him</u>—ending with the bumpkin facing the corner on the upper left diagonal *while* the two other men face their own near l. diag.
A2	The <u>umpkin sets to & right hand turn 1st left-diagonal woman</u> <u>then sets to & left hand turn the woman at other end of long left diagonal</u>	*while* <u>end men set to & right hand turn the left diagonal women</u> (i.e. one on the middle of the side) <u>then set to & left hand turn the woman in corner</u>
B1	<u>The same diagonal three reel on same route, starting right shoulder to 1st woman</u> set to
B2	With 4 counts <u>the outside ranks dance forward toward centre</u> then with 4 counts <u>all set *while* the bumpkin surrenders hat (or crown) to facing (top) man (or the latter takes hat from bumpkin)</u> Then with 4 counts <u>the middle and top ranks pass by right shoulder *while* the other rank falls back</u> and then with 4 counts <u>all set *while* those around</u> the new man in the middle (<u>the new bumpkin) take hands ready for circle.</u>

AABBx5 Repeat with hat passing down and bottom ranks switching, and continue with alternate ranks switching so after 6 times through all return to original place.

— John Gardiner-Garden, *Dance Delights*, 2020 —

For an in-depth study of the four earliest descriptions of a long version of this large matrix dance, see my entry on **Country Bumpkin (1)** in my *Dancing through the Ages,* Volume VI: 1750-1800. There I present the instructions for **The Country Bumpkin** offered in *Campbell's 14th book of new and favorite country dances & strathspey reels*, London [c.1799], for **The Bounky** in the 1805 Blantyre manuscript, **The Bumkin** in the anonymous *Companion to the Reticule,* London, c.1815, and **The original Country Bumpkin,** in R. & J. Lowe, *The ball-conductor,* 2nd edition, Glasgow, 1822 (with same text and diagrams in *Anderson's Ball-room and solo dance guide*, Dundee, c.1897). The dance being described in these manuals would seem to have been very popular in Scotland, and this is indeed stated in the anonymous c.1815 *Companion to the Reticule.* At the end of the *Companion*'s dance description we read: **thus concludes the Bumpkin, as danced al over Scotland prior to the year 1815** and the work's preface ends with the note that: **The figure of the universally admired Bumpkin alone is given at the end of this collection, in the hope that, having been longest in disuse, it may be amongst the first of the National Dances to be revived.** The dance even seems to have been enjoyed in early 19th century Australia—thus Annabella Boswell (her married name) wrote in her childhood diary on the 19 June 1843 that at a party at her uncle's Lake Innes House (outside Newcastle, north of Sydney):

> **There was again a large dinner party, and after-dinner speeches with much cheering, followed by music and dancing, in which Mr Macleay, and my aunt, my uncle, and my mother joined I had never seen mamma dance before, though she often sings while she teaches us some reel steps. Mr Macleay showed us an old country dance called "The Country Bumpkin" which amused us very much. I cannot give a very instructive description of it, but it is danced by six ladies and six gentlemen, the gentleman in the centre of the circle wearing a hat which he puts on one of the others, who then takes his place, and so on. I danced with Mr Salwey, who is most amusing.**

For more background on the above dance account see the 'Australia' section in Part 1a of *Dancing through the Ages* Volume VIII. The popularity of the tune and the dance is indeed attested also in other sources and the innumerable choreographic possibilities offered by this 3-by-3 matrix were evidently being explored by many in the 19th century. We find, for example, the fancy 'Reel of nine' recorded by Willock in c.1860 and David Anderson in the 1890s (see my entry on **Reel of Nine** in my *Dancing through the Ages* Volume X).

I will not here go further into the tradition behind or the history of the original long-version Country Bumpkin matrix dance (see my *Dancing through the Ages* for that), but turn now to the dance I offer in the tabulation above. It is not the dance any of the above sources describe, but my own version. It differs from the historical versions in that it allows multiple sets to dance in their own place, has the 'Country Bumpkin' hat switching feature come around with every playing of the tune, and make sure ever reel starts right shoulder and is preceded with turning the first corner right by the right and the second by the left.

Before leaving this dance I might note that some of the ways in which dancers would have fun with the longer historical versions of this dance can be used in my version. The dancer in the middle was referred to in the Blantyre and *Companion* as the **King**, said by a contemporary commentator to wear an Opera hat, and required in the Lowe manual to wear a **cocked hat.** This was clearly a 'bumpkin' acting above his station. The Campbell text says that at the end of the sequence **the gentleman of the top line then takes the hat off the gentleman of the middle line** and the *Companion* also says a new dancer becomes king by **taking the hat.** The storyline would seem to be that the one in the middle is a bumpkin putting on graces, wearing a posh hat and pretending to be important, and he doesn't voluntarily relinquish his aristocratic emblem but has it snatched off his head. This storyline seems also consistent with Lowe's account, for although the Lowes have the bumpkin pass the hat voluntarily to the facing man, it is like an abdication: **the first bumpkin crowns the succeeding one with the hat.** I would suggest you play up this storyline in my dance.

To distinguish my short version of the 'hat' dance from the longer historical versions, after trying out many long clumsy names for my dance, I settled on a nice short name suggested by dance friend Katherine Tammaro: The Short Country Bumpkin.

For two very different dances that went under the name 'Country Bumpkin' see my entries under **Country Bumpkin (2)** and **(3)** in *Dancing through the Ages,* Volume VII: 1800-1825.

~ The Social Obligations Minuet ~

(a longways canon)

Form longways set for as many pairs of couples as will.

Dance as progressive criss-crossing duple minor sequence, all starting simultaneously.

> 1st cnrs (1M2W—followed by 2nd cnrs 2 bars later) do:
> **A1** set w. 1 min. step r, l; 1/2 r.sh. gypsy / **A2** t.s. l.; 1/2 r.h. t.
> **B1** complete r.h. t.; t.s. l. / start l.h. turn; complete l.h. turn
> **B2** t.s. r.; start 2 h. t. / complete 2h t.; bow to that cnr, bow to new
> *All x n.*

Play any 24 bar not-too slow minuet, e.g. 'Mr Priest's Minuet' in E. Pemberton's *An essay for the further improvement of dancing,* London, 1711.

Intro.		*while...*
A1	1M2W set with 1 minuet step to <u>right</u> and 1 to <u>left</u>	1W2M <u>do nothing;</u>
	1M2W <u>1/2 right-shoulder gypsy</u>	1W2M <u>set</u>
A2	1M2W <u>turns single left</u>	1W2M <u>right-shoulder gypsy;</u>
	1M2W <u>1/2 right-hand turn</u>	2nd corners <u>turns single left</u>
Long B1	1st corners <u>complete right-hand turn</u>	2nd corners <u>start right-hand turn</u> (in 1/2 mill)
	1st corners <u>turns single left</u>	2nd corners <u>complete right-hand turn</u>
	1st corners <u>start left-hand turn</u>	2nd corners <u>turns single left</u>
	1st <u>complete left-hand turn</u>	2nd corners join, <u>start 1/2 right-hand mill</u>
Long B2	1st corners <u>turn single right</u>	2nd corners <u>complete left-hand turn;</u>
	1st corners <u>start 2-hand turn</u>	2nd corners <u>turns single left</u>
	1st corners <u>complete 2-hand turn</u>	2nd corners <u>start 2-hand turn</u> threading their open arms thru those of the others, <u>right over left under;</u>
	1st corners 6 counts to <u>bow to each other</u> then take 6 counts to turn 90 degrees and <u>bow to new corner</u> on new diagonal, the man now starting from the W's side the W from the M's side	*While* <u>2nd corners complete 2-hand turn</u> into progressed improper place
2A1	1M recommence sequence with new 2W on new diagonal	*While* 1W and 2M who had danced previous sequence together <u>bow to each other</u> then <u>bow to new corner.</u>

— John Gardiner-Garden, *Dance Delights*, 2020 —

2A2-2BB	Dance the sequence through a second time till dancers have progressed again and arrive back on original home side
xn	Continue, each time through the sequence alternating starting side as well as progressing one place up or down the set

In this choreography I have created a variant of the *menuet à deux* that can be enjoyed canon-wise on the diagonal in a proper longways set. I recommend a playing tempo that is a little faster than most modern players' instinct but it is still at the slow end of the range for a period minuet dance. The dance offers a challenge not just in the way the diagonal roles need to dovetail, but also in the way dancers start successive sequences from alternate sides of the set. This was not unknown in traditional choreography- see my entries on **Bobbing Jo (1)** and **A Mayden Fayre / Once I loved a Maiden Fair** in Volume III of *Dancing through the Ages.* It is, nevertheless often tricky to sustain and tricky to manage changes of roles at the end of the column. To make the latter easier I recommend always starting with an even number of couples in the set and all starting simultaneously, i.e. with the whole column starting as a series of active improper duple minor sets. That way, dancers will not need to change sides when they arrive at each end of the set. They need simply rest out one turn and re-enter the set from the same side as that on which they exited and rested.

I chose Mr Priest's Minuet as it is a great tune of the right length and structure which can bear being played at the lively tempo most suited for the dance and which we don't often have occasion to play/hear as the namesake dance to which it is set in its 1710 source, **Mr Priest's Minuet** (presented in my Dancing through the Ages Volume V) needs 12 well-rehearsed dancers. Here the tune can be enjoyed after just a quick teaching of the dance.

There is no need to add 2 bars to the end of the tune the last time through the tune as the last figure of the sequence is just a bowing off with former corner and bowing on to new corner, so the music can end at the end of a B2 and the 2nd corners can just forfeit doing the corner bows which the 1st corners will have done, and all, with the final dotted minim, can just face their partner for a bow.

This is the kind of dance for which you might invite someone who you think you should really at some stage be asking for a dance but with whom you don't necessarily want to dance, because in between the opening and closing bow to partner there need be no eye contact at all with your partner. The dance sequence itself provides for no interaction at all with partner. The closest you get to your partner is a brief crossing over or under of hands as a result of you both hold the hand of a corner, but at that time the focus is on your corner not the partner who is only incidentally crossing your path. After pointing this out to the dance group that was kindly test-running the dance for me, and calling for suggested dance titles, dance friend Ceri Teather suggested 'The Social Obligations Minuet', and I've been pleased to go with that as the name does straightaway give away the secret that you won't be dancing with your partner. Unfortunately it also doesn't alert the listener/reader to the essential nature of the dance figures as a standard couples minuet ones canonised within a longways set. If you think it needs a subtitle to hint more at the nature of the dance you might add—**a longways canon**. You can't really call it 'The minuet canon' as that raises the expectation that the tune might be a canon, which it isn't, or able to be made into a canon, which it can't easily (unless you are Bach).

~ The Spanish Brawl ~

Form a circle of couples

Start left foot free.

Dance sequence as many times as will, alternating between circle variant and couple's variant with progression, and ending with circle variant.

Play the late 16ᵗʰ century tune 'Gagliarda di Spagna' with repeats intro. then tune x n.

possibly alternating between the tune in Cm

Alternate between this **Circle variant**
1A1 Holding hs in circle double l.; r / **1A2** Repeat, ending releasing hs.
1B1 w. hs on own hips all facing in set l&r; full t.s. 1D l. / **1B2** cntrpart r.
1C1 All holding hs 3 steps in as hs rise up & stomp r.f.; set r, l.
1C2 Retire w. 3 steps and stomp l.f., set l., r. *while* facing ptner.

and this **Couples' variant**
2A1 Not holding hs M sideways in W out w. D l. & clap; D r. & clap returning to line.
2A2 Repeat.
2BB As in circle but facing partner (set l,r; ts D.l./ cntrpt).
2CC As in circle (f: set r,l/cntrprt) but facing partner and while taking final set l.& r. ½ cw 2h t. and open out in progressed position in inward-facing circle.

After alternating a few times back and forth return to the circle variant to finish, bowing upon facing partner at end of 1C2

And the tune in Gm

and then after a few alternations return to the tune in Cm to end.

	~ Circle variant ~
1A	All circle left with a double left and right with a double right,
1A2	Repeat
1B1	With hands on own hips all set left and right with 2 *fleurets* (quickly stepping left-right-left, right-left-right *while* kicking feet out and shading left and right as you do so), then do a full turn single left with and ornamented double (left-right-leftright-left&).
1B2	Counterpart starting to the right with right foot.

— John Gardiner-Garden, *Dance Delights*, 2020 —

1C1	All 3 steps in (left-right-left) while raising joined wide-spread hands to chest level and on 4th count stomp and free right foot (a stamp bouncing foot back up) then with next 4 counts set right & left kicking and shading as before.
1C2	Retire with right-left-right-stamp left, then set left & right *while* facing partner and releasing hand, man facing acw around l.od. woman cw.
	~ Couple's variant ~
2A1	Double left (men going sideways into circle *while* women go sideways out) with a clap on 4th count in front of left shoulder then a double right (back into line, men facing along l.o.d. women against) with a clap on 4th count in front of right shoulder.
2A2	Repeat.
2B1	With hands on own hips facing ptner set with 2 *fleuret* shading left and right, then full turn single left with ornamented double left as in circle variant
2B2	Counterpart starting right foot.
2C1	Holding partner's hands take 3 steps directly towards partner as wide-spread joined hands rise up to chest level and, with chests almost touching stamp right then set right and left
2C2	Fall back with right-left-right-stamp/hop &lift left, then *while* setting left & right ½ cw 2-hand turn each other and open out in progressed position in inward-facing circle.
Etc	and continue with an alternation of circle variant and couple's variant, ending with circle variant.
AABBCC x n.	

I wrote this simple dance to with a tune that appears in several c.1600 Italian dance manuals as *Gagliarda di Spagna* (see my entries on **Gagliarda di Spagna (1)** and **Gagliarda di Spagna (2) & (3)** in Volume II and III respectively in my *Dancing through the Ages*, 2020. Although for the 1581 Caroso, 1602 Negri and 1614 Santucci choreographies there presented the tune needs to be played relatively slowly and without any of the strain repeats shown her, the tune lends itself to being played quickly and with strain repeats as shown, so to give me an excuse for playing it as such on my hurdy-gurdy I wrote this dance. As the tune ends up having a structure and feel very similar to **Branle de Montirande** (though they are slightly different lengths), for which I wrote a circle dance presented in this book, and to open the possibility of playing this tune in medley with *Branle de Montirande*, I decided to write this dance also as one that can be done by as many couples as will in a circle. The pattern I have devised here is a little simpler than that for *Branle de Montirande*, but interest can be added by alternating between doing the step pattern in a communal circle and doing it facing a partner and progressing on to new position in the circle and new partner.

You will note that this *Gagliarda di Spagna* tune is not in 3/4 or 6/4, the rhythm you would normally expect for a galliard. As I explain in my historical work (cited above), this is because the tune probably really was a 'Galliard from Spain' and there was at the time a form of the Spanish galliard known to be in double time. I have called my dance 'Spanish Brawl' because the tune is said to be *di Spagna* (from Spain) but the dance I've set to it is in a French 'branle' style and the period English term for a branle was 'brawl'.

~ Stars of Joy ~

Form a single circle of 12 couples, partners facing each other holding right hand in right (can also be done as Sicilian circle of 24 couples)

Start left foot.

Dance the progressive sequences as many times as will, or as the anthem is played, or x 6 to return to original opposite in original place.

If doing as a single circle for 12 couples:

2 bar intro. Step l.- bow, step r.- bow

A1 Full r.h. t. w. l.h. in air (slow l; slow r , med., med; quick2-3)

A2 Full l.h. t. the one behind w. counterpart

B1 w. 15 steps, starting r.h. to next, chain 4 hs / w. next (5th in chain) slow r. step into r.allemande hold and 3 quick steps ½ cw; counterpart b.

B2 Counterpart starting l.h. to same and allemanding 5th in chain 1&r.

AABBx2 Repeat sequence till w. original ptner in home place.

If doing as a Sicilian circle with 24 couples: footwork as above but instead of A part h. turns make mills for 4, instead of 4 changes of grand chain, do 4 ½ mills, and instead of back-allem. hold take wrist or forearm star hold put free hand on or just behind own outside hip.

Option to **repeat all** (intro, AABBx3).

Play 2 bar intro. then essential Ode to Joy from Beethoven's Symphony no.9 AABBx3 to return to partner in place then repeat introduction and AABBx3to dance all again then hold last note for concluding bows.

then AABB another 2 times

	Figures for couples in a single circle	Figures for Sicilian circle (i.e. couples facing each other in a double circle).
Intr. 2 bar	M bow for 4 counts; W bow for 4 counts.	
A1	Full right-hand turn opposite with slow step left, slow step right, medium left, right, and quick leftright-left while reaching out to take left hand with person who was behind.	With left hand in the air and with slow step left, slow step right, medium left, right, and quick leftright-left right hand mill
A2	Counterpart: left-hand turn the couple behind with counterpart, staring right foot and ending right hand to original opposite.	Counterpart: with right hand in the air and starting right foot left hand mill the couple behind.
B1	With 15 quick walking steps chain 4 hands (starting with one partner and taking 4 steps for each of the first hands 3 for the last), starting right hand past the one just turned	Starting right hands across with original opposites take 4 walking steps to mill ½ cw with them, then 4 walking steps to mill ½ acw with the next on-coming couple.

— John Gardiner-Garden, *Dance Delights*, 2020 —

	and ending right foot free as you approach right shoulder to 5th opposite in chain Take a slow right step in towards this new opposite as right elbows are linked and with your left hand take their right hand behind your back to make a back allemande hold, and with 3 quick steps turn ½ cw as a couple, then with slow step right turn about and slide out of that hold into left forearm hold, and with 3 quick steps turn ½ acw, ending sliding into holding left hands ready for:	With a slow right step in towards new opposites to take right forearms across, and with left hand on own hip or behind own back and with 3 quick steps turn ½ cw, then with slow step right slide out of that hold and take left forearms and with right hand on own hip or behind own back and with 3 quick steps turn ½ acw, sliding out towards end to hold left hand in left ready for:
B2	Counterpart of B1: With 15 quick walking steps chain 4 hands, starting left hand past the one just turned in left allemande hold and ending left foot free as you approach with left shoulder a new opposite (no. 8, 4 places short of home), then take a slow left step into a left back allemande hold with this new opposite and with 3 quick steps turn ½ acw, then with slow step left turn about into right back allemande hold, and with 3 quick steps turn ½ cw, ending sliding into holding right hands ready to recommence:	Counterpart of B1: starting left hands across with the same group take 4 walking steps to mill ½ acw with them, then 4 walking steps to mill ½ cw with the next on-coming couple. With a slow left step in towards new opposites take left forearms across, and with right hand on or behind hip and with 3 quick steps turn ½ acw, then with slow step left slide out of that hold and take right forearms and with left hand on or behind hip and 3 quick steps turn ½ cw, sliding out towards end to hold right hand in right, left hand coming up into the air and left foot free ready to start the whole sequence again.

AABBx2 to go twice around the circle.to arrive with partner in original place having	

2 b.	Facing the one or ones last turned but

Introduction (AABBx3) to go around another 2 times and meet partner again in home place.

The above dances have been crafted to fit the theme from the fourth and final movement of Ludwig van Beethoven's Ninth Symphony, completed in 1824. Beethoven wrote the music to accommodate, with a few additions, Frederich Schiller's 1785 poem 'An die Freude' ('To Joy') which the poet had intended at the time to be a celebration of the brotherhood of man. The poem became very popular and was translated from German into several other languages. In 1972 the Council of Europe officially adopted the prelude to the 'Ode to Joy' from Beethoven's 9th, as the European anthem. Conductor Herbert von Karajan was asked to write instrumental arrangements for solo piano, wind instruments and symphony orchestra and increased the tempo from Beethoven's crotchet =120 to minim = 80. In 1985 it was adopted as the official anthem of the then European Community, and in 1993 as that of the European Union.

There has never been an official lyric to accompany the anthem, though Shiller's poem is often sung to it by German speakers, and other lyrics have been created in other European languages). Given the multiplicity of modern European languages and a widely shared Roman-Latin heritage, in 2004 Austrian Professor Peter Roland of the Europa Academy in Vienna proposed the following Latin lyric be officially adopted. It has not yet been adopted but it strikes me to be full of merit and relevant too to hope-filled humanity beyond Europe.

Est Europa nunc unita	Europe is united now
Et unita maneat	United it may remain
Una in diversitate	Our unity in diversity
Pacem mundi augeat.	May contribute to world peace.
Semper regnant in Europa	May there forever reign in Europe

— John Gardiner-Garden, *Dance Delights*, 2020 —

Fides et iustitia	Faith and justice
Et libertas populorum	And freedom for its people
In majore patria.	In a bigger fatherland.
Cives, floreat Europa	Citizens, Europe shall flourish
Opus magnum vocat vos	A great task calls on you
Stellae signa sunt in caelo	Golden stars in the sky are
Aureae, quae iungant nos.	The symbols that shall unite us.

What do we call this dance? Do we go for something obvious but a little matter-of-fact like 'European (Union) Anthem dance', or 'European (Union) flag dance', or the 'Ode for Joy dance' or do we go for some lines from the above poem? If so do we use the Latin **Europa unit**, or **Una in diversitate**, or **Stellae signa sunt in caelo** and sound grand but mysterious or do we use the English translations 'Unity in diversity' or 'Golden stars in the sky' and risk sounding overly sentimental? Do we go for something poetic such as 'Celestial dance' and allude simultaneously to the flag of the European Union, to the dance's making of stars in an ever changing circle, and to that 2,000-year-long metaphor that threads through European literature, from Plato in the 5th century B.C., through Lucian and Plotinus in the 2nd century A.D. Victorinus in the 4th century A.D. and Dante in the 14th century, to Dorat and Davies in the late 16th century and to Milton in the 17th century? Do we go for something prosaic but descriptive such as 'Twelve stars in a circle' or 'Twelve stars'? Having put the dilemma to a dance class, I was very taken by the 'Stars of Joy' suggestion made by a dancer in my class. Perfect I thought. It combines the 'stars' in the anthem lyric and flag with the 'Joy' in the English translation of the title of the 1785 poem, as a setting for which Beethoven had written the tune, and in the English name for the resulting song.

With respect the dance, to echo in the dance the twelve stars in circle that feature in the European flag, to capture the 'hoped for unity' of the various lyrics, and produce a dance that is easy for people to join in on, I settled (after much consideration) on a simple dance in a circle, on the periphery of which you are continually making different types of stars. You can do the dance starting with either 12 couples in a single circle or 24 couples in a Sicilian circle (alternatives given in summary box and table), or you can build up to these formations, starting with fewer numbers.

You might start the dance with just a few couple in a single circle, progress on 4 places each sequence, and then as others see how it works, more couples can join in and start turning each other right and left and then linking into the chain. When you get to 12 couples (i.e. 24 dancers) making 12 star-like hand turns each way, take note of who your partner is and what your location is, then do the dance 3 more times to end back with them in starting place.

You can do a similar build up with the Sicilian circle version but those joining in will have to be experienced dancers as this verion will be more challenging. I've never actually led this version, so you can be the first!

You can change from a 12 couples single circle to a 24 couple Sicilian version by, during a reprise of the introductory 2 bars, having 12 ready and waiting partners join in on the outside of the single circle. If doing so, make sure the men join in in such a way they have a dancing woman on their right and women in such a way that they have a dancing man on their left.

You can do a version of the above figure with some pairs dancing in tandem and some singles still dance, so some of the 'star' become 3 hand rather than two. Eventually, when you have 24 couples dancing (12 facing acw 12 cw) you have the Sicilian circle formation, with minor sets of 4 dancers. Then all the stars are 4 hand ones, and the flag looks even brighter.

If matching the dance to the official instrumental version of the EU anthem played AABB twice and if the playing is louder, then you might want to save the hand in the air for the turns at the beginning of the second playing. Although three playings of the tune will return dancers to their partner and home place, it might not be enough to satisfy dancers, so you should feel free to then offer the introduction again to repeat the opening bows and dance the whole sequence another 3 times to return home a second time. When ending, you might hold the final note or add a coda.

— John Gardiner-Garden, *Dance Delights*, 2020 —

~ Sweet Bunch of Daisies ~

Form
circle of couples.

Dance as a progressive circle mixer

Long A W in and take hs in circle; M in and raise joined hs over W's head / all basket l. // M out; W raise hands onto M's sh. / all basket r.

Long B Fall b. into single circle; M swings r.h. b., up and pass ptner under to reform circle facing out / fall b.; M swings l.h. b. and ch. places w. cnr to reform circle facing in // bal. f&b in circle; M pass or cw twirl W from l. to r. h. / repeat

B waltz corner around set ending opening out with W on right side of M

ABAxn Repeat as many times as will.

Play Anita Owen's c.1894 song 'Sweet Bunch of Daisies' intro. then AABxn.

8 bar Aa	With 2 waltz steps <u>W in and take hands in circle</u> then with 2 waltz steps <u>M in, take hands and raise joined hands over W's head to make hands-inside basket</u> <u>All basket 4 waltz steps to left</u>
8 bar Ab	With 2 waltz steps <u>M out</u> then with 2 waltz steps <u>W raise hands</u> over M's heads or <u>onto M's shoulders</u> to make hands-outside basket <u>All basket 4 waltz steps to right</u>
8 bar Ba	With 2 waltz steps <u>all fall backward</u> into holding hands in a single circle then with 2 waltz steps M swing's his right hand out as he faces W on right, raises his right arm and changes places with that W going under and all reform circle facing out. With 2 waltz steps <u>all fall back</u>; M swings left hand back as he faces W on left, raises his left arm and changes places with her and all reform circle facing in
8 bar Bb	All <u>balance f&b</u> in circle then <u>M</u> pass (and/or cw <u>twirls</u>) <u>W from left to right</u> hand <u>Repeat</u> for W to arrive back with original partner
8 bar C	all <u>waltz corner around set ending opening out with W on right side of M</u> so all the W have progressed 1 place acw around the circle.
ABCxn	Repeat sequence three more times till women are all back with partners.

This dance is very close to a choreography I prepared for a production in 2017 of Elizabeth Scott's play *The Rational Dress Society*. The dance which I thought might be perfect for that production was a combination of 1890s dance figures set to the 1890's music hall song 'Sweet Bunch of Daisies'. This song was popular in Britain, America and Australia, and was actually used or the Spanish Waltz in a Quadrille context in a Quadrille tune suite published in Allan's (c.1894) Australian Music Books no.3 (H. Kendall's Kalgoorlie suite for the Albert's Quadrille—that suite's piano score is reproduced at the end of this entry). The words and music for **Sweet bunch of daisies** seem to have been composed by Anita Owen who copyrighted them in 1894, and the lyric seems to have been as follows:

**Sweet golden daisies, oh, how dear to me, / Ever I hear them, whisp'ring, love, of thee,
Murmuring softly, in a silent theme, / Of love's bright morning, now one sad, sweet dream.**
Refrain:
**Sweet bunch of daisies, brought from the dell, / Kiss me once, darling, daisies won't tell.
Give me your promise, O sweetheart do; / Darling, I love you, will you be true?**

**Sweet, withered daisies, treasured more than gold, / Bring; back to mem'ry those sweet days of old,
When we together strolled through forests green, / Gathering daisies growing by the stream.**
Refrain etc.

— John Gardiner-Garden, *Dance Delights*, 2020 —

~ Tempest through a Looking Glass ~

Form 4 couples in horseshoe. 2 top (no.1) couples facing down, between aisle of 2s in becket formation on side.

Start either foot

Prepare for walking (and possible slipping in circles)

Dance as duple minor

Play any set of 32 bar walking tunes, intro. then AABB x n.

A1	1s down 1 place, face out, arch over and b. w. neigh.s
A2	Mirror circles (1s up), star other way
B1	1s down in file, twirl neigh. to face up; rear arch over, return (all *while* 2s go 8 steps up, t. & b. 8 steps)
B2	Mirror star (1s up), circle ¾ other way and 1s ½ double *chassé croisé while* 2s slip up.
All x n	

A1	1s (tops) go <u>down 4-in-line 1 place and bend line back</u> (by mirror wheels as couples) to face neighbours / 1s with near side couple <u>arch out</u> over sides <u>and</u> reverse <u>back</u>.
A2	Mirror <u>circle</u> on each side, starting with 1s going <u>up</u> (left side go acw, right side cw) / near hand <u>star</u> the other way (starting 1s <u>down</u>).
B1	<u>1s go 4 steps down</u> single file <u>holding neighour's</u> inside <u>hand then twirl as couple to face about</u> (couple below keeping joined hands high) *all while* 2s on side <u>go 8 steps</u> single file <u>up</u> and turn inward ½ about <u>1s do ½ wave with rear couple arching</u> forward <u>over front couple</u> as front reverses back under return, then 1s with neighbour return <u>4 steps up</u> the middle *all while* 2s on side <u>return with 8 steps</u> single file <u>down</u>.
B2	Give near hand to new opposites and mirror <u>star</u> new side neighbours, starting with 1s going <u>up</u>, <u>then</u> briskly slip <u>circle</u> in same group, starting with 1s going <u>down</u> and finishing releasing hands when just ¾ through the circle so 2s can slide a few steps up their own side of the set and 1s can cross in as a couple with neighbouring couple ½ double *chassé croisé* (couple on relative left going behind) *while* travelling down the set a little.
Etc.	

The allusions in the title of this dance are significant.

The 'Tempest' alludes to the family of dances which in the course of the 19th century was variously called 'La Tempête' or 'The Tempest'. These were invariably 'double' contras, with pair of first couples progressing side-by-side down through or between pairs of second couples. In Jørgen Gad Lund's 1823 version presented in my *Dancing through the Ages*, volume VII as **La Tempête (1)** and in most of the later versions which were called 'The Tempest' and which have been presented in *Dancing through the Ages*, volume VIII as **The Tempest (1), (2)** and **(3)**, the 2s lined up not in front of the downward facing 1s, but to the side, facing the other 2s across the set. So it is with this dance. As in these versions of the dance, when the 1s reach the bottom of the set and have no one to face they can fall onto the near side line, ready, after once out, to start back up as 2s and conversely when the 2s reach the top of the set and have on one to face they can fall into facing down the middle, ready, after once out, to start travelling down as a 1.

This 'Tempest' is 'through a looking glass', because unlike all those historic versions, in this one all the action is mirror image. There is also an allusion in this expression to the title of one of Lewis Carroll's best love nonsense stories. Lewis Carroll loved puzzles and this dance proposes a solution to the puzzle of how to have mirror action throughout a dance which has 'Tempest' like formation and figures, and still have it work on several different axes and be socially and physically satisfying.

The dance can be enjoyed by as many as will, but if you have more than about 16 couples wanting to dance, you will have to, as you do in any uneven duple-minor contra, either drop the expectation that everyone will get to be 1s for the same amount of time, or play a lot more 8 lots of 32 bars.

If you want to make sure everyone gets a turn at being 1s all the way down, start the dance with 4 minor sets – i.e. 4 couples on each side and 4 rows of 1s – 16 couples all together. You will all get back to place after 8 times through 32 bars.

If you want to make sure everyone gets to dance from every position, then start with just 3 minor sets – i.e. 3 couples on each side and 3 ranks of 2 couples in the middle, and make it that the 1s don't chassée across the set after the last circle, they just walk down the set a little taking hands where they are with their neighbours, ready to start the dance from a new side – and eventually a new top position. After 14 times 32 bars everyone will be home. With more music this will also work with 5 or 7 minor sets, but unless you introduce a switch at top, bottom or somewhere on route if you have an even number of minor sets starting, you will return to the same top position as before, and some of the people you dance with will be in the same position as before.

I'm debted, as so often is the case, to the Bordonian Heritage Dancers for helping me test out the timings and flow on this Looking Glass Tempest and for Jason Tankard for encouraging me to give the 2s a counterpart role to the 1s down and back action in B1- and thus resulted the 2 'whiles' that are now in the instructions at that point. If space is limited at the top and bottom of the set the 2s can promenade in file in an arc that takes them across the set and back (as if the set was for them a circle). This addition not only gives the 2s a little more dancing than they would otherwise have, gives the dance greater 'depth' and reinforces the 'through the looking glass' effect, but it also helps the 2s be ready to present the appropriate 'near hand' for the subsequent star that opens B2.

In 2019 I changed the order of the action for the 1s as they go down the centre with neighbours and back so that the rear couple arch over straight after the 'California twirl', as that means that after their twirl the lower couple can just leave their joined hands raised ready for the arch and that as the 1s return up the middle there is no figure to distract them from looking for the hand they need to take for their new star on the side—which is helpful as if the first couples don't take and make that start in time they will not be able to make enough of a circle back the other way before they have to do the ½ *chassé croisé* with each other.

~ Wachet auf / Sleepers awake ~

Form longways proper set of as many as will

Dance as arranged with 4 counts or steps per bar and ';' marking 4 counts half way through a bar and '/' marking 8 counts, the end of a bar or half way through a strain.

Play, from Johann Sebastian Bach's 1731 cantata (no.140) based on Philipp Nicolai's 1599 hymn *Wachet auf, ruft uns die Stimme,* the 12 bars given below AABCDE xn

A1 1s cast off; start ½ fig. of 8 up /
1s (possibly collecting up-facing 2s on inside h. on way thru. to do side-by-side cast off) complete ½ fig. of 8 ending between 2s in upward facing line-of-4

A2 1s release ea. others h. and wheel w. neigh. to side ending improper below 2s; 2s start ½ fig. of 8 down /
2s (possibly collecting down-facing 1s on way thru. to do side-by-side cast up) complete ½ fig. down ending all improper progressed holding hs in side lines; lines f. to greet ptner

B All 4 step b. on r.f. to turn ¼ cw and ½ l.h. mill ending M turning ptner acw under raised l.h. into single file facing up (men behind ptners in order from top 1W, 1M, 2W, 2M) /
all in file up; fall b.

C 1W, 1M; 2W, 2M take turns (at 4 count intervals) to cast to home place *while* everyone not casting off goes up and b. file 2 more times (so 1W cast *while* file goes up, 1M cast *while* file goes down; 2W cast *while* file goes up, 2M cast *while* no-one else goes anywhere)

D Snowball r&l (starting 1s giving r.h. to ptner, 4 counts per h.)

E 1s r.sh. pass *while* 2s complete the r&l w. a ½ r.h. t; 1s go outside below *while* 2s retaining r.h. in r.h. lead up one place /
1s 2h t. 1½ and open out facing up retaining inside hs *while* 2s join l.hs. below r.h.s and t. 1x cw.

All x n.

in Cm low octave:

or Cm high octave:

— John Gardiner-Garden, *Dance Delights*, 2020 —

A1	With 4 quick walking steps <u>1s cast off</u> then with another 4 quick <u>steps start ½ figure of 8 up</u> With 8 quick steps 1s (<u>possibly collecting up-facing 2s</u> on inside hand <u>on way through</u> in order <u>to do side-by-side cast off</u>) <u>complete ½ figure of 8</u> ending between 2s in upward facing line-of-4.
A2	With 4 steps <u>1s release each others hand and wheel with neighour back to side</u> ending improper below 2s proper <u>then</u> with 4 steps <u>2s start ½ figure of 8 down</u> With 4 steps <u>2s</u> (<u>possibly collecting down-facing 1s</u> on inside hand on way through <u>to do side-by-side cast up</u>) <u>complete ½ figure down</u> ending all improper and progressed holding hands inside lines then with 4 steps lines go forward to greet partner
B	All 4 <u>step back on right foot to turn ¼ cw and</u> with another 4 steps <u>½ left hand mill ending M turning partner acw under raised left hand into single file</u> facing up (men behind partners in order from top 1W, 1M, 2W, 2M) All <u>in up-facing file</u> take 4 steps <u>up</u> and with 4 steps fall <u>back</u>
C	<u>1W, 1M; 2W, 2M take turns</u> (at 4 count intervals) <u>to cast to home place</u> *while* everyone not casting off goes up and back file 2 more times (so 1W cast *while* file goes up, 1M cast *while* file goes down; 2W cast *while* file goes up, 2M cast *while* no-one else goes anywhere)
D	<u>Snowball rights and lefts with 4 counts per hand and starting 1s giving right</u> hand to partner,
E	With 4 steps <u>1s right shoulder pass</u> *while* <u>2s complete the rights and lefts</u> with a ½ right hand turn <u>then</u> with 4 steps <u>1s go on outside below</u> *while* 2s retaining right hand in right lead up one place <u>1s 2h turn 1½ and open out facing up retaining inside hands</u> *while* 2s join left hands below joined right hands and in tight crossed arm hold turn 1x cw
AABCDE x n Repeat as many times as will.	

W*achet auf, ruft uns die Stimme* (which might translate, 'Wake up, the voice calls us', giving rise to its alternate English name 'Sleepers Awake'), is the name of a hymn written by Philipp Nicolai in 1599 as part of a collection of hymns contemplating eternal life in response to the plague taking hundreds of lives while he was a Lutheran pastor in Unna Westphalia. It is also the name of a 7-movement cantata (no.140) based on this hymn that Johann Sebastian Bach wrote specifically for the 27th Sunday after Trinity, a date that occurs only in years when Easter falls early—so the occasion for it comes around only rarely. Bach only arranged one performance of it his lifetime, in the Nikolaikirche in Leipzig on 25 November 1731. The 12 bar theme which I've set this dance is from the middle 4th movement of the Cantata, and is one of three movements which are said to have been based on or inspired by Nicolai's 'Wachet auf', but I must confess failing to be able to hear any of Nicolai's original tune in this tune. Considering it therefore more a piece form 1731 than from 1599, I have endeavoured to match it with a dance in a social dance form popular in 1731 (longways proper, duple minor) and using figures popular at that time (figure of eights, lines-of-four across up-and-back, files of four up and back, rights and left etc). I was keen, however, to achieve a dance that would not only fit the music but compliment it, that would not only be in a contemporary form, but play with transformations of shape possible within that form, in the way contemporary masters such as Bray and Esses would play with these possibilities, and that would not only use period figures, but use them in new interesting ways and offer near flawless transitions between them. I was keen also, although the dance was to start and finish proper, to have most of the interactions (whether giving hand or eye) between dancers of opposite sex. I was also keen to have the interactions evenly distributed between partner and corner, and to have the end of the dance tie into the beginning. As the tune did not inspire me to think in terms of baroque *belle danse* foot work, as much as the modern English country dance 'dance walking' step, I decided to build the dance around the expectation that the dancers would take 8 quick plain dance walking steps for every bar (one every crotchet).

— John Gardiner-Garden, *Dance Delights*, 2020 —

The resulting dance ends up having some interesting features.

The A strains feature a figure, the ½ figure of eight, that would normally be set to 8 counts of its own, lying across the middle 8 counts of a 16-count strain—the 1s ½ figure up in A1 and the 2s ½ figure down in A2. By going across the phrase I hope to add to a sense of breathless flow.

The B strain features am accommodation of the open crotchet for a single step back on the right foot in order to turn ¼ acw to present left hands, or at least shoulders, before doing a ½ acw mill that ends with dancers turning over their left shoulder (M 5/8 while turning W under his raised left hand 1¼) into an upward facing file—all in the first bar. In the second bar the partners release the left hand that is still momentarily joined, so all can go up 4 counts and 4 counts back.

The C strain is a 'fountain' figure. In this figure I have combined two ideas. This first is of having the 1W, 1M, 2W and 2M taking turns, 4 counts apart, to cast home—women casting over their right shoulder, men over their left. The second is of having those left in the file going up and back two more times, echoing the 4 counts ascending melody going up and echoing the 4-count descending melody falling back. The two can work perfectly together as the women, who are positioned forward of their men in the file, end up starting their cast off when the file is most 'back', while the men, who are starting their cast off from behind where their partners were, end up starting their cast off when the file is most 'forward'. The result at the end of the cast is that partners end up level with each other. To facilitate entry into the next figure, the 1s might after their cast off turn to face each other and over the next 8 counts raise their right hand slowly, and the 2s after their cast off might turn to face up towards the 1s and over the next 8 counts raise their left hand slowly.

The D strain features a duple-minor 'right and left' chain, but not as it is normally done in this period. I have it 'snowball' from the top. Although I have no evidence for this exact figure from the time of Bach's writing in the early 18th century, the figure was described as an option by masters such as Gennaro Magri and Thomas Wilson end of the 18th and beginning of the 19th century respectively, and a snowball grand chain for four couple can be found in Renaissance dances and in **Nonesuch** from the mid 17th century (see Volume IV). Snowballing the 'right and left' in the context of this dance can have three advantages. Firstly, the 2s don't have to be entirely ready as the figure can be initiated by the 1s and the 2s just respond. Secondly, the four dancers end up always giving hands to members of the opposite sex. Thirdly, as the 2s will complete the figure 4 counts after the 1s, it can help blur the boundaries between figures and by having some of the figure overlap into the next musical phrase contribute to the sense of seamlessness. The latter is particularly relevant when it comes to the D and E strain of this tune, as those strains do flow so seamlessly one to the other. It is also particular useful in this dance as the 2s can use the beginning of the E strain not only to complete the last right hand pass of their chain (while the 1s are crossing right shoulder), but, if they retain right-in-right with their partner, use the second lots of 4 counts in E to lead up the middle of the set (while the 1s cast down the outside).

The end of the E strain features a full 2-hand turn for partners that goes 1½ about so there is no daylight between the opening out of it on a proper inside hand facing up and the cast off that begins the repeat of the sequence. It will give the 1s that final woosh that makes them feel as if they are indeed 1s enjoying something extra, in a dance that is otherwise rather even in its spread of action. If the 2s want (and this is my preference), after leading up right hand in right they can face and join left in left beneath the joined rights and turn cw once about on the crossed arms, keeping elbows bend so as to leave maximum space for the 1s to do their 2 hand turn, and then the 2s can push/fall back in place, just in time for the new 1s above them to cast off around them.

~ Waltz Futsal ~

Form 3 couples start in each half of a rectangular field with a toy ball in the centre ready for 'kick-off'. In Boston-Ball two cpls in semi-circles marked to each sideline and one in the semi-circle marked for the goal. In 'Waltz Futsal' no need for side semi-circles, just a cone in each corner of field and 4 cones marking goals at each end.

'Waltz Futsal' (John G-G's rules):
- If the ball crosses the sideline, a sideline couple picks it up, hands it to the couple who last touched the ball and swaps places with them, the new sideline couple get to roll the ball in.
- If the ball crosses a baseline outside the goal posts and if the last person to touch the ball was an attacker, a defender takes ball in front of their own goal, if a defender an attacker gets a corner kick.
- If a goal or own goal is scored all three defending couples have to swap over with couples on the sideline.

Start either foot and **dance** *ad libitum*

Play any moderate-tempo waltz.

Needed: a soccer ball whether real, toy (better) or a 'Hover ball' (the best—see notes below) and 8 chairs or cones to mark the four corners of a rectangle almost as big as the hall and to mark goals at each end.

Start with 6 on-field couples divided into two teams (one perhaps distinguished by sashes), three on each base line. Remaining couples stand with partner just beyond sidelines, half on one side half on other.

An umpire is not essential as the game can be self-managing but an umpire may help direct play and couple swaps, keep a tally of goals by each side (even as sides members change and as couples end up changing teams), may help the MC determine when to end game, and can announce the winning side.

Theoretical aim: to contribute to a side scoring the most goals before an end is called.

Real aim: to be all inclusive (i.e. passing the ball within your side, prioritising swapping in of couples who have not yet danced), survive and have fun!

Rules

Couples
- on the field must waltz continuously (even if faultingly when trying to trap or kick the ball) and avoid kicks that endanger heads or hall) and if an on-field couple tires, stops waltzing or kicks the ball too high or hard, they have to swap with a sideline couple.
- on side-line do not need to hold each other or waltz, but partners need to be with each other, and they may need to take sashes from a departing couple when swapped in.

If the ball crosses the sideline, a sideline couple picks it up, hands it to the couple who last touched the ball and swaps places with them, the new sideline couple get to roll the ball in.

If the ball crosses a baseline outside the goal posts and…
- o if the last person to touch the ball was from an attacking side, the defending side takes possession of the ball in front of their own goal and the attacking side have to fall back to their own half.
- o if the last person to touch the ball was from the defending side, the attacking side get possession of the ball for a corner kick and players of both sides can be anywhere.

If a goal or own-goal is scored all three defending couples have to swap over with couples on the sideline, the scoring team have to fall back to their own half and the new on-field side take possession of the ball in the centre of the field.

End when MC judges all have participated sufficiently. There no need for half time change of sides.

Options for playing further games after an initial one's completion include:

- Change ball from a small toy practise one to a normal one
- Change partners, whether by random repairing or by getting all couples around the perimeter and having the women move on one place.
- Change music, whether to a waltz of a different character or tempo, to different kind of triple time tune (e.g. to a mazurka, redowa or polska) to an entirely different rhythm (e.g. to a polka).
- Form same sex couples, have same sex sides and makes sure you always swap same sex in for one going out. If gender numbers are not even you can have a mixed-gender couple so long as they are dancing in each other's role, so on one side all the normal male roles are dance by women and on the other vice-versa.

This dance was inspired by one called 'The Boston-Ball' which was described on the cover of a music folio in my possession entitled **Boston-Ball (Valse Lente) Par A. Pryor Sous-Chef de Sousa-Band Paris. Cette Valse est aussi publiée sous le titre: Love Thougts** [should be 'Thoughts' as inside score], published by Libraire Hachette & Cie, Paris, 1898. The dance there described was said to have been **Le Grand Succès du 'Nouveau-Cirque'** ('The great success of the 'New Circus'') and I presented that folio's dance instruction and piano score in my entry entitled **The Boston-Ball / Waltz Futsal** in my 2020 *Dancing through the Ages*: Volume X: 1875-1900. There I also offered full context to the dance, a reconstruction of the dance being described, and, because the dance being described seemed to be more theatrical than socially practical (a French joke version of an American cotillon dance game), I offered a version of 'The Boston Ball' soccer dance which I called 'Waltz Futsal'.

Here I present just my 'Waltz Futsal'. It can work well in a real-life ball context and to nearly any waltz. Tabulated above are the rules I devised for its debut at the Sunday Victorian Masquerade on the last evening of the Jane Austen Festival Australia 2019 at Canberra's grand Albert Hall on 14 April 2019. On the dance's debut we set the game to un-interrupted playing of the 'The Boston Ball' musical suite 'Love thoughts', which although subtitled *Valse lente* we found best played at moderate tempo. We have on two subsequent occasions danced the game to other waltz tunes in smaller venues, adapting the goal and sideline position markers. I do not represent here the Pryor suite which I reproduced in full in my *Dancing through the Ages*: Volume X entry, as we are not here reconstructing the 1898 dance so much as simply taking inspiration from it and accordingly I recommend you use whatever waltz tune set you like. I do, however, for your interest present further below the front page of the music folio with its beautiful illustration of ballroom soccer in process (staged using the theatre shows actors).

When it comes to the soccer ball, it can be a real one of normal size, but dancers would have to agree to avoid high or hard kicks. Alternatively, it can be small toy one, which is less likely to do too much damage inside, but it too is likely to go high and complicated the game. Best of all, if you have a nice smooth floor, might be something I have bought called a 'Hover ball' which is soccer-ball patterned dome with a cushioned perimeter that glides just above the floor on a cushion of air, and can be kicked without it leaving the floor. It's battery operated and if the hall lights are turned down you can enjoy the swirl of its lit-up dome as it spins across the floor.

LE GRAND SUCCÈS   DU " NOUVEAU-CIRQUE "

BOSTON-BALL (VALSE LENTE)

Par A. PRYOR, Sous-Chef de Sousa-Band

Cette Valse est aussi publiée
sous le titre : **Love Thougts**.

PIANO, net ~~~~~~~~ **2** *fr.* »
PIANO A 4 MAINS, net. **2** *fr.* **50**
ORCHESTRE, net ~~~~ **2** *fr.* »

(Cliché Femina).

Dans une pantomime jouée au Nouveau-Cirque, où sont figurées quelques scènes de l'éducation américaine, un groupe de jeunes gens et de jeunes filles apparaissent à un moment donné en toilette de soirée, et disputent une partie de *Boston-Ball*. Qu'est-ce donc que le *Boston-Ball* ? C'est un amusant jeu de salon sportif où le boston, tel qu'on le danse ordinairement, joue le principal rôle. Le *Boston-Ball* ne nécessite pas grande installation et peut se jouer dans un salon, même de dimensions restreintes. On trace à terre un rectangle, puis, à l'intérieur du rectangle, six demi-cercles se touchant l'un l'autre, un sur chacun des petits côtés, deux sur chacun des grands côtés. Il reste ainsi entre les demi-cercles un espace vide. Au milieu des petits côtés on dispose un arceau à peu près de dimension quadruple d'un arceau de croquet et le jeu est ainsi complétement établi. Voici comment on joue :

Six couples de bostonneurs occupent chacun un des demi-cercles et forment deux camps opposés. Chaque camp occupe un des demi-cercles appuyés sur les petits côtés du triangle et les deux demi-cercles qui touchent. Au milieu de l'espace libre on place une grosse balle. L'orchestre attaque une valse lente, les joueurs se mettent à bostonner jusqu'à ce qu'un coup de tambour de basque annonce le commencement de la partie. A ce moment, deux couples, un de chaque camp, qui ont été désignés à l'avance, quittent leur place et se dirigent vers la balle en bostonnant. La balle appartient au premier couple qui l'a touchée et le couple opposé revient à sa place.

A partir de ce moment, le couple qui s'est assuré la balle, doit s'efforcer de la faire passer, en la poussant d'un petit coup de pied, sous l'arceau du camp ennemi qui figure le but. S'il réussit de suite son camp marque un point et la partie recommence.

Mais supposez au contraire qu'un coup de pied mal dirigé ait envoyé la balle dans un des demi-cercles occupé par un adversaire ou même un partenaire; alors le couple qui avait maintenant la balle revient à sa place et cède le milieu du jeu à celui qui l'a reçue. Celui-ci pousse doucement la balle dans la partie libre du jeu. Là elle est à lui et il la conserve jusqu'à ce qu'il ait marqué un point pour son camp ou commis la même faute que le couple précédent, etc., etc., mais en aucun cas les couples ne doivent s'arrêter de bostonner.

Le boston-ball, très simple et très amusant, ne manquera pas de faire fortune cet hiver dans les salons. Notre photographie représente une des premières parties qui aient été jouées en France.

Au premier plan, miss Myora Isler, une jeune américaine, bostonneuse émérite qui conduit tous les soirs la partie au Nouveau-Cirque, a la balle en bonne position pour marquer un but, à droite l'arbitre est déjà prête à l'annoncer.

~ The Waratah Polka Mazurka ~

Form couples around
l.o.d., outside foot
free.

Dance as arranged

Play AABBAA CC
DD D'D' CC EE A

A1	2 short p.mazurka / 1 long p.mazurka **A2** Cnterpart starting over sh.
B1	2 long p.mazurka **B2** Repeat *AA Repeat all above*
C1	1 short p.mazurka; 1 p.redowa and point / long p.mazurka
C2	Counterpart starting over sh.
D1	3 short p.mazurka then 2 p.redowa **D2** Cnterpart starting over sh.
D'1&2	Repeat D1&2 **C1&2** As before
E1	1 short p.mazurka, 2 p.redowa /1 short p.mazurka, 1 p.redowa, point
E2	Cnterpart starting over sh. but instead of final point end w.2 stamps
A1	As before but after 3 hobbles do 3 step cw 1½ pivot then with 2 steps and close spin W cw out under M's raised l.h. to face and bow.

	To 'The Celebrated Waratah Polka Mazurka' by Daphne, No.55 Paling's Ballroom Music, W.H. Paling & Co, Sydney, 15th edition [no date, but perhaps 1893 reissue of 1878 original].
A1	2 short polka mazurkas (each 1 glide-cut-hop hobble and glide-cut-leap polka redowa to turn ½ cw)
	1 long polka mazurka (3 glide-cut-hop hobble and a glide-cut-leap polka redowa to turn ½ cw)
A2	Counterpart starting over sh.

— John Gardiner-Garden, *Dance Delights*, 2020 —

B1	2 long polka mazurkas
B2	Another 2 long polka mazurkas
AA	As in previous AA
1C1	1 short polka mazurka then 1 polka redowa and point long polka mazurka
1C2	Counterpart
D1	3 short polka mazurkas then 2 polka redowas
D2	Counterpart (starting over shoulder)
D'1&2	Repeat D1&2
2C1&2	As in 1CC before
E1	1 short polka mazurka the 2 polka redowas 1 short polka mazurka then 1 polka redowa, point
E2	Counterpart (starting over shoulder) but instead of final point end with 2 stamps
A/coda	As before but replace last bar with 3 bars and after hobbles 2 slow stamps to face & bow

I presented this dance in my entry **Polka Mazurka (3) / The Waratah** in my *Dancing through the Ages*, Volume X: 1875-1900, Part 2b, Canberra, 2020, but the choreography is my own. I included the dance in that historical dance series because it illustrated the way period polka mazurka steps might have been used when dancing freely to a period polka mazurka suite such as Daphne's 'Waratah Polka Mazurka' piano score, published and republished in Australia in the last decades of the 19th and first decade of the 20th century. Here I present the choreography simply because it is an exciting sequence to very pleasant music.

With respect the music, as I reported in my *Dancing through the Ages* entry, many editions are held by the Australian National Library. None of the early editions have dates, but the copy in my personal possession and which I have appended in facsimile to this entry is 'The Celebrated Waratah Polka Mazurka' by Daphne, No.55 Paling's Ballroom Music, W.H. Paling & Co, Sydney, 15th edition', and looks like it was printed in the 1890s, and one of the earliest, possibly the first edition, includes a dedication to 'the Australian XI'— meaning the Australian national cricket team. The first Australian team to tour England was an all-Aboriginal team that did so in 1868 but that team was not called 'The Australian XI' and a date of 1868 is a bit early for a score that was still being published in the new century. For a date closer to the end of the century, we might take 'The Australian XI' to be a reference to the Australian side that toured England in 1890 or 1893, but it is unlikely anyone would compose a polka mazurka in the 1890s as the dance was no longer fashionable (even though a suite might be reprinted then). I think the most probable scenario is that the suite was written and published in 1878, that the early dedication was intended to be to the first official representative national team, called 'The Australian XI' that toured England in March 1878, and that the suite was reissued annually, meaning my 15th edition was released c.1893.

With respect the dance, there are no dance or step instructions accompanying this or any edition of the score and it's possible that it was intended purely as a listening piece or a piece to which dancers might at home improvise a polka mazurka pattern. You could freely improvise a dance to this suite using polka mazurka and polka redowa variants of the kind I have discussed at length in my *Dancing through the Ages* Volume IX: 1850-1875. However, as with 'The Australian Polka Mazurka' piano score to which I set a dance in my entry in that Volume IX under **Polka Mazurka (1) / The Australian**, the music is so suggestive of when to do a short polka mazurka (1 hobble step, 1 polka redowa to turn ½ cw), when a long polka mazurka (3 hobble steps, 1 polka redowa to turn ½ cw), when just polka redowas, and when just point or stamp, that you might want to try the sequence that I have mapped out above using just those ingredients.

Waratah Polka Mazurka.

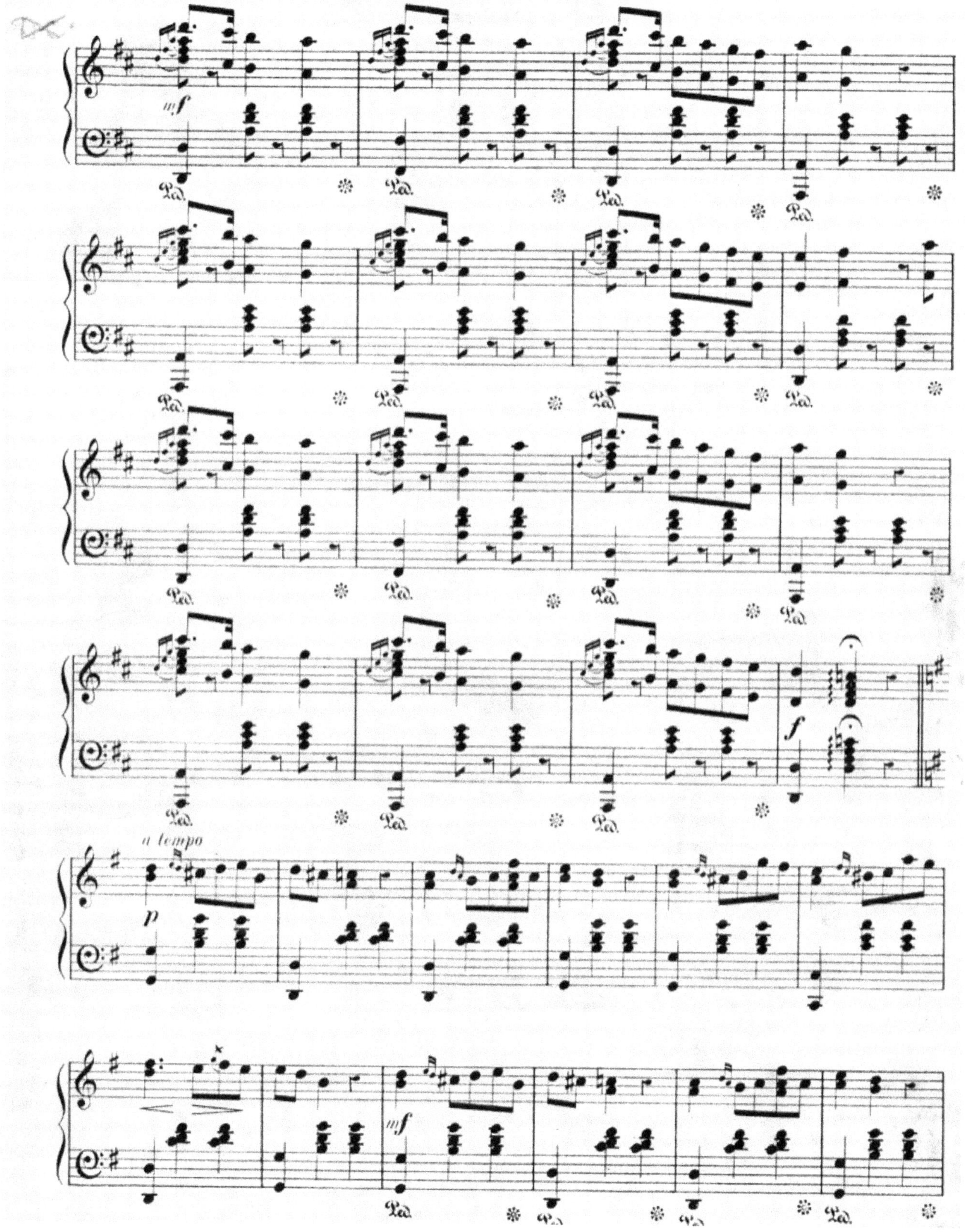
DC
mf
Ped.
f
a tempo
p
mf

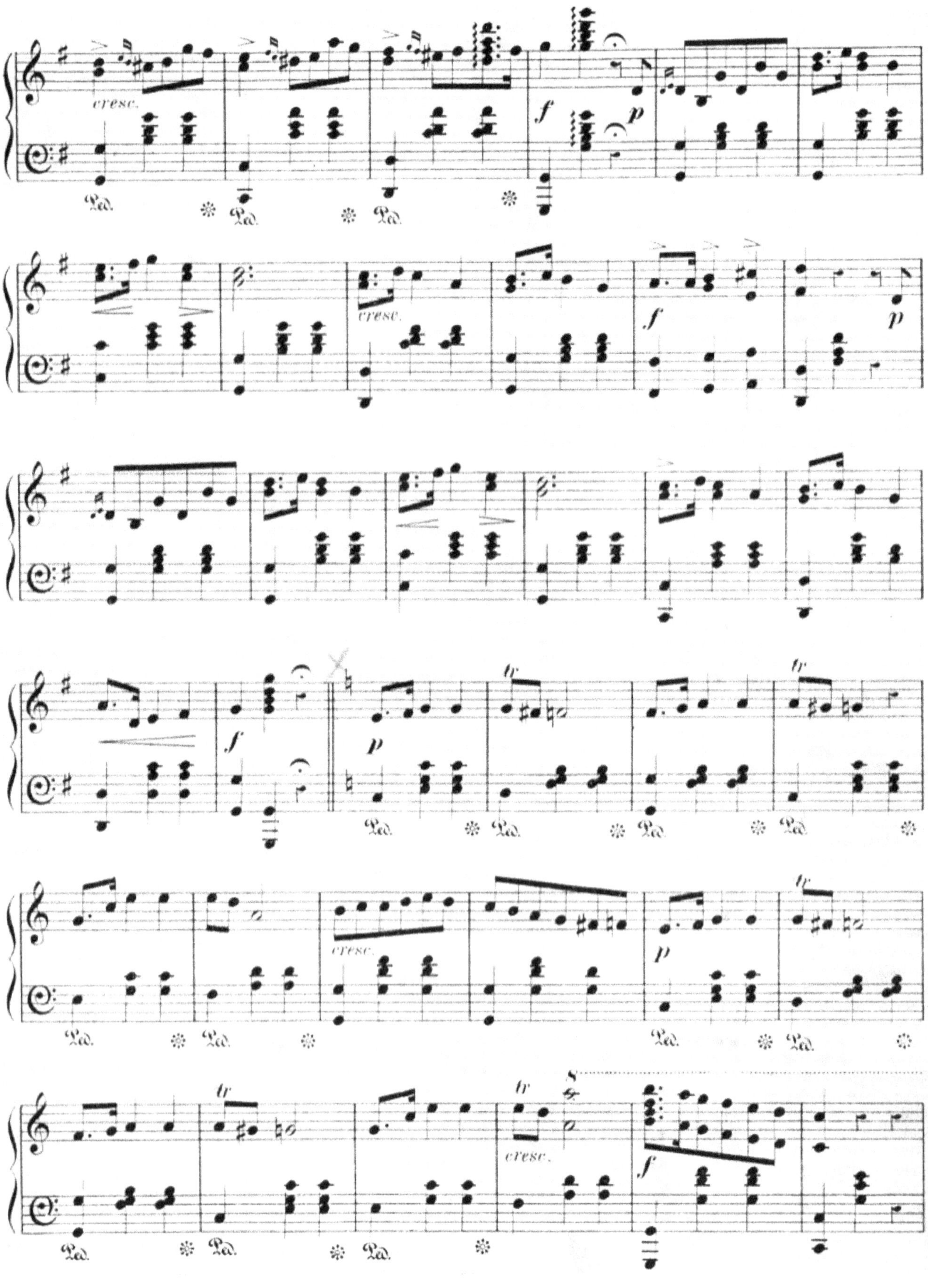
cresc.
f
p
tr
Ped.

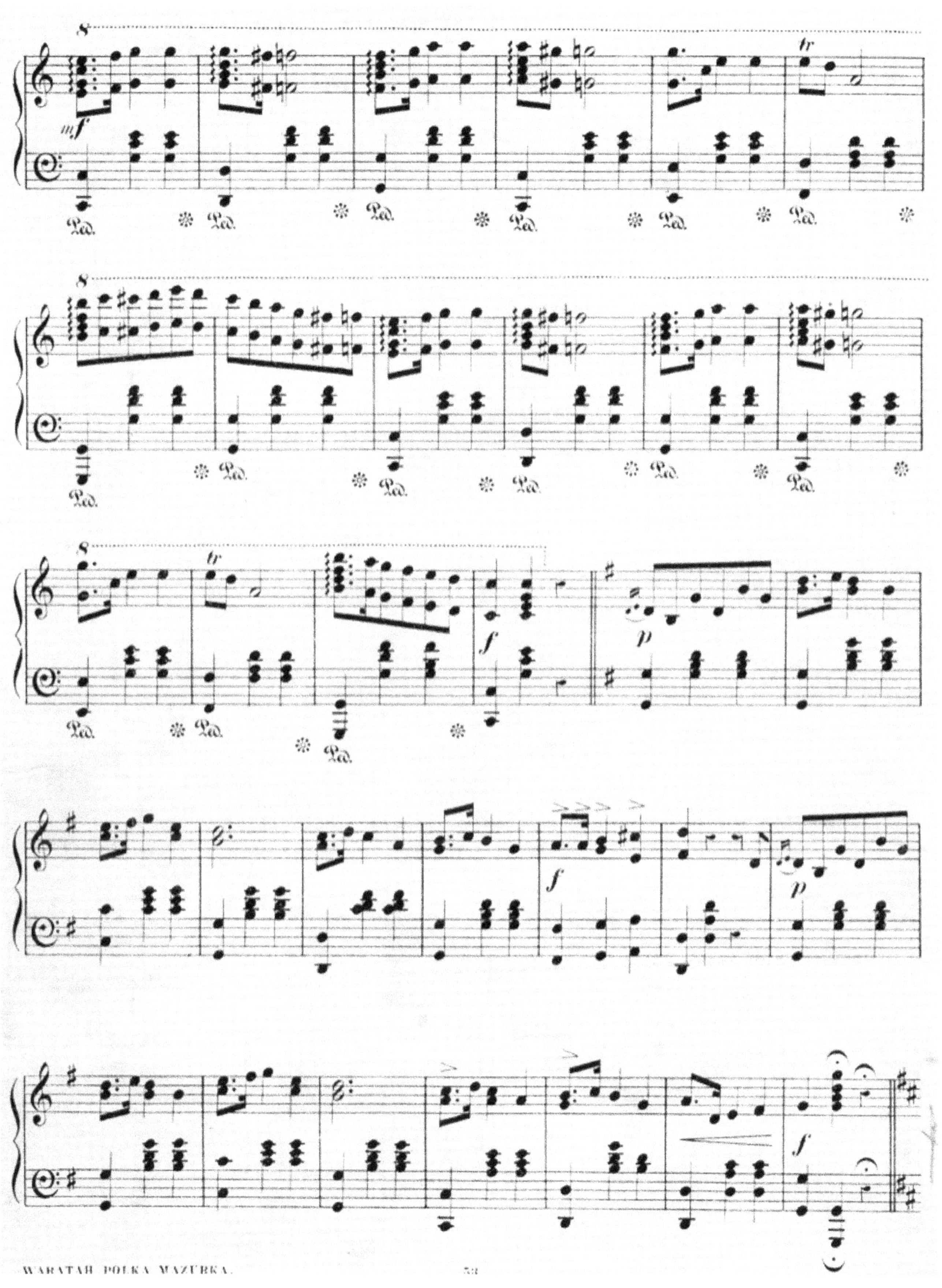
WARATAH POLKA MAZURKA.
53

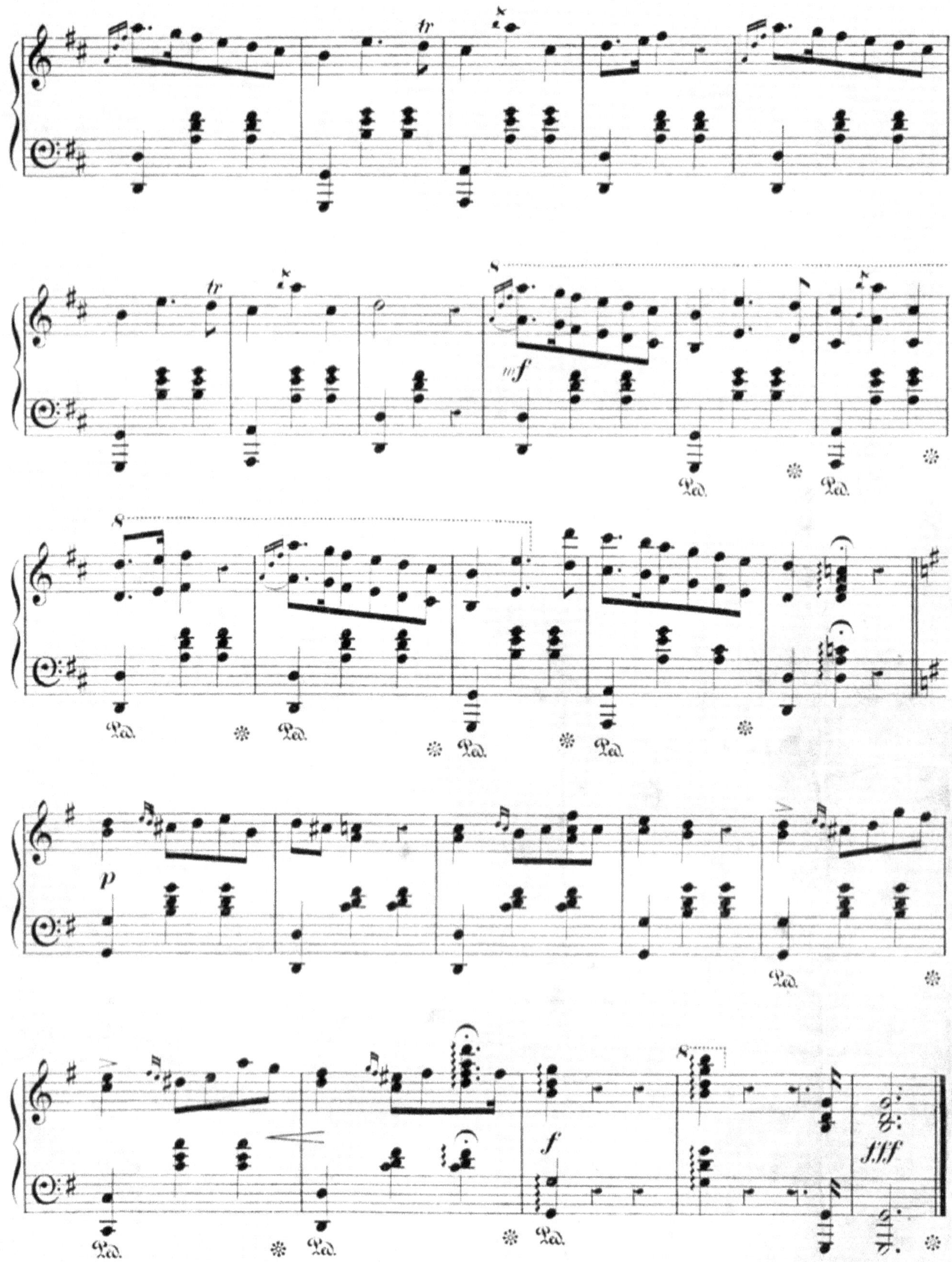
tr
mf
Ped.
p
f
fff

~ The Wind-Up Galop ~

Form couples in ballroom hold.

Start outside foot, M's l.f. W r.f.

Dance as many times as will.

Play any 32-bar polka or galop set, but particularly appropriate may be Charles Godfrey's wonderful 1871/2 'The Wind-up Galop', reproduced in facsimile at the end of this dance entry, played AABB AACC DDCC AABB E.

A1	Sideways along l.o.d. w. 2 click-step-steps; ½ acw t. w. polka, M acw pir. W under raised l.h. w. 2 steps / cntrprt over sh.: but cw t. and *pir.*
A2	2 steps (M's 2nd through middle, W's together), 1 polka to ½ cw t.; cntrprt / w. 2 polka steps both t. under lead hs; w. 1 polka W t. under again, w. 1 polka M again.
B1	8 galops & t. / 4 galops & t.; 2 galops & t., 2 pivots
B2	Cntrprt.
All x n.	

A1	Sideways along l.o.d. with <u>2 click-step-steps and ½ acw turn</u> (M back) with 1 polka step <u>then M pirouettes W acw under his raised left hand</u> *while* both take just <u>2 steps</u> <u>Counterpart</u> over shoulder: i.e. 2 clicks then ½ cw turn and M cw turn W
A2	In ballroom hold M does a 1/2 grapevine for 2 steps *while* W does a slow step-together, then both do a polka step to turn ½ cw, then repeat in reversed roles (W on inside crosses through with her second step *while* M goes sideways along l.o.d.). <u>With 2 polka steps both turn under leading hand, then with 1 polka step W turn under again and with 1 polka step M turns under.</u>
B1	<u>8 galops</u> along l.o.d., lifting and turning on last glide rather than closing <u>4 galop</u>, turning on last, <u>then 2 galops</u> turning ½ cw on last, <u>and 2 pivots</u> turning fully cw.
B2	<u>Counterpart</u>
AABB x n Repeat.	

Most curiously, this dance was for a long time the only new dance I had in my 'bottom draw' which did not have its own tune. I always intended to get around to writing a tune as a setting for the dance, but then, to my amazement, discovered on sale a piano score published in London about 1871/2 by Cramer Wook & Co. It was by the leading British composer Charles Godfrey (1839-1919) and was called *The Wind-Up Galop*. I purchased it, pianist friend Sally Taylor, with her husband Peter on guitar, brought it to life and I had the great fortune to discover that it worked perfectly for my dance—whether by itself, or in a medley with such other dances of my creation as the Bordonian National Polka 1 and 2. For more on Godfrey and this score see my entry under Godfrey in Part 5 of Volume IX.

I might now return to the dance. You can literally wind-up your partner then let yourselves tear away. Through a series of hobbled heel-clicks, cross-steps, pirouettes and tumbles in the A part you build up the energy which is then discharged in the B part as an explosively, but eventually fading, direct current of galop.

The inspiration for the click-step-steps in the first four bars of A1 was Elias Howe's 1862 description of **L'Hongoise** (2) (see entry in *Dancing through the Ages* Volume IX) and for the alternation of 'grapevine' roles in A2 from Gilbert's 1890 **Cross Step Polka** (see entry in *Dancing through the Ages* Volume X, although here I'm assuming a quicker tempo than for Gilbert's dance so have changed his 2 step-hops to just 2 steps and his 'step-together-step-lift' to a polka step). The ideas for the recurrent (so to speak) twirling of the women under the M's left arm and the reduction from 8 to 4 to 2 galops and then pivot, were simply ideas

— John Gardiner-Garden, *Dance Delights*, 2020 —

I worked out as feasible, nicely balanced and neatly making use of built-up momentum while offering appropriate trajectory for that which follows. As many women seem to enjoy turns on the spot, I gave the woman the opportunity to do quick 2 step pirouettes in A1 and a quick 1 polka step turn straight after a 2 step one in A2. I created a more forgiving M's role, but gave him, after a 1 bar rest, the last quick turn of the A part so that he might be able to use the resulting momentum and trajectory to sweep up the woman with his right arm and drive her off into the B part's galops.

DEDICATED TO MADAME LOUISE MICHAU

THE

WIND - UP

GALOP

BY

CHARLES GODFREY.

(A & P. 10,800)

2
A1
GALOP.
fz p
G
D
fz p
Em
D
cres:
A7
A2
f
D
G
D
G
D7
Em
A7
B1&2
cres:
f
ff
G
D7
G
D
G
p
ff
C
G
D7
C. GODFREY, Wind-up Galop.
(A & P. 10.800)

C. GODFREY, Wind-up Galop.   (A & P. 10,800)

C. GODFREY, Wind-up Galop. (A & P. 10,800)

5
D2
C7
F
Gm
G7
C
C1&2
p
C7
F
C
G7
C
Dm
G7
C
Repeat this C
G7
C
Dm
G7
C
D.C. to Galop.
C. GODFREY, Wind-up Galop
(A & P. 10,800)

6

— John Gardiner-Garden, *Dance Delights*, 2020 —

~ Winifred—the Baden Berlin Bohemian ~

Form couples scattered around the l.o.d.

Dance AABBCC sequence with one partner then progress to new partner for repeat of sequence.

Play tune by S. Milbourn Jnr (piano score with coda further below):

A1	**La Badoise**: Both clap side-own hs, w. ptner 3x; repeat / just M wag r.finger 3x, l.finger 3x; t.s. w. 2 steps & 3 stomps // Repeat w. just W doing 2nd half.
A2	**The Kreuz with scuff and step-hops:** Polka f. along l.o.d., swing inside f. thru (w. scuff) and back; ch. hs & polka against l.o.d, swing new inside f. / 4 turning step hops // Repeat
B1	**The Berlin w. points and polka:** Polka prom. f., point inside f.-hop *while* t. in and about; prom b., point new inside f.-hop *while* turning to face / turn as cpl w. 4 polkas
B2	**The Berlin with points and coquette:** As before but instead of 4 polkas take 2 *glissades*; 1 polka ½ cw; cnterpart.
C1	**The Bohemian:** h&t, ½ cw t. w.1 polka; repeat other f. / 4 galops & t.; 4 galops // cntrprt **C2** Repeat

AABBCC Repeat all (with or without new partner).

A Reprise **The Badoise** x 1 but w. both doing 2nd half together // reprise **The Kreuz** x 1 but after 3 step-hops do 1 polka step

8 bar finale: turn as cpl w. 8 pivots / M turns W out; bow.

These are the Robert Bruce words set to the tune:

A1:
Merry hearts and / youth are ours,
Swiftly fly the / careless hours,
Now that sober / old clock glows
Ah! Ah! Ah! / Ah! Ah! Ah!
In and out, and / to and fro,
Glancing feet to / to music go,
With each step fresh / joy we know,
Ah! Ah! Ah!

A2:
Moments flit like / busy bees,
Honey laden / all are these,
Let us then their / honey seize,
Yes! Yes! Yes! / Yes! Yes! Yes!
On they go, and / on go we,
Care with daylight / we may see
Now's the time to / happy be,
Yes! Yes! Yes!

— John Gardiner-Garden, *Dance Delights*, 2020 —

A1	—1st 8 bars	**La Badoise**	Man clap thighs-clap own hands, man with partner clap 3 times, then repeat man wag right finger in menace or chastising 3x, same with left finger 3x then turn single left with 2 steps & 3 stomps
	—2nd 8 bars	—2nd time	Repeat but with woman leading the clapping and finger wagging and ending both facing along l.o.d. taking inside hand.
A2	—1st 8 bars	**The Kreuz Polka**	As couple promenade on inside hand with 1 polka step forward along l.o.d., swing inside f. thru (w. scuff) and back, then change hands & polka against l.o.d, swing new inside foot Turn as a couple twice about with 4 slow step-hops, ending sliding back onto inside hand
	—2nd 8 bars	—2nd time	Repeat
B1	—2nd 8 bars	**The Berlin var. 1**	As above but instead of scuffing inside foot forward and back, point it then withdraw it while hopping to face about and instead of turning as a couple with step-hops, turn with 4 plain polka steps.
	—2nd 8 bars	—2nd time	Repeat
B2	—1st 8 bars	**The Berlin var. 2**	As above but instead of 4 polkas take 2 *glissades*; 1 polka ½ cw; cnterpart, and at end retain ballroom hold
	—2nd 8 bars	—2nd time	Repeat
C1	—1st 8 bars	**The Bohemian**	With outside foot heel-and-toe, ½ cw turn with 1 polka; repeat with other foot 4 galops along l.o.d. (the last unclosed) & turn cw ½ about; 4 galops (all closed and no turn, leave weight on back foot)
	—2nd 8 bars		Counterpart (heel and toe with other foot, galop and turn, galop with no turn).
C2	8 bars 8 bars	—2nd time	Repeat C1 action with option of man going forward by himself to new woman on last 4 galops while woman cast over right shoulder with 4 steps into arms of new partner.
AABBCC		*Repeat* all the above with new partner if you have progressed and with woman leading on first time through *Badoise* sequence, man leading second time.	
A1	—1st 8 bars	Reprise **La Badoise** but this time with man and woman doing all the action simultaneously, and ending taking each other in ballroom hold	
	—2nd 8 bars	Reprise **The Kreuz Polka** but instead of turn with 3 slow step-hops and 1 turning polka step leading into …	
8 bar **finale**		4 bars turning as a couple with 8 pivot steps then, 2 bars to turn W out and 2 bars to bow to each other.	

— John Gardiner-Garden, *Dance Delights*, 2020 —

This dance is a medley of 4 dances that were popular all around the western world in the 1890s. Individually these short-sequences dances can be a little tedious if repeated without variation with the same partner, but as a medley they can offer a pleasant sufficiently-varied dance. For a full discussion of each of the four dances see the relevant entries in Volume X of my *Dancing through the Ages,* namely my entry on **The Baby Polka / Finger Polka / La Badoise** (that occupies the A1, on **The Kreuz Polka**, a type of Berlin Polka that with its repeat occupies the A2, on **The Berlin Polka / La Berline / Alsatian Polka / Polka Militaire** two different variants of which, with their repeats, occupy B1 and B2, and on **The Bohemian Polka / Heel and Toe**, a sequence that has to be repeated in counterpart in order for dancers to return to original side so, in order to repeat fully, occupies the whole of C1 and C2. The place alluded to in the various titles indicate the extent of the area to which people were prepared to ascribe the dance's origin or practice— from Baden in the south west of Germany to Berlin in the north east to Bohemia to the west of Germany.

I have arranged these four tunes to go to a musical suite by S. Milbourn Junr. entitled Winifred (my copy of which I have reproduced below). It was published c.1894 in Adelaide, Australia, by P.A. Howell, under the heading *The New Kreuz Polka,* probably because it was intended to be a setting a 'Kreuz Polka'. That the suite was written in Australia is suggested by the dedication 'to Mrs R. Barr-Smith, Torrens Park'—the latter being in Adelaide. The words by the famous Scottish poet Robert Bruce were set to the AA part of the melody.

I have set the four dances to the parts of the Milbourn suite that best support them, and have put the dances in an order that builds the excitement, from the man and woman alternating action in place in A1, to foot scuffing and turning step-hops in A2, to point-lifts and turning with polkas in B1, to the point-lifts and turning with a 'coquette' passage (2 galops, polka, 2 galops, polka) in B2, to heel-&-toeing, ½ turning and 4 galops, turn, 4 galops etc in C1 and C2. If you repeat all this with the same partner you can vary the beginning by having the lady go first with the bow-clap etc, and when you return to the A1 to end the dance you can have both the man and woman do the bow-clap etc simultaneously. If playing the full coda offered in the piano score you are welcome to end with 6 bars of progressively more rapid turning and with 2 bars of turning out.

— John Gardiner-Garden, *Dance Delights*, 2020 —

WINIFRED.

Words by ROBERT BRUCE.

Music by S. MILBOURN, Ju

INTRO.

POLKA.

Merry hearts and youth are ours,
Moments flit like bu - sy bees,
Swiftly fly the care - less hours,
Honey la - den all are these,
Now that so - ber old clock glowers
Let us then their hon - ey seize,
Ah! Ah! Ah!
Yes! Yes! Yes!

In and out, and to and fro,
On they go, and on go we,
Glancing feet to mu - sic go,
Care with daylight we may see
With each step fresh joy, we know,
Now's the time 'to hap - py be,
Ah! Ah! Ah!
Yes! Yes! Yes!

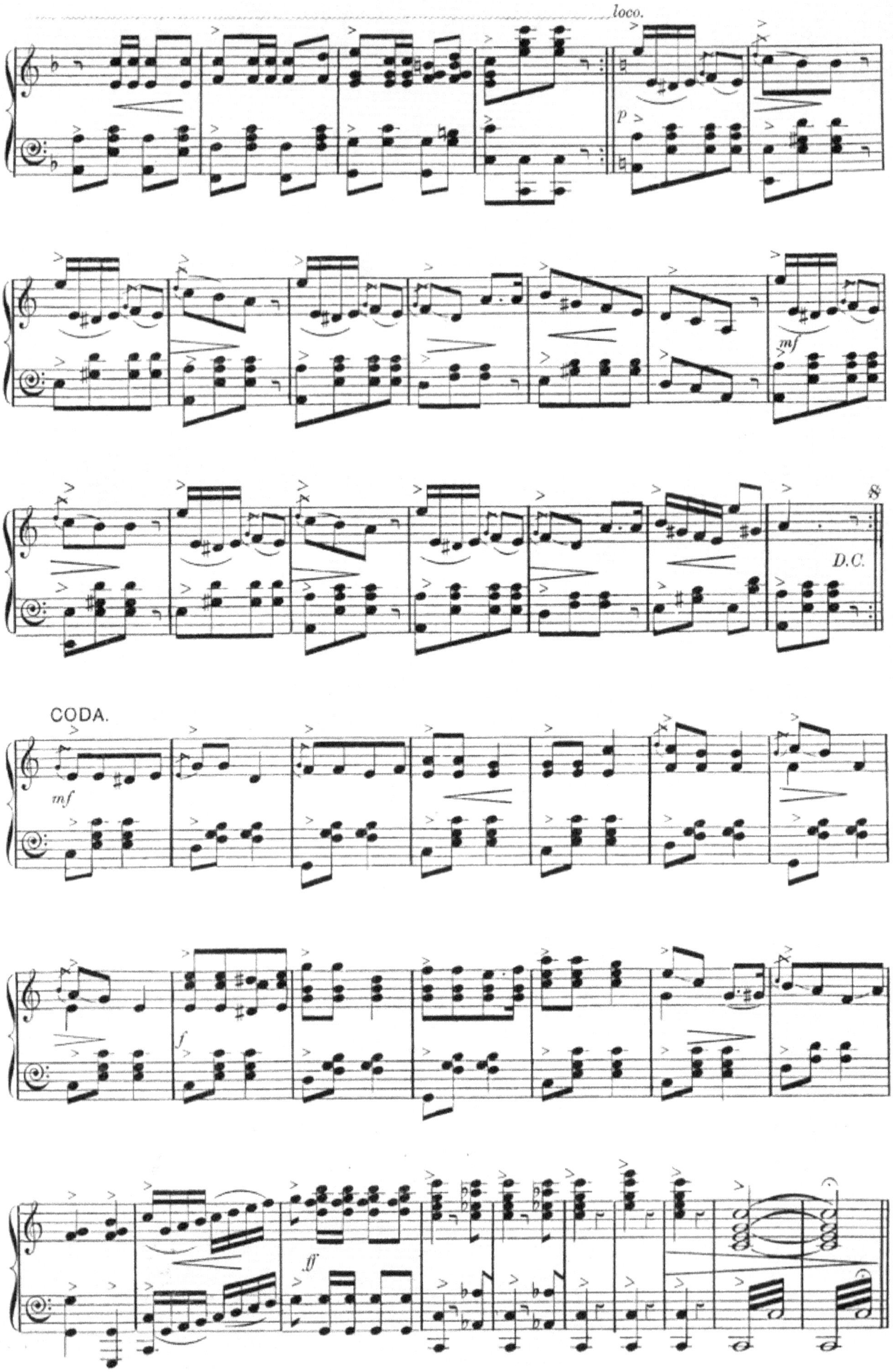
loco.
p
mf
D.C.
CODA.
mf
f
ff

~ The Zig-Zag Mazurka ~

Form couples facing along l.o.d. in low promenade hold, l.hs joined over r.hs

Start weight on r.f., l.f. free.

Dance as many times as will.

Play any slow waltz or mazurka.

A1	Prom. f. on alternate l,r,l,r diagonals w. 3 hop-drop-kicks and 1 click-click-click (r.f. free) / Counterpart, finishing holding r.hs
A2	Starting outside (l.) f. free, r.h. t. w. 3 hop-drop-kicks then click-click-click (r.f. free) sideways r. catching l.arm on ptner's waist / R.f. free t. w. 3 click-step-steps, then w. triple clicks slide into l.h.s
B1	Starting outside (r.) f. free, l.h. t. w. 3 hop-drop-kicks then w. triple clicks (l.f. free) pull sideways l. catching r.arm on ptner's waist / L.f. free t. w. 3 click-step-steps then w. triple clicks slide into r.hs.
B2	Starting outside (l.) f. free, w. 1st hop-drop-kick t. cw on r.h., w. 2nd M t. over outside (l.) sh. and w. 3rd W over outside (r.) sh., then joining l.hs over r.hs t. acw w. triple click (r.f. free) / Counterpart: - finishing swivelling to both face f. along l.o.d.

All x n.

A1	<u>Promenade forward on alternate</u> left, right, left and right <u>diagonals with 3 hop-drop-kicks and 1 click-click-click</u> (hopping 3 times on left foot) <u>Repeat but starting on right diagonal</u> and finishing with a click-click-click on left diagonal while hopping 3 times on right foot and dropping l.h. to finish facing holding r.hs
A2	Starting with outside (left) foot free and hopping on inside (right) foot, <u>right hand turn with 3 hop-drop-kicks and then with 1 click-click-click</u> (a 'triple click' hopping 3 times on left foot) <u>pull</u> directly right <u>sideways</u> towards and belly-to-belly past partner, finishing <u>catching l.arm on partner's waist</u> and putting right hand in the air. With outside (right) foot free and hopping on left, <u>turn with 3 click-step-steps, then with 1 click-click-click</u> (hopping 3 times on left foot) <u>slide out into holding</u> partner's <u>left hand</u>.
B1	Starting with outside (right) foot and hopping on inside (left) foot, <u>left hand turn with 3 hop-drop-kicks and then with 1 click-click-click</u> (hopping 3 times on right foot) <u>pull</u> directly left <u>sideways</u> towards and belly-to-belly past partner, finishing <u>catching r.arm on partner's waist</u> and putting left hand in the air. With outside (left) foot free and hopping on right, <u>turn with 3 click-step-steps, then with click-click-click</u> (hopping 3 times on right foot) <u>slide out into holding</u> partner's <u>right hand</u>.
B2	<u>The Knott:</u> Change from right hand cw turn to crossed hands acw swing with 3 hop-drop-kicks, the first one both going forward cw on right hand, the second man turns over outside (left) shoulder, and the third woman turns over outside (right) shoulder, and then joining left hands over right hands with click-click-click (hopping 3 times on left foot) swing acw. <u>Knott the other way:</u> Drop the right hand and change from left hand acw turn to crossed hands cw swing with 3 hop-drop-kicks, the first one both going forward acw on left hand, the second man turns over outside (right) shoulder, and the third woman over outside (left) shoulder, and then joining right hands over left hands with click-click-click (hopping 3 times on right foot) swing cw—finishing swivelling a little to both face forward along l.o.d.
	AABBxn Repeat as many times as will or put into a medley with other mazurka sequences.

— John Gardiner-Garden, *Dance Delights*, 2020 —

In this sequence I was attempting to combine a figure (the waist-waist tour) and a step sequence (different 'hop-first' mazurka steps followed by a 'triple-click') I had not used in any earlier dance. As with **The Lacework Mazurka** with which this dance can make a nice pair, I settled on the given choreography for 3 main reasons.

Firstly, it distributes evenly across the 32 bars actions that are on the spot and ones that move forward, turns that go cw and ones that go acw, holds that are close and ones that are distant, step sequences that change feet and ones that don't, and phrases that tire and those that are forgiving.

Secondly, the step pattern has a certain memorable logic to it - each 4 bar phrase starting with 3 fancy 'hop-first' steps (hop-drop-kick steps if at a distance from partner, click-step-steps if close beside partner) and finishing with a 'triple click' (hopping 3 times on the same foot while doing travelling heel-clicks).

Thirdly, the foot and weight flow fits well with changing need—e.g. the foot that is free before every 'tour' is on the most useful side for executing that tour—which for all these tours is the 'outside'.

~ Die Zwelf Monet ~

Form couples holding inside hand.

Start outside foot, M's left foot W's right.

Dance sequence a suggested as many times as will.

Play any 24-bar common

Taking throughout 1 double every 2 bars, so 4 in every strain:
A1 Prom. f. w. 2 low doubles (ea. bar step-2-3-hop) / swing arms b.& f.
A2 prom. while with free hs M waives and woman puts on tummy / lean & push purposely forward with 2 doubles.
B1 face, b-to-b; bring trailing hs through, prom.
B2 M guide W acw around / kiss and fall b.
C1 M t. W cw 2x under raised inside h. / separate from ptner, clap & return
C2 M t. himself under raised inside h. / W goes f. to new M *while* M casts out (vomits) and takes new ptner
All x n.

time tune. Below I present an An Dro from Brittany which, although not a tune of medieval German origin, has a suitable ancient folk feel and was the tune I had in mind when composing the song for the dance.

In Volume I of my *Dancing through the Ages* series, I consider a dance I called the 'Enigmatic German Dance'. Many Dutch and German illustrations of peasant dancing in the 15th, 16th and 17th century depict couples promenading enthusiastically around their dance space with swing arms, twirls and kisses. Sometimes these illustrations come in multiple plates and seem to depict various stages of the one dance or dance occasion. Such a series is the wood block set Sebald Beham calls *Die Zwelf Monet*. In *Die Zwelf Monet* Sebald would seem to be suggesting in this particular series that the months of the year are like the flow of a peasant dance. The first wintry months of the year are like a steady-low procession forward. March seems to herald a new baby, the happy man waiving *while* his partner visibly pregnant after the courtship 7 or 8 months earlier in July and August. The heavy work of ploughing in April seems to be represented a forward leaning promenade and the lively promenade ends spring. The onset of the summer seems to be represented by expansive arm swinging, and its end by a return to promenading (though I recommend a facing kiss to seal the courting months). Then comes autumn and it seems no coincidence that the man in October is carrying a threshing flail. December and the man vomiting clearly represents the excesses of Christmas. Is it possible, that the artist was also, consciously or unconsciously, depicting an actual dance sequence? In my *Dancing through the Ages* Volume I argued that here, as in many other c.16th century collections of images of German peasants dancing and contemporary paintings from that region and time that seem to show couples in different phases of a dance, the answer is yes.

In the table that follows I have suggested a dance which might satisfy the images, and which when set to the song I have invented, might tell the story of a peasant's year. I have tried to create a lyric that captures something about agrarian life during each month and hints at the figure that the dancers need to perform, so that the song can serve as a form of dance call. Thus the table I underline the words in the lyric that might most remind dancers of the suggested dance figure: In **January** 'trudge' reminds the couple to promenade, in **February** 'warm by the glow' to swing arms back to face as if before a fire, in **March** 'celebrate ... rebirth' for man to waive and woman to look pregnant, in **April** 'plough' for both to lean forward, in **May** 'choose' to swing arms back so partners can see each other, in **June** 'watch' to face again, in **July** 'the maids all around', for the women to go fully around man, in **August** 'love's unbound' to kiss partner, in **September** 'race' to quickly twirl woman twice, in **October** 'thresh and winnow' to separate from partner, in **November** 'turns' reminds the man to turn once under his own hand, and in **December** 'drink' for the man to mime vomiting.

— John Gardiner-Garden, *Dance Delights*, 2020 —

Aa	**January and we <u>trudge</u> through snow** <u>2 quick doubles forward</u>	**1. Fabianus Jenbr.**	Bb	**July youths dance the / maids all <u>around</u>.** With 2 doubles <u>man raises his right hand and arcs woman acw around him</u>		**7. Iacob Hewmon**
	February we <u>warm</u> by the glow 2 doubles <u>forward</u>, this time <u>swing joined arms back to face and forward</u>	**2. Mathias Hornuns**		**August crops <u>ripen</u> and / <u>love</u>'s unbound** With 2 doubles <u>woman completes orbit of man</u> and they <u>come face-to-face to kiss and fall back</u>)		**8.Laurencius Augstmon.**
Ab	**March we <u>celebrate</u> / Spring's re<u>birth</u>** 2 doubles <u>forward, man waiving joyfully to friend with free hand, partner holds tummy as if pregnant</u>	**3. Herr Greg- orius Mercz**	Ca	**September's harvest's a / <u>race</u> against rain** With 2 doubles <u>man swings joined inside hands forward to turn woman twice cw under his right hand</u>.		**9.Egidius Herbstmon**
	April we <u>plough</u> and / till the earth 2 doubles <u>forward but arms down and leaning forward as you make longer stride</u>	**4. Marcus April.**		**October we <u>thresh and</u> / <u>winnow</u> the grain** With 2 doubles <u>couple separate with a double away & clap, rejoin with double in</u>.		**10. Simon Weinmon**
Ba	**May and we <u>choose</u> / the season's queen** 2 doubles <u>forward, swinging arms back to face on 1st and forward to go back-to-back on 2nd</u> (but free arm low).	**5. Philipus Mei.**	Cb	**November and the / year <u>turns</u> t'wards end(e)** With 2 doubles <u>man turns acw under own raised right hand</u>.		**11. Marinus Wintermon**
	June and we <u>watch</u> / the fields grow green 2 doubles <u>joining trailing free hands and bringing them through as front hands are released</u>.	**6. Iohannes Brachmon**		**December we party / with <u>drinks</u> and friends(e)** With 2 doubles <u>woman goes forward to new man *while* man casts out over his left shoulder</u> (miming vomiting) <u>and takes a new partner</u>.		**12. Nicholau- s Christmon**

Inspiring me to attempt to reconstruct a dance out of Beham's *Zwie Monet* was an 'Elisa von Sophey' paper '16th Century German Peasant Dance from Period Woodcuts: Two Dances from the Beham Brothers', presented at the Known World Dance Symposium 2009 and posted in a revised form on-line. Elisa suggests these images may represent the following dance:

Section A	6 counts	4 alman doubles forward
Section B	8 counts	2 alman doubles forward
	8 counts	Clockwise circle back-to-back, ladies lead
	8 counts	2 alman doubles forward
	8 counts	Counterclockwise circle back-to-back, men lead
Section C	8 counts	2 alman doubles forward, turn to face
	4 counts	Men guide ladies (ladies back up)
	4 counts	Ladies guide men (men back up)
Section D	16 counts	4 *salterelli tedesci*

Although inspired by Elisa's suggestion I was not entirely convinced by all her suggestions and as you will have noticed from my above table and discussion, my 'reconstruction' ended up quite different. I agreed that the first 4 images seem to depict promenading using an 'almain double' (i.e. a step-2-3-slight hop), but it is possible that the figures accompanying the first 3 pairs of doubles are intended to be the same. It is possible that images 6 and 7 depict, as Elisa suggests, some form of back-to-back turning (a possible antecedent of the allemande turning we find 200 years later?), but it is also possible they depict some other action that involves a momentary back-to-back hold. It does seem likely, as Elisa suggests, that image 9 was cut from a stamping of the image which formed part of a 16 panel dance woodcut by Sebald Beham from 1537 so should be reverse (as in my table that follows)—instead of outside hands joined and man wearing his sword on his right, inside hands joined and sword on the left, but backing each other is not the only figure that might account for the raised inside hand. It is possible, as Elisa suggests, that the final images show some form of lively *pas de Breban* or *salterello* travelling round the dance space, as concluded many courtly dances of this period, but I am not convinced that the wearing of the laurel wreath in image 12 represents virginity or a wedding or victory in the worse nose competition, as Elisa suggests. I see simply representing the bacchanalia of Christmas. The vomiting might then represent the overindulge of Christmas time (particularly when excess food and drink are combined with dance).

One compromise I have made in creating this 'reconstruction' concerns feet. In a contemporary courtly French or Italian dance partners favoured same foot action, and in modern day German folk dance partner favour opposite foot. In 'Die Zwelf Monet' feet do not seem to have been the main concern of the artist or of his subjects. Some images show dancers on same foot, others on opposite. Some show dancers in perfect time with each other, others out of time. For the sake of my choreography I have chosen to have partners in time on opposite (i.e. mirror) feet. I also suggest including two figures not depicted in any of the given images but depicted in other period illustrations of the German dance—kissing at the end of B2 and separating sideways then rejoining instead of just promenading in the second half of C1 and C2, the last being able to be used to progress men forward onto a new partner. The latter helps make the dance useful in a modern social context.

My dance 'reconstruction' is not entirely serious—the presence of too many uncertainties and the absent of originally-intended music make this impossible (and I do not, accordingly include this reconstruction in Part 4 of this Volume). My 'reconstruction' may, however, (along with Elisa's) help suggest to the reader that there were possibly 'real' dances behind the cavorting being depicted in such woodblocks and may encourage people to experiment for themselves with ways to bring such images to life.

In larger continuous format Sebald Beham's *Die Zwelf Monet* looks like this:

www.ingramcontent.com/pod-product-compliance
Lightning Source LLC
Chambersburg PA
CBHW080843270326
41928CB00014B/2881